D1480658

I SWEAR BY APOLLO

Dr. Ewen Cameron and the CIA-Brainwashing Experiments

The Allan Memorial Institute

I SWEAR BY APOLLO

Dr. Ewen Cameron and the CIA-Brainwashing Experiments

By Don Gillmor

Eden Press
Montréal

I SWEAR BY APOLLO
Dr. Ewen Cameron and the CIA-Brainwashing Experiments
by Don Gillmor

ISBN: 0-920792-72-3

Page design: Lynette Stokes
Inside photographs: photograph of the Allan Memorial Institute by David
Laforge; photographs of Ewen Cameron, Heinz Lehmann, and the 1957 port-
rait of a typical patient stay at the Allan (photographers; Fred Poland and
Paul Taillefer) are from Canada-Wide Feature Service Limited; All other
photographs are from the *Montreal Star*/Public Archives of Canada.

Printed in Canada at Metropole Litho Inc.
Dépot légal — deuxième trimestre 1987
Bibliothèque nationale du Québec

Eden Press
4626 St. Catherine Street West
Montreal, Quebec, H3Z 1S3
Canada

Canadian Cataloguing in Publication Data

Gillmor, Don
    I swear by Apollo : Dr. Ewen Cameron and the CIA-brainwashing
experiments

ISBN 0-920792-72-3

1. Cameron, Ewen, 1901-1967.   2. Psychiatrists--
United States--Biography.   3. Psychiatric ethics.
4. Psychiatry--Research--Canada.   I. Title.

RC339.52.C34G44 1987   616.89'0092'4   C86-090238-2

ACKNOWLEDGEMENTS

I would like to thank the following for their valuable contributions: Debra Schram for her editorial, financial, and moral support; researcher Heather Moe for her organizational efforts, insights, and research contribution; my publishers and editors, Pamela Chichinskas and Lynette Stokes; The Canada Council; Rod Young and Bennett McCardle at the Public Archives of Canada; Heinz Lehmann; Joseph Rauh; and James Turner.

AUTHOR'S NOTE

Much of the material in this book was taken from over seventy interviews conducted with colleagues of Ewen Cameron; doctors, nurses, students, social workers, and government officials. Many of these people wished to remain anonymous, most often citing professional reasons. Psychiatry prides itself on being a discreet profession. When it comes to secrecy, one doctor told me, the Mafia have nothing on the psychiatric profession. A number of Cameron's colleagues have an opinion of him that is made up of very disparate thoughts; "He was a great humanist" coexisting with "He was a dangerous and misguided autocrat." They were nervous that perhaps only the negative opinion would survive in print. The psychiatrists who worked with or under Ewen Cameron have been picked over by the media and are a cautious lot. For these reasons, many comments are attributed simply to "a colleague" or "a former resident."

TABLE OF CONTENTS

*"The place where optimism most flourishes
is the lunatic asylum."*

Havelock Ellis

INTRODUCTION

In early September, 1967, at the age of sixty-six, Dr. Ewen Cameron climbed to the summit of Street Mountain in the Adirondacks near his home in Lake Placid, New York. He sat down to admire the view below him. Here, on a warm September day, he succumbed to massive cardiac arrest. There were rumours about his death. Some people speculated that he knew he had heart trouble and that he went up the mountain to die. It was a gesture well within his dramatic range.

Ewen Cameron died one of the most respected psychiatrists on the continent. Born and educated in Scotland, he became an American citizen in 1942, which he remained throughout his life, despite working in Canada for twenty-eight years.

He had been, respectively, president of the Quebec, Canadian and American Psychiatric Associations. In 1961 he co-founded and became the first president of the World Psychiatric Association. For twenty-one years he was chairman of the department of psychiatry at McGill University in Montreal and director of the Allan Memorial Psychiatric Institute, a teaching hospital co-administered by McGill and the Royal Victoria Hospital. As the Allan's first director, he created a teaching facility and psychiatric institution that became internationally renowned. It was the first "open door" psychiatric facility on the continent, a forward-looking counterpoint to the locked-ward asylums of the day. Cameron's "open door" policy stipulated that no doors in the Allan would be locked. He said that even if one ward was locked, society would judge the institution by that ward. He attracted impressive figures to staff the Allan, sold Montreal as the site for prestigious conferences, fought successfully for elusive research funds, and publicized the problem of mental health to both the government and the public with the skill of P. T. Barnum. He possessed an evangelical zeal to eradicate mental illness within his own lifetime. He attracted few friends, a lengthy list of admirers, a handful of enemies, and the enduring respect of most of the medical profession. He is acknowledged as the father of Canadian academic psychiatry.

On August 2, 1977, ten years after Cameron's death, his reputation became the subject of some debate. A front-page headline in *The New York Times* read, "Private institutions used in CIA effort to control behaviour." The article outlined a Central Intelligence Agency program, conceived in 1950, to develop brainwashing techniques; techniques they suspected the Chinese already possessed.

Details of various projects, most of which involved research into the uses of LSD (Lysergic Acid Diethylamide), a powerful hallucinogen, were outlined in the *Times* article.

Most of the researchers had been approached through a private medical research foundation called the Society for the Investigation of Human Ecology (SIHE). One of the researchers who received SIHE money was Ewen Cameron. The *Times* piece read, "Dr. Ewen Cameron, of the Allan Memorial Institute of Psychiatry at McGill University in Montreal, conducted several experiments on behaviour control, including the effects of isolation and sensory deprivation on humans for the CIA between 1955 and 1960. The work was paid for by the Society for the Investigation of Human Ecology . . . An associate in the research said in an interview that he was unaware that the research had been paid for by the CIA."

Leonard Rubenstein, a colleague of Cameron's was quoted as saying:

> It [Cameron's research] was definitely related to brainwashing
> . . . they had investigated brainwashing among soldiers who
> had been in Korea. We, in Montreal, started to use some
> of these techniques, brainwashing patients instead of using
> drugs.

Sidney Gottlieb, a CIA pharmacologist, later described the Society for the Investigation of Human Ecology as "a funding mechanism so that involvement of the CIA's organizational entity would not be apparent in projects we were funding." The *Times* reported:

> By the early 1960s the CIA had grown uncomfortable about
> the experiments. A 1957 report by the Inspector General
> noted that the chemical division "had added difficulty in

obtaining expert services and facilities to conduct tests and experiments. Some of the activities are considered to be professionally unethical and in some instances border on the illegal."

The Society for the Investigation of Human Ecology was disbanded in 1965.

*   *   *

In 1979, American journalist John Marks published a book entitled *The Search for the Manchurian Candidate* that detailed the extent of the CIA's behaviour-control program. Through the Freedom of Information Act, Marks had gained access to sixteen thousand pages of CIA documents that described the internal workings of the program. In a chapter on brainwashing, Marks described Cameron's work at the Allan, expanding on the theme presented in *The New York Times* piece. He outlined a course of experimentation that used massive electroshock, powerful hallucinogens such as LSD and a treatment Cameron called "psychic driving," which used extended repetition of cue statements to effect a change in behaviour.

In Marks's book, Cameron's work with LSD was presented largely through the experiences of a former Canadian patient, Val Orlikow, the wife of David Orlikow, a member of Parliament from Winnipeg. On December 11, 1980, Val Orlikow brought suit against the CIA, soliciting the services of Joseph Rauh, a prominent Washington civil rights lawyer who had defended Arthur Miller and Lillian Hellman during the McCarthy trials. At the crux of Orlikow's suit was the question of research versus treatment. Mrs. Orlikow alleged that she had gone to the Allan Memorial Institute seeking treatment for *post partum* depression and instead was subjected to brainwashing experiments financed by the CIA. She was eventually joined in her suit by eight other Canadians, all former patients of Cameron's.

Cameron's career and reputation became the issues over which the battle raged. Rauh attacked Cameron's work as unethical and charged that the CIA had knowingly funded unethical research. The CIA responded that they were "simply buying goods off the shelf," and that Cameron was doing the research anyway. The Canadian psychiatric profession, partly founded on Cameron's administrative efforts, very quietly took on the task of restoring Cameron's reputation with occasional forays into print. They stated that a sense of perspective was needed, that Cameron's work was ethical within the context of the times. Taking money from the CIA, especially money laundered through a private foundation, was no crime if the work was ethical, they argued.

Supporters point out that Cameron was doing nothing new, or at least very little that was new. Other researchers had already used similar techniques. Detractors suggest that Cameron's breach of ethics was of a quantitative rather than a qualitative nature; that he was prepared to take existing techniques past the point of responsibility, endangering his patients welfare.

The Canadian government was compelled to join the fray when a newspaper report detailed the extent of governmental financing of Cameron's work. Between 1948 and 1964, Cameron had received more than five hundred thousand dollars in mental health grants from the federal government to support his research, some of which was an extension of the work he had done with SIHE money. Also there has been some public outcry about why the Canadian government wasn't doing more for its citizens in their fight against the CIA. Rauh had, in fact, charged the Canadian government with withholding correspondence between themselves and the U.S. government that has a bearing on his case. "I thought the Canadian government would be on my side," Rauh said in *Maclean's* magazine. "Boy, did I make a mistake." External Affairs Minister Joe Clark declared that the government had "acted as much as we can."

In 1985, Justice Minister John Crosbie commissioned Halifax lawyer George Cooper to supply an independant legal opinion "as to the government's potential legal liability, and also an opinion as to whether the government may be under some duty towards the patients of a kind which falls short of legal liability." Cooper conducted a circumscribed investigation and concluded that his client, the Canadian government, has no legal or moral culpability resulting from its funding of Ewen Cameron's work. His findings were published in the spring of 1986 as "The Opinion of George Cooper" and distributed across the country.

Almost a decade after the disclosure in *The New York Times*, nothing has been settled. Orlikow's case has yet to come to trial, nor will the outcome of her suit necessarily resolve the issue. What is before the courts is the issue of damages. Have the nine individual plaintiffs suffered as a result of the treatment they received from Cameron almost thirty years ago? Cameron's reputation and research abilities and the role of the CIA will be brought in to reinforce both sides of the legal issue, but much of the weight of the decision lies on the plaintiffs' medical histories.

It was hoped that Cooper's report would bring all the facts to light, but that has not been the case. Rauh immediately labelled the report "a whitewash," and pointed to the fact that Cooper had not interviewed a single patient of Cameron's, or in fact anyone who was not a government employee.

Although the Cooper report was only the legal opinion of an individual attorney, it was published by the Department of Justice, distributed across the country and presented to the press, taking on, in the public's mind the weight of a government investigation on the scale of a royal commission. Justice Minister Crosbie commented that it was an independant investigation and as such did not necessarily represent the views of the Canadian government. He welcomed anyone to come forward with new evidence on the issue. Cooper's report became little more than a catalogue of background information that either side could arbitrarily refer to.

Although brainwashing and the CIA played a part in the events in Montreal in the 1950s, at the centre of the action is Ewen Cameron's enigmatic personality and remarkable career. "He was easy to respect," said a colleague, "but hard to like. I never heard the word *love* associated with Ewen Cameron's name." More than seventy of Cameron's colleagues were interviewed for this book, and over the course of these interviews their responses took on a pattern. Most began by praising Cameron, then they voiced some grave doubts or personal reservations, and eventually concluded that, overall, he was a great man. Seriously flawed perhaps, but that often goes with the territory.

According to those who worked with him, Cameron was described, variously, as warm, distant, dedicated, evil, heroic, pathological, vindictive, and fair almost to a fault. A tyrannical, democratic, eagle-beaked loner who brooked no opposition, welcomed the views of others, and pushed forward the frontiers of psychiatry while ruthlessly expanding the psychiatric empire he was building in Montreal. He had an almost magical clinical touch with his patients and an addled persistance for wrong-headed therapy.

Many of Canada's practising psychiatrists are graduates of teaching programs that Cameron instituted. Many of the heads of university psychiatric departments, hospital directors, and internationally respected researchers owe some of their success to Ewen Cameron. Under his tutelage, the Allan Memorial's program became the second-largest graduate psychiatry program in the world, next only to the Menninger Clinic's. It also won a significant reputation for psychiatric research. Almost everyone who worked or trained at the Allan Institute gained from their association. They are now re-examining their teacher and peer in the light of recent disclosures, in an attempt to ascribe to him his proper place in Canadian psychiatric history.

There are many questions still unanswered. Was Cameron aware of the CIA's funding? What was the nature of the Canadian government's financing? Was the work ethical? But other issues are raised as well. Cameron has been labelled a "mad scientist" (by John Marks, among others) and a "dedicated humanist" by many of his former colleagues and on the face of the evidence, neither claim is demonstrably false. The extremes Cameron approached in his research, regardless of his motivation, raises questions about the nature of the treatment of patients and the relationship between mental illness and research and between psychiatry and society. Cameron was determined to build a better world and he was prepared to use whatever measures he thought necessary to accomplish this aim. He was a complex man who was given to crudely wrought solutions. "His goals you could admire," said a colleague, "but it was difficult to live with his methods."

Psychiatrists, for the most part, are hard-working, goal-oriented, and ambitious. Of Cameron's peers who are still living, some of whom are past eighty-years-old, none have retired. It is a demanding and frustratingly imprecise occupation that is still struggling for recognition and research funds. On one psychiatrist's office wall at the Allan there is a *New Yorker* cartoon that shows a bearded psychiatrist looking pensively upward. A patient is lying on his couch. "Why did I go into psychiatry?" the psychiatrist asks. He answers himself, "The voices told me to." The owner of the office concurred with the cartoon. "There are a lot of nuts in this business," he said.

CHAPTER ONE

ESTABLISHING
THE ALLAN MEMORIAL INSTITUTE

Donald Ewen Cameron was born on December 24, 1901, in Bridge of Allan, Scotland. A small town twenty miles north of Glasgow's industrial grit, it sits in the low rolling hills and scattered spruce of the Scottish midlands. Cameron's father, Duncan, was a Presbyterian minister, a stern propponent of his chosen brand of Calvinism. As a boy, Ewen caddied for his father, walking quietly behind him on the golf course under the cloud cover characteristic of Scottish summers. The damp air and forced march to the morning's eighteen holes produced a powerful appetite in the adolescent boy. At one in the afternoon, when Ewen's pangs of hunger increased in intensity, his father would announce, "And now, Ewen, we will go another nine holes." Years later, Cameron remembered his hunger and remarked on the experience and his subsequent distaste for golf.

After graduating from Stirling and the Glasgow Academy, Cameron attended the University of Glasgow, where he was a competitive student. He received a "blue" in the punishing game of rugby, excelled in the four-mile race and graduated Alpha Kappa Kappa in 1924. He began a stint as resident surgeon at the Glasgow Western Infirmary, leaving later that year to become a resident physician at the Glasgow Royal Mental Hospital. He received his M. B., Ch. B. in 1924, and in 1925 was promoted to the position of assistant physician at the Glasgow Mental Hospital.

In 1925, he attended the University of London, where he received his diploma of psychological medicine, and he did some consulting with the Berkshire Industrial Farm. He left London for Baltimore, Maryland, in 1926, to become assistant psychiatrist at the Phipps Clinic at Johns Hopkins Hospital. Continuing his climb through the academic ranks, he became an instructor in psychiatry there within two years, holding a Henderson Research Scholarship.

In Baltimore Cameron worked under Adolf Meyer, perhaps his greatest influence. Like Cameron, Meyer was a minister's son. He was also a pragmatist who worked to improve the lot of mental patients, using any approach that seemed to him sensible and practical. Meyer stressed that a doctor had to understand a patient's social environment, and, he viewed a patient's disorganized state as a personality disfunction rather than the result of brain pathology.

Although Meyer helped form the American Psychoanalytic Association, he did not fully accept all their principles of analysis. He did not adhere to any single school of psychiatric thought, urging a broad perspective instead. He lectured to many generations of students, stating that "Your point of reference should always be life itself and not the imagined cesspool of the unconscious."

Meyer's approach was integrative, although his critics argued that it lacked discrimination. He failed to offer a solid theoretical basis for understanding the psychodynamics of individual patients. His contribution to psychiatry was primarily as a teacher and practical innovator. He instituted child-guidance clinics, stressed aftercare for patients as opposed to merely discharging them from the hospital, argued for the use of common sense in psychiatry, and developed psychiatric social work. (His wife, Mary Potter Brooks, became the first psychiatric social worker when she began visiting the families of patients to learn more about their backgrounds.)

Cameron eventually received the Adolf Meyer Memorial Award for "meritorious contributions in behalf of improved care and treatment of the mentally ill, inside and outside the institution," in 1957.

Later in 1928, Cameron went to Zurich where he worked as a psychiatrist under Hans W. Maier. It was there that he met A. T. Mathers, then provincial psychiatrist of Manitoba. It was this connection that led to Cameron's first serious post as a practising psychiatrist.

In 1929, Cameron went to the Brandon Mental Hospital in Brandon, Manitoba, arriving to witness the onset of the dustbowl and the worst depression in Canadian history. In the academic purgatory of the prairies, Cameron was aware that the only way to keep his professional profile from sinking out of sight was to publish in psychiatric journals. During his years in Brandon, he published a number of articles on depression, schizophrenia and psychotic behaviour, developing his first inquiries into experimental method as it existed in psychiatry. In a 1933 paper, "Mensuration in

Psychoses," he suggested that there was a growing need for more exact methods of measurement in psychiatry. He felt that psychiatry was entering the scientific era, an idea he developed further in his book *Objective and Experimental Psychiatry*. He wrote:

> Whether we recognize it or not, the influence which most strongly beat upon those of us who passed into psychiatry . . . was the humanitarian. Sympathy, patience, insight, rapport — these were the magic words. They must remain so, but as a means to an end and not as an end in themselves. . . . So many of our concepts are mere traditions . . . an increasing number of us experience a feeling of growing distrust by purely descriptive and intuitive concepts of human behaviour and find it more and more difficult to content ourselves with facts or assertions save where they will withstand experimentation and will not fail us on prediction.

Cameron lamented his isolation at the Manitoba outpost and the concomitant lack of contact with other psychiatrists. This was before the advent of the Canadian Psychiatric Association, so there was no professional Canadian network other than a loose membership implied by subscription to professional journals. He instituted mobile clinics to serve remote farms and communities on the prairies, promoted the idea of an objective, experimentally viable method of dealing with mental illness, and prepared himself for the pyschiatric major leagues.

In 1936, he left the academic internment of Brandon for a research appointment at Worcester State Hospital in Massachusetts. At Worcester he would become the resident director of research and the first psychiatrist in North America to use insulin coma therapy, a treatment already introduced in Europe to treat schizophrenia.

In 1938, Cameron accepted the position of professor of neurology and psychiatry at the Albany Medical School. At Albany he was in charge of the Mosher Memorial, one of the first psychiatric departments to be established in a general hospital in North America. Here, Cameron was exposed to the newest developments in psychiatry and achieved a measure of prominence.

*   *

When Cameron arrived at Montreal's Windsor Station in 1943, it was an elegant and airy building with a vast open floor and a buttressed greenhouse roof. Dr. T. E. Dancey, senior district military psychiatrist for Montreal, met him at the station amidst the wartime bustle. Montreal was a cultural oddity, a hybrid city that owed its European charm to the French and its economic base to the English. It was also an urban rallying point for the war effort and hotel rooms were consequently hard to come by. Dancey pulled some strings to get Cameron lodgings at the University Club.

A tall man with the angled expression of a benign hawk, Cameron had come to chair the department of psychiatry at McGill University and to become the founding director of the Allan Memorial Institute, a psychiatric facility co-administered by McGill and the Royal Victoria Hospital. A Rockefeller grant had been the financial impetus behind the Allan, and Cameron had been brought in on the recommendation of Dean Johnathan Meakins and Wilder Penfield, the famed neurologist and Montreal's reigning medical star. Penfield gave Cameron two pieces of advice when he arrived: become a Canadian citizen and learn to speak French. Cameron did neither. He retained his American citizenship, unwilling, perhaps, to surrender its political advantages in the international medical world. He developed a patriotism for neither country, scorning nationalism as an outmoded concept that had caused enough trouble. As a Scottish-born American, Cameron was only allowed to live outside the U.S. for five years without forfeiting his U.S. citizenship. He resolved the dilemma by setting up residence in Lake Placid, New York, and commuting one hundred miles daily to Montreal.

Cameron showed little tolerance for unilingual francophones. The government money required to support the two languages offended both his pragmatism and his Scottish sense of thrift. He once told a bilingual colleague, "Look, Doc, that's ridiculous, two languages . . . It's a waste of money." He was unable to grasp French-Canadian culture, dismissing it as a lot of sentimental nonsense. Cameron unconsciously joined the ranks of the "Westmount Rhodesians," an anglophone enclave where residents sipped gin, wore old school ties, and dismissed the "pea soupers" as a colonial nuisance that had to be endured.

Upon Cameron's arrival in Montreal, Wilder Penfield approached him with a proposal to combine neurology and psychiatry into a splinter discipline called neuropsychiatry. To Penfield's surprise, he was rebuffed. The decision established Cameron's autonomy, distancing him from the towering shadow of his patron. His action captured the attention of the medical community. It was characteristic of the curious pattern of political adroitness and diplomatic disaster that would mark Cameron's career in Montreal. Relations between the two men cooled, eventually degenerating into acrimony over a rumoured funding dispute.

Although Montreal was a medical mecca in 1943, due to the reputations of McGill University's School of Medicine and of Wilder Penfield, the department of psychiatry had yet to achieve similar stature. In the days of Philipe Pinel (1745-1826), psychiatry had declared itself "in its infancy" and it seemed permanently relegated to the role of newcomer. When Cameron arrived in Montreal, treatment for mental illness hadn't made all that many strides since Pinel. There was really only one community psychiatric service for the English-speaking population, the Mental Hygiene Institute, and one provincial mental hospital, the Verdun Protestant Hospital (now called the Douglas Hospital). In September 1943, Cameron predicted in *The Montreal Star* that the Allan would quickly become one of the most prominent psychiatric institutions on the continent. It was a bold prediction considering his position.

He had a tiny staff, fewer students, and a fifty-bed facility in a donated mansion still undergoing renovations. He had confidence, an elusive charm, and the linear persistance of a nineteenth-century empire builder. He talked of the increased understanding of mental disorders, effective means of treatment, and the exciting possibilities that psychiatry held for the future. "We shall focus our efforts upon research and treatment," he told the *Star*.

The Rockefeller Foundation had awarded a grant to McGill for the establishment of a psychiatric department partly in anticipation of the expected need for psychiatrists to deal with war-induced disorders. The stress of dislocation, death, bereavement, and the horrors of the front was evident in returning soldiers in the form of neuroses. People were turning to the psychiatric profession to aid in the rebuilding process. It was a chance to field-test the psychiatrists' oft-questioned abilities.

The medical profession, however, hadn't entirely welcomed psychiatry into its fold. Psychiatric residents were sometimes mocked by other medical students. "We're opening up a cadaver this afternoon, perhaps you'd be good enough to come over and show us where the ego is located?" Psychiatry was a poor cousin that was hard-pressed to produce uniform procedures and terminology for the very things they purported to treat. The general public's perception of psychiatry at the time didn't extend much past parlor room Freudian controversy. Freud was tittilating, stylish, and provided the casual thinker with a theme that not only claimed some academic support but was potentially embarassing as a topic of dinner discussion.

The actual day-to-day work of the psychiatrist was a gritty mixture of custodial care and the application of only a few effective treatments. There was an acute lack of funding for both the care of patients and for research.

Early Canadian mental institutions were constructed on the outskirts of towns and were little more than warehouses for the disturbed detritus of society. Often administered by religious organizations, they combined the budding efforts of science with the stern catechismal fostering of the Church. Dr. J. R. Unwin, a psychiatrist trained in Britain, recalled the mental facility where he did his residency. "It had three thousand patients. I was in charge of four hundred of them. These great, grey stone buildings full of people we couldn't really do a hell of a lot for. The wards were full of suicides, schizophrenics, and criminals. The Sisters really ran the place. You'd make your rounds and buzz the locked door and one of these grim faced harridans would appear. 'Everything all right here?' you'd ask. 'Quite, doctor,' they'd answer. Sometimes you'd want to check on a specific patient. 'I'll just nip in and look at Mr. Billings,' you'd say. 'Mr. Billings is just fine, doctor,' they'd say ominously, then close the door. Quite spooky really."

Cameron wanted to eliminate these snakepit institutions and locked-door asylums. When he arrived in Montreal there were two such psychiatric institutions already. Sick Catholics were sent to St-Jean de Dieu Hospital in east-end Montreal, a facility so mammoth it once had its own railway system to shunt its several thousand inmates between buildings. Their Protestant counterparts were deposited in Verdun Protestant Hospital in nearby Verdun.

Cameron's abolition of locked doors at the Allan was considered a risky proposition. The Allan was located in the heart of the city, a short walk from the expensive homes of English businessmen and the bustling retail centre. The public may have been warming to psychiatry, but they still had a Victorian regard for the insane. Cameron's first task was to sell his brand of institution to the middle class. He did it with a combination of political perception and media savvy.

Cameron molded the Allan Memorial into a unique facility that corralled the aims of formerly separate spheres — teaching, research, and service for the mentally ill — under a single roof. As well as Cameron's innovative open-door policy, which he called "giving responsibility back to the patient," he instituted a psychiatric day hospital. Patients were able to go to the Allan for treatment during the day and return home to their families in the evening. It was an enlightened move away from incarceration in large hospitals. Both of these innovations were widely copied and the Allan eventually became the model of psychiatric reform in North America.

*   *   *

The Allan Memorial Institute occupies a mansion on the lower reaches of Mount Royal, a hill that thrusts up from Montreal's downtown core. The mansion was built in 1867 by Sir Hugh Allan, a shipping magnate who could watch the profitable activities of his fleet from the comfort of his mansion's watchtower. His former residence suffers from the unfortunate name "Ravenscrag" as well as an undeniably gothic presence, a combination that easily summons to mind the dark lunacy of Poe.

As Sir Hugh's home, the mansion was impressive. Modelled on the Italian Renaissance style in grey limestone, it contained thirty-four bedrooms, two large drawing rooms, a capacious ballroom, a billiard room, and a library. Immediately behind the house were the stables, a squat building with a stone horse's head jutting out over the main door. Tucked among the trees on the heavily wooded grounds were the gardener's cottage, a conservatory, a vinery, and a peach house. During its heyday, a host of second-string royalty passed through Ravenscrag. Queen Victoria's younger son, the Duke of Connaught, stayed during his colonial adventure with the Fenian Raiders. His son, Prince Arthur of Connaught, was a later guest. Prince Fushimi of Japan, brother of the Emperor, stayed for a spell upon his return from visiting King Edward VII. Indeed, Ravenscrag was once the focal point of Montreal society, the site of graceful teas, dignified recitals, and lavish entertainments.

Hugh Allan was a businessman who expanded his father's modest shipping line into a diversified empire. He gained a reputation as an unscrupulous Scots autocrat with a penchant for driving a hard bargain. A typical example of Allan craftiness was his bid to secure the charter to build the first railway across Canada. Allan apparently headed two opposing business groups competing for the charter while he shovelled campaign funds to then prime minister John A. Macdonald, whose decision it was to award the contract. Allan's unwieldy position lead to a collapse of the deal, which, it was later revealed, involved bribery and double-dealing. These were described in gleeful detail in a series of personal letters to which *The Montreal Herald* gained access and subsequently published. Allan quietly retreated from the railway business, and he died in 1882. It was his son, Sir Montagu

Allan, who, with his wife, donated the family home to the Royal Victoria Hospital in 1940 "as a free and unrestricted gift."

Three years later, forty thousand dollars were spent on the renovations needed to accomodate a teaching hospital. Rooms were divided, ceilings lowered, and linoleum laid over the gleaming hardwood floors. Ballroom, billiard room, and drawing rooms were converted and muted hospital tones were applied over the stately colour schemes once chosen by Lady Allan. Only the library was unaffected, an oaken enclave in the maelstrom of institutional progress. Thirty years earlier the Italian Futurists had screamed for the razing of Venice, which they claimed was a dying, fetid symbol of the past. They wanted to erect a modern industrial testament to the twentieth century on the site. If the renovators of the Allan didn't have quite the antagonism toward the past that the Futurists had, nor did they reverence it. It was a forward-looking time, and the past held little of value for the psychiatric profession. When it opened in 1944, the Allan Memorial Institute had the shining, slightly Art Deco look of a modern facility, pointing to a future free from the dark, granite gloom of nineteenth-century madhouses.

Cameron moved quickly to bring about his prediction that he would make the Allan an internationally recognized institution. The way to achieve this status was through research. In 1944, a behavioural laboratory was established in the stables, its function being to study human behaviour by means of sound and visual recordings. Karl Stern, an eminent German psychiatrist, established a gerontologic unit that same year and, in 1945, a laboratory for psychological studies was opened under Dr. R. B. Malmo. A year later, Dr. Lloyd Hisey established an electrophysiological laboratory and Dr. Robert Cleghorn opened an experimental therapeutics lab. Units on vasculographic studies, pharmacology and transcultural studies followed. Every corner of the Allan was taken up with research, treatment, or teaching. Closets, stairwells, and attic space continued to be converted for the use of Cameron's growing team of researchers.

In psychiatry at the time there were sharply divided schools of thought. The often bloody in-fighting that resulted was partly why psychiatry had trouble establishing a credible presence in the medical world. Cameron marshalled all the major schools and put them together under one roof. "He brought in all these different groups," remembers Alena Valdstyn, a former nurse at the Allan, "and they fought like hell." By 1953, a modern wing was built that extended out behind Ravenscrag. However, it barely accommodated the expanding teaching program and burgeoning research activities.

Cameron organized a network of psychiatric hospitals in Montreal, beginning with an association with the Mental Hygiene Institute. What began as an alliance to pool resources eventually became a coalition called the McGill Psychiatric Training Network that included eight Montreal hospitals. The network established a diploma course in psychiatry in 1945, and had only six students. By 1964, when Cameron left the Allan, there were one hundred and seventeen post-graduate students in the program.

The Allan and Cameron were firmly at the hub of this network, which also organized funding. Applications from Montreal hospitals for government funds were channelled through Cameron's office.

Dr. Brian Robertson, current director of the Allan Memorial, described the evolution of the network he inherited:

> Cameron was a unique man for a rather unique time. Psychiatry was becoming established as an academic discipline. He had the vision and the ability to understand what was needed. He had to have first-class teachers; he knew he had to accommodate the huge range of expertise, from psychoanalysts to neurochemists. He knew that he needed research. He had a very free hand because money was available and mental health was not as government-dominated or bureaucratized as it is now. So you have an organization that started with a very coherent vision. Cameron occupied a very dominating role in the organization itself and at McGill and in the community. He was the man who made it happen, thus his power was much greater than mine could ever be.

Although Cameron developed an eclectic teaching program that exposed students to a variety of psychiatric schools of thought, he did not initially include training in psychoanalysis at the Allan. Then, in the early 1950s, he noticed that he was losing students who were going to New York to study psychoanalysis. Cameron was not an analyst himself, having shunned its jargon as cabalistic and its methods as plodding and impractical. "Analysis was too slow for Cameron," said a colleague. "He was in a hurry." But he recognized its political worth and brought in a group of eminent analysts to set up a teaching program at the Allan, effectively staunching the flow of students to the U.S. Dr. Clifford Scott, one of the analysts Cameron imported from England, said, "Cameron wanted analytical training in the department on the one hand for status and secondly so he could control analytic training in Canada as he had controlled the standards of psychiatric training in Canada." Another colleague agreed, "Cameron wanted to control analysis, not promote it."

Cameron gave the analysts room to work but he had difficulty empathizing with their methods. He thought they were a bit flighty. On one occasion, an analyst offered Cameron a Freudian diagnosis of a patient. Cameron responded, "Doc, you're flying in mid-air. Why don't you come down to earth." Sceptical of analytic conjecture, he was looking for more empirical evidence. The man was diagnosed as suffering from Oedipal feelings:

"This man hates his father," the analyst said.

"Why?" Cameron asked. "Did his father beat him?"

Cameron had a dynamic energy that was infectious. He set his watch fifteen minutes fast, kept three secretaries busy typing his memos and correspondance, put in fifteen-hour days, and walked so fast that nurses joked of buying roller skates to keep up with him. His patient rounds resembled a papal tour; a retinue of residents and nurses trailed in his wake like competing cardinals. He was an expert motivator, demanding and getting the best from his staff. Dr. Dancey recalls, "He had an ability to make you work for him. You knew you were being manipulated but you did it anyway."

No detail escaped him. His former secretary, Dorothy Trainor, attested, "He permitted no sloppiness. If your slip was showing or your stocking had a run in it, you'd hear about it." His own appearance, though, was of little interest to him. For photo opportunities and fund-raising forays into West-mount's economic base, he could muster a crisp blue suit and smartly shined shoes. On the ward, his mind was elsewhere and his cuffs were often frayed, shoes scuffed, and socks mismatched. On occasion he would walk out of his shoes, testimony to both his pace and the split seams of his battered loafers. He dressed, commented a nurse, "like the east-end of a horse heading west."

When he was there, the Allan was vibrant. Dorothy Trainor swore she could tell if he was in the building as soon as she came through the door; there was an electricity in the air. He arrived before his staff and often stayed until nine in the evening, making rounds before he left. On weekends he phoned every ward and asked for a report. He was omnipresent.

Cameron's ambitious goals for the Allan needed huge injections of capital. The building itself required constant renovation to accommodate new plans. There was expensive equipment to be bought, assistants to be hired, and the salaries of assorted heavyweights to be paid. Cameron quickly proved to be a master at securing funding. Foundations, government agencies, and private donors contributed generously to Cameron's expanding programs. Even when money was not readily available, Cameron was prepared to proceed with his plans. Clifford Scott, a psychoanalyst and an expatriate Canadian living in London, was lured to the Allan with the promise of an extended appointment. "We have the necessary funding to provide you with a salary for the next five years," Cameron told him. Satisfied with these terms, Scott agreed to an appointment and made arrangements to have his Rolls Royce shipped to Montreal. Upon arrival he discovered that his Rolls did not deal well with the Canadian climate, running for about thirty-six trouble-free hours before something expensive broke down. He also discovered that Cameron only had financing for the first year of Scott's salary. He and other analysts who had been recruited from Europe weren't overjoyed at the news. They took up a collection from the students and pooled it into a resource fund to be tapped should they have to seek other employment. Cameron eventually was able to come up with long-range financing, to the relief of both the analysts and their students.

Although he was the consummate political creature, Cameron had few social skills. He was a gifted lecturer, an inspired fund raiser, and could speak publicly on anything he had an opinion on, a field with few restrictions, but he lacked the ability for small talk. He never entertained and the Allan's annual Christmas party was the only social event he attended, smiling uncomfortably for an hour or so while he tried not to look at his watch. Seeing Cameron standing awkwardly at the Christmas party looking like a thirteen-year-old at his first dance, a resident approached him to chat. "How was Mrs. Simms when you left her?" Cameron asked, his sole attempt at party conversation.

Voicing an ill-thought-out pleasantry, Cameron once mentioned to a colleague that if he was ever in the Lake Placid area, to look him up. Misinterpreting the comment as an invitation, he visited Cameron at his residence, apparently becoming the only person ever to do so. "It was very awkward," he remembers. "He wasn't a great conversationalist unless there was something specific to talk about. We just sort of sat. His family was there, one son played chess by himself in the corner."

With most of the doctors and residents, Cameron was aloof. Dr. J. R. Unwin, once Cameron's chief resident, said, "He didn't socialize or ask anything about anyone's personal life. He toured the wards like a bishop and the residents were the altar boys." Yet Unwin denied that Cameron was an autocrat. "He discussed each patient in detail and asked everyone what they thought. He'd turn to you and say, 'Well, Doc (Cameron called all doctors 'Doc.'), what do you think?' and then ask the nurses for their opinions."

A Rockefeller Foundation observer, in Montreal for a progress report on a grant they had given Cameron, noted his aloofness, adding that it seemed to "nourish his need for power." The power that Cameron wielded helped maintain a distance from his co-workers. No one ever slapped Ewen Cameron on the back and asked him if he wanted to go out for a beer. "People were aware of what Cameron could do to advance their careers." One former resident said, "The residents were like little boys trying to please their father." He solicited everyone's opinion but he did not react well to criticism. "Cameron knew how to use power and he wouldn't tolerate any assaults on it. A male patient once spat on Cameron when he was talking to a women's auxiliary group in the hallway. He had the man thrown out of the institute."

The nurses who worked at the Allan recall a less severe man. "We loved him," said one nurse. "He had a wonderful sense of humour. He made you work though." His relationship with the nurses was a mixture of paternalism and flirtation. He called them all "lassie." Alena Valdstyn, nursing director at the Allan for nine years, said, "There was a magnificence about Cameron; patients wanted to be touched by him, even the patients of other doctors."

"He was an ideas man," says Dr. Carlo Bos, a colleague still at the Allan. "He carried around these library cards full of ideas he'd thought up at night. One morning, I remember, he came in with about forty of them."

Cameron loved gadgets and when a reasonably portable, twenty-pound recording device came along he purchased it. He dictated his ideas into this dictabelt, a clumsy prototype to the cassette recorder, on his way to work in the morning. He would barrel north on Highway 87 in his black Cadillac, the sun barely up and the road to himself, with one hand on the wheel and the other on the microphone. When he arrived at eight a.m., he gave the belts to a secretary to transcribe.

Cameron was a man of action; he got things done. He raised the necessary money, hired the right people, arranged conferences, and got papers published. Nothing piled up on his desk. Correspondence was returned promptly, contacts made and maintained, problems addressed as they came up. His reputation for quick action spread and doctors in other parts of the country began to refer difficult patients to him. In psychiatric parlance, patients who did not respond to prescribed techniques were failures. Failures began to arrive at the Allan from other parts of Canada, the northeastern U.S. and, occasionally, Europe.

Cameron himself travelled widely, he attended conferences, delivered papers and visited other psychiatric institutions. A Greek colleague asked him after he'd returned from a trip to Greece, what he had thought about the ruins in Athens. Not much, it turned out. They were, after all, ruins.

In 1950, Cameron helped to establish the Canadian Mental Health Association and served as Chairman of the Scientific Planning Committee. Two years later, he was elected president of the American Psychiatric Association, a lofty honour, where he made his mark by implementing a number of dramatic reforms.

Cameron recruited students from abroad and, by 1953, students in his program came from eleven different countries. Recalling this era, Dr. Robert Cleghorn, the psychiatrist who succeeded Cameron in 1964, wrote, "There was a general feeling that psychiatry was leaping ahead; hope abounded and McGill was felt to be in the forefront not only in Canada but the world."

Sir David Henderson, a Scottish doctor who had taught Cameron in Edinburgh, visited the Allan and attended a lunch in Cameron's honour. He surveyed the institute his former student had built and turned to his lunch companion. In the booming voice of encroaching deafness he said, "He's done very well for a man who hasn't overcome his adolescent troubles."

CHAPTER TWO

THE NUREMBERG CODE

In the wake of the criminal excesses of the Nazis in the Second World War, an international tribunal was set up at Nuremberg to establish guilt and dictate punishment. One of the first Nazis to be tried, in October 1945, was Rudolf Hess. Hess's defence attorney, Von Rohrscheidt, requested that the defence be allowed to appoint a psychiatric expert from a Swiss university to examine Hess. Von Rohrscheidt hoped that Hess would be declared insane and thus be declared unfit to stand trial. The tribunal rejected Von Rohrscheidt's request, establishing instead their own commission of psychiatric experts from the Allied countries. Ewen Cameron was appointed as assistant to American representative Nolan Lewis.

In 1944, Hess had parachuted alone into England, on his own initiative. His aim was to talk Winston Churchill into an early surrender, thus curtailing the needless bloodshed that would mark what Hess felt to be the inevitable Nazi victory. He told his English captors that the Nazi air raids on London pained Hitler deeply. As an impromptu envoy, Hess explained that if only England were aware of Hitler's respect and compassion for their nation, they would come to a speedy agreement with him. The English listened to his ramblings and then assigned Major Douglas Kelly, an army psychiatrist, to his case. In prison, whenever he was questioned on uncomfortable issues, Hess claimed that he suffered from amnesia, and he periodically experienced paranoia. Kelly had a year to examine him, but failed to make a clear diagnosis. He noted the amnesia and paranoid tendencies (Hess saved samples of food and medicine later to be used as evidence that the British were trying to poison him), but declared in his report that he remained unconvinced that all Hess's symptoms were genuine.

The American psychiatric team at Nuremberg, including Cameron and the eminent French psychiatrist Dr. Jean Daley, stated in their assessment, filed on November 20, 1945, that "Rudolf Hess is not insane at the present time in the strict sense of the word." Their opinion was echoed by the British and the Russian teams and by Hess, who declared himself sane and responsible for his actions, and who admitted that he had faked his amnesia. Hess stood trial and was found guilty of crimes against humanity and was incarcerated at Spandau prison, where he remains, its only prisoner, guarded by a rotating cadre of Allied soldiers.

One of the methods used to ascertain Hess's mental health was a series of Rorschach prints, ink-blot designs that are interpreted by the patient. Copies of Hess's Rorschach tests made the psychiatric rounds in the years following the war, enabling various North American psychiatrists to make their own judgments on the celebrated case. Dr. Heinz Lehmann and Dr. Donald Ross of the Verdun Protestant Hospital in Montreal received copies of the tests, and in October, 1947, sent their results to Cameron. Ross diagnosed Hess as schizophrenic, Lehmann submitted the opinion that Hess's Rorschachs "pointed to a diagnosis of schizophrenic personality disintegration."

Because of the uniqueness of the case, Hess's diagnosis was widely debated. One critic of the diagnosis was Clifford Scott, an analyst colleague of Cameron's at the Allan. Scott wrote an article entitled "The Psychiatric Tragedy of Rudolf Hess," that claimed Hess was obviously schizophrenic. The article argued that Hess was treated as an experimental subject rather than a human being; that he was studied rather than treated. Scott concluded that the Nuremberg Commission psychiatrists were guilty of "the sin of omission — they omitted to treat the patient." This quote was underlined in heavy black pencil on a copy of Scott's article that exists among Cameron's personal papers.

Scott wasn't the only critic of Hess's treatment. Winston Churchill, in *The Second War: The Grand Alliance*, wrote:

> Reflecting upon the whole of the story [Hess's], I am glad not to be responsible for the way in which Hess has been and is being treated. Whatever may be the moral guilt of a German who stood near to Hitler, Hess had, in my view, atoned for this by his completely devoted and frantic deed of lunatic benevolence. He came to us of his own free will, and, though without authority, had something of the quality of an envoy. He was a medical case and not a criminal case, and should be so regarded.

No consensus was ever reached on the Hess case and he was reputed to have outgrown whatever personality disorder he had at the time of his trial. "These types of cases often have a tendency to straighten out some time in their fifties," Dr. Lehmann said. All that remains on which to judge Hess are his Rorschach tests, a tool that has lost some of its currency as a diagnostic technique. Although still used, it is usually to corroborate a diagnosis that has been made using other means.

In 1945, the political stakes resting on Hess's sanity were high. A plea of insanity would have absolved Hess of any moral responsibility — an issue that was at the heart of the Nuremberg Trials. Hess was one of the first Nazis to be tried, and the order had been partly determined on the basis of media impact. Were Hess to be declared insane, it would diminish the Commission's moral clout.

Certainly there was a degree of stage management in the proceedings at the Nuremberg Trials. In a series of government memos marked confidential, a distinct game plan was mapped out regarding the objectives, press treatment, and pitfalls to be avoided at the trials. It was recommended that major war criminals be given "fair but expeditious trials, emphasizing the moral guilt of the Germans by building up the trial as an historic event." Among the instructions listed in the memo were, "Do not give the impression that the outcome of the trial is a foregone conclusion," and "Do not report passionately or preach; let the facts speak for themselves whenever possible and give the impression that it is up to the Germans to draw their own conclusions."

As Hess had been examined by the British for a year before Nuremberg, news of his case had percolated through the psychiatric world prior to Cameron's opportunity to examine him. There was, says a colleague, a climate of doubt surrounding the legitimacy of Hess's disorder. "The feeling was that the Nuremberg psychiatrists had a bias before they examined Hess, a pre-formed notion that he knew what he was doing. They were not inclined to find him psychotic." The colleague recalls thinking it was odd as Hess had once experienced a transient psychotic episode, pointing to a diagnosis of schizophrenia.

Back in Montreal, Cameron reported that Hess was a strange case and that he had had trouble communicating with him. Hess's co-operation with the examining doctors was fleeting. Cameron's most vivid impression of Nuremberg was the ability of one of the Russian psychiatrists to predict that Hess would become lucid when he took the stand. Hess did just that, renouncing his insanity as fraudulent to the court. The colleague felt that Cameron wished he had made the prediction himself.

Cameron wrote a paper on his experience entitled "Nuremberg and its Significance." In it he stated that the Nazi regime could never have established itself in a healthy society. The question of an individual's responsibility to society was of ongoing interest to Cameron and he warned against the type of hierarchy the Nazis had constructed — one that replaced individual responsibility with blind loyalty. Great numbers of Nazis at Nuremberg had declared that they had done nothing wrong, that they were only following orders. Cameron understood the subtle development of the Nazi regime, warning that "it is clear that it is not simply against future conspiracies of evil men which we have to guard ourselves, but it is ourselves, against weaknesses in our social order, in our ways of living against which we have to be on continued guard."

In the second year of the Nuremberg trials, from October 1946, to July 1947, the tribunal dealt with the doctors who had staffed the concentration camps. This second set of trials, often referred to as the Medical Trials, investigated human experimentation and genocide that took place in German concentration camps, and the doctors responsible.

Nazi ideology was partly based on a biomedical vision of the racial purity of Aryan people. To legitimize that vision it was necessary for doctors to play a prominent role in the Nazi Weltanschauung, searching for biological evidence to support the claim of Aryan superiority.

The Nazis were meticulous record-keepers and through surviving records and the testimony of concentration camp survivors — a number of whom were doctors themselves — a horrifying account of medical atrocities was presented to the world. Millions had died in the gas chambers and thousands of others had died by phenol injection, usually administered by the doctors themselves. For the deaths by injection, a death certificate was issued listing a false cause in an attempt to cover up the murders.

The extent of the doctors' experimentation came out during the trials, revealing a program of experimental abuse unprecedented in medical history. A series of experiments carried out for the benefit of the Luftwaffe (the German Air Force) investigated the effects of cold water on downed pilots. Prisoners were immersed in freezing water until they died; the time required to do so was duly noted by a researcher. Experiments were also conducted on the effect of sitting naked in snow for fourteen hours. Some prisoners were shot in order to study the effects of untreated gunshot wounds, and others injected with typhus or other toxic substances so the effects could be observed.

In a November 1942 letter, Heinrich Himmler wrote to Field Marshall Erhard Milch, Inspector General of the Luftwaffe, that a pocket of opposition among the doctors had been noted. "In these 'Christian medical circles' " Himmler wrote, "the standpoint is being taken that a young German aviator should be allowed to risk his life, but that the life of a criminal . . . is too sacred and one should not stain oneself with this guilt." Nevertheless, Nazi doctors, even those from "Christian medical circles" carried out terminal experiments on prisoners, often trying desperately to rationalize their work as being of scientific value.

Not all Nazi doctors had trouble with their role as state-sanctioned murderers. Josef Mengele, the most notorious of the Nazi doctors, seized the situation as an opportunity to make a scientific reputation for himself. His work with twins, involving endless measurement of their respective features and eventually death and dissection for most, was his main area of interest. But he also tinkered with the question of blue eyes and the unfortunate lack of them in some cases (including his own). Mengele injected the eyes of seven-year-old boys with methylene blue to test the possibilities of a cosmetic approach to Aryan determinism.

Dr. Bruno Weber, head of the Hygenic Institute on the outskirts of Auschwitz, carried out chemical brainwashing experiments for the Gestapo. The Nazis were frustrated with their crude and often unsuccessful methods of torturing prisoners — usually Poles — to extract information about comrades in the Resistance. It was suggested by the Gestapo that drugs might be effective. They believed that the Russians had used drugs to obtain confessions at the Moscow show trials in 1936 with chilling effect. There, hardened Bolsheviks delivered grovelling confessions to crimes they could not have committed and for which they were subsequently executed.

Weber was given the task of coming up with a drug that would be effective in obtaining confessions from hardened Polish prisoners. Working with Dr. Viktor Capesius, the Chief S.S. pharmacist, Weber tried various barbituates and morphine derivatives. They were observed giving "a coffee-like substance" to four prisoners, two of whom died that night. It was widely believed that mescaline was one of the substances used in Weber's experiments.

Similar experiments were conducted at Dachau under the direction of S.S. doctor Kurt Plotner. Plotner covertly administered mescaline to prisoners and noted the effects. A member of Plotner's research team, Walter Neff, was later interrogated by the American Office of Strategic Services (OSS) who had been looking for a "truth drug" themselves. What was currently held to be a "truth drug," sodium pentathol, had been demonstrated as unreliable. After talking to Neff, the OSS prepared a report entitled "Technical Report no. 331-45, German Aviation Research at the Dachau Concentration Camp." The report was submitted to the head of the truth-drug committee, Dr. Winfred Overholser, at St. Elizabeth's Hospital and was not made public. Not until 1951, when the CIA began in earnest its research into the interrogation potential of LSD, did the results of the Dachau experiments surface.

As a result of the medical nightmare of the German concentration camps the prosecutions' closing arguments at Nuremberg on July 14, 1947, included a proposed set of rules for future human experimentation. This set of rules, suggested in what amounted to their final form by Dr. Leo Alexander, a Boston psychiatrist who was a consultant to the prosecuting team, were presented to the military tribunal and subsequently adopted by the American Medical Association as the Nuremberg Code. The first and most important tenet of that code reads:

> The voluntary consent of the human subject is absolutely essential. This means that the person involved should have legal capacity to give consent; should be so situated as to be able to exercise free power of choice, without the intervention of any element of force, fraud, deceit, duress, overreaching or other ulterior form of constraint or coercion; and should have sufficient knowledge and comprehension of the elements of the subject matter involved as to enable him to make an understanding and enlightened decision. This latter element requires that before the acceptance of an affirmative decision by the experimental subject there should be made known to him the nature, duration, and purpose of the experiment; the method and means by which it is conducted; all inconveniences and hazards reasonably to be expected; and the effects upon his health or person which may possibly come from his participation in the experiment. The duty and responsibility for ascertaining the quality of the consent rests upon each individual who initiates, directs

or engages in the experiment. It is a personal duty and responsibility which may not be delegated to another with impunity.

Nine other points were outlined that supported the notion of voluntary consent and the responsibility of the researcher in conducting experiments on humans.

Despite the widespread media attention given the trials and the adoption of the Nuremberg Code by the American Medical Association, it appeared to have little effect on the medical practices of the time. It wasn't until the early 1970s that the concept of informed consent was applied widely in North American research. The Nuremberg Code was never adopted as legislation and thus had no binding legal powers. Violators couldn't be prosecuted. Many doctors felt that it was simply an extension of the Hippocratic oath; a specific clause to deal with human experimentation that still ultimately left the doctor with his own conscience as judge.

Heinz Lehmann, a Montreal psychiatrist who was practising at the time of the code's adoption, suggested that it was more of a moral statement than a practical guideline. The code clarified certain principles for the researcher but no specific body was empowered to enforce them. The Nuremberg Code really was a political monument, erected to note the barbarous actions of the Nazi doctors. The magnitude of their deeds — the slaughter of millions — was incomprehensible and the code became a sort of moral epitaph.

The Nuremberg Code was updated in a succession of further medical codes. Great Britain's Medical Research Council issued a memorandum on clinical investigations in 1953, and, in 1962, issued a more extensive memorandum entitled, "Responsibility in Investigations on Human Subjects." Both these documents expanded on the theme presented at Nuremberg and outlined specific questions doctors should ask themselves before embarking on research with human subjects. The World Medical Association produced "The Declaration of Helsinki" in 1964, at the Eighteenth World Medical Assembly in Helsinki, Finland. It was revised in 1975, at the twenty-ninth meeting in Tokyo. It is the latter Helsinki document that has become the modern blueprint for medical ethics and clinical research on human beings. Although it is a much more comprehensive document than the Nuremberg Code, it incorporates all of the basic ideas laid out in 1946. The chief difference is that the Helsinki Declaration was supported by laws and agencies designed to enforce its dictates.

Without the clout of legislation, the various medical codes that preceded the Helsinki Declaration were ineffective in guaranteeing patient rights. Henry Beecher, a Boston psychiatrist, wrote in a 1966 paper, "There is a disturbing and widespread myth that 'codes' (all of which emphasize, above all else, consent) will provide some kind of security." Beecher argued that codes cannot allow for the contingencies of individual cases and pointed out that in dealing with the mentally ill, informed consent is not always possible. If the patient is deeply disturbed, a detailed explanation of his treatment may not register. The most important point Beecher made involved the notion of trust. "If suitably approached," he wrote, "patients will accede, on the basis of trust, to about any request their physician may make." In the 1950s there was still a strong element of paternalism in medicine and the fallibility of doctors had yet to be rigorously questioned or perhaps more importantly, litigated against. Most patients would do whatever their physician advised.

In the same paper, Beecher succinctly identified a major cause of unethical practices in medical research; the pressure to produce scientific papers. He wrote:

> Every young man knows that he will never be promoted to a tenure post, to a professorship in a major medical school unless he has proved himself an investigator. If the ready availability of money for conducting research is added to this fact, one can see how great the pressures are on ambitious young physicians.

Jockeying for position within the medical community could, theoretically, leave patients vulnerable to the personal and professional ambitions of the researcher.

Although Nuremberg failed to have a practical impact on medical ethics, it did have a significant impact on Cameron. It was a pivotal event for his own theories on social psychiatry and it was another political feather in his cap. Although he was not a senior figure at Nuremberg, he was, nevertheless, one of only ten psychiatrists, representing four countries, to examine a central Nazi figure. It was a great boost for his career, coming only two years after his appointment in Montreal.

CHAPTER THREE

PSYCHIATRY
THE NEW RELIGION

As the son of a Scottish Presbyterian minister, Ewen Cameron was witness to a considerable amount of flinty morality while he was growing up. The nineteenth century Presbyterian faith his father espoused didn't make too many allowances; sin wasn't graded on a scale and you weren't judged by degree. There was right and wrong, and no opportunity for absolution at the end of a corrupt life. And generally speaking, all lives were corrupt; it was the nature of man. The dour, ruddy-faced congregation who listened to the senior Cameron's fire and brimstone every Sunday accepted this as one more piece of bad news in a life long on hardships.

But Ewen rejected his father's religious beliefs. Dr. Brian Robertson, current director of the Allan states:

> Cameron rejected it completely; he was very much against organized religion. He felt it was the survival of a primitive morale. But you can't shed the Old Testament Jehovah that you've learned in the Scottish cirque, you can't get rid of [it] in one generation. You might modify it with psychoanalysis — which Cameron did not believe in — you might modify it in some sublimated form, but you rarely part with that view of the world, you can't get rid of it over a generation. Cameron believed he could.

As a scientist Cameron dismissed the crutch of organized religion as medieval dogma designed for superstitious peasants. He felt that science and religion were competing for the hearts and minds of men. Nowhere would the struggle be more dramatic than in Montreal, which boasted the scientific beacons of Wilder Penfield and McGill University as well as a permeating Catholic presence.

When Clifford Scott arrived from England to assume a post at the Allan Memorial in 1954, Cameron took him on a tour of the city in his enormous black Cadillac. Gliding through the historic section of Montreal, Cameron pointed to Notre Dame Church, "There's the competition," he said.

However, it can be argued that the beginnings of western psychiatry were built on a religious foundation. In 1409, Father Joffré, a Spanish priest in Valencia, walked to Mass one Sunday morning and came across the spectacle of a deranged man being tormented by a crowd of people. The man was mentally ill and, as such, the object of suspicion and derision. Father Joffré was moved by the scene and petitioned his parishioners to contribute money towards the care of the mentally afflicted. Enough money was raised to build the first insane asylum in the western world. The Church thus became the first institution to assume moral responsibility for the mentally ill, a disenfranchised group who were poorly understood and subject to medieval stigmas.

In twentieth-century North America, the state has taken over the task of administering to the sick, easing the church into a minor role. Quebec in the early part of this century was an exception. Five hundred years after Father Joffré's compassion became church policy, Quebec still held to his model. The Catholic Church ran most of the hospitals, orphanages, mental asylums, and welfare agencies in the province. In the 1940s, it was the single most powerful force in Quebec. The Church administered the educational and social welfare systems and had a hand in labour unions, the news media, politics, and the arts. The nuns of Providence ran the St-Jean de Dieu Hospital, that housed as many as six thousand psychotics, neurotics, alcoholics, mad aunts and disturbed sinners. The church was the arbiter of right and wrong and reserved the right to extend its role of moral interpreter in every aspect of Quebec life. The curriculum in schools was tailored to a Catholic viewpoint, forcing an ecclessiastical perspective on the study of mathematics, philosophy and history.

The Church was able to operate largely free of state interference on the basis of an unwritten concordat with Maurice Duplessis's Union Nationale government. Duplessis, the premier of Quebec, modelled his government's role in social welfare on that of seventeenth-century France. The state encouraged and supported the initiative of non-government concerns to deal with the expensive problem of social welfare, supplying funding when necessary, but without taking on the role of overseer. Duplessis was acutely aware that the limited funds he made available to the Church for this purpose were a fraction of what it would cost the province to assume the role of benefactor. If the Church wanted the lame, the old and the insane, they were welcome to them. It was a happy trade-off; few of those afflicted represented votes, but all of them represented souls.

Duplessis awarded the institutions a minimal *per diem* rate based on the patient population. At the time of Cameron's arrival in Montreal, it was approximately seventy-five cents per day per patient. With that stipend, the hospital had to feed, clothe, shelter, and treat the individual. Seventy-five cents went further in 1943 than it does now, certainly, but it nowhere near covered the distance asked of it. The shortfall was made up by a draconian administration and the commercial instincts of enterprising nuns.

The Allan Memorial Institute opened in 1944, the same year that Maurice Duplessis's Union Nationale party took power in Quebec for the second time, having enjoyed a three-year term before being ousted by the Liberals in 1939. Maurice Duplessis was adept at integrating religious and cultural concerns and recognized the political uses of the Catholic Church. He recognized that a devout Catholic's unquestioning obedience to the Church could be translated into politics. Religion and culture were the overriding nationalist concerns in French-Quebec then, and Duplessis played on the fears that both could be threatened by a predominantly anglophone federal government in Ottawa unless he was able to go to bat for them. The rest of his power stemmed mostly from a political machine that used unlimited patronage and was prepared to practise corruption and intimidation during elections. When whisky, a new radio, or a cigar failed to win votes, violence was sometimes substituted as a vote gathering strategy. Indeed, campaigning required singular measures with Quebec's divided electorate. For example, a road through the Gatineau Hills was deliberately paved to service the Union Nationale's party faithful while avoiding the homes of errant Liberals. Engineered by electoral loyalties, it wound through the hills, erratically charting the geographical strengths of the Union Nationale; it proved to be one of the least safe highways in the province.

Duplessis and the Catholic Church co-existed like the crocodile and the Egyptian Plover — an impudent bird that, according to legend, flies into the jaws of the crocodile to remove leeches and food remnants from its teeth. These services appeal to the crocodile's self-interest; aware of the benefits, it refrains from snapping its jaws shut. In the same way, Duplessis's and the Church's relationship was symbiotic; the Church, for it's part, was given the freedom to educate as it saw fit and council its flock without government intervention. In return, Duplessis had the Church's tacit support.

By the 1950s, a number of factors conspired to loosen the Church's grip on the province. The urbanization of Quebec, the most dramatic such transformation in the country, helped to erode the rural power base of the Church. An emerging French nationalism, which stressed politics and economics as well as religion and culture, was drawing intellectuals away from the Church into a secular movement. Church attendance dwindled, fewer young people were drawn into the clergy as a career, and, consequently, its ranks thinned. University graduates instead chose professional careers, and lay people were increasingly called upon as teachers, replacing retiring brothers and nuns.

In the mid-fifties, there was some public dissension about the alliance between the Church and the government. In 1956, Abbé Gerard Dion and Abbé Louis O'Neill of Laval University published a condemnation of the "political immorality" in the province of Quebec in an obscure clerical publication, *Ad Usum Sacerdotum*. The article was picked up by *Le Devoir*, a major Montreal newspaper. It stated boldly that the church had grown tolerant of electoral abuses and was complacent about the corrupt Duplessis government. It was the first public criticism by clerics of a regime that used a mixture of paternalism and cattle prods to run the province, and which boasted the Church as an uncomfortable partner. The article caused a good deal of controversy and led to heated debates over just when Quebec "was going to emerge from the seventeenth century."

In 1959, a teaching brother, Jean-Paul Desbiens, wrote a letter to *Le Devoir* under the pseudonym Frère Untel, criticizing the Church's role in Quebec education. André Laurendau, editor of the paper, invited Desbiens to elaborate on his views. The result was a book entitled *Les Insolences du Frère Untel (The Insolence of Brother Anonymous)*, which appeared in 1960. Untel levelled charges at both Church and state:

> We are afraid of authority, we live in a climate of magic, where under penalty of death we must infringe no taboo, where we must respect all the knowledge, all of the conformities.

The book was strident in its criticism and suggested a series of reforms. It quickly became a bestseller, selling over one hundred thousand copies in Quebec. Unfortunately, Desbiens didn't remain anonymous for long and was shipped to Europe for a study trip by his angry superiors.

In 1961, a former patient of St-Jean de Dieu Hospital, Jean-Charles Pagé, published a book entitled, *Les Fous crient au secours (The Mentally Ill Cry for Help)*. It exposed the abuses at the Catholic mental facility, St-Jean de Dieu, and signalled the end of the church's hold on social welfare in Quebec. It also prompted the Bédard Commission, an investigative board of inquiry commissioned by the provincial government, to examine every mental health facility in Quebec.

When Cameron arrived in 1943, however, the clergy was still firmly in the driver's seat. The lack of government interest in mental health facilities extended to the Allan. "Duplessis's Quebec was a one-man dictatorship," said a doctor/psychiatrist who had worked at the Allan in the 1950s. "He ran a lot of things but he left a lot of things alone. Cameron could operate free of bureaucratic interference and still get some money from them. The government didn't ask any questions."

Cameron was struck by the Catholic presence in Montreal. Their impressive structures dominated the city's architectural landscape. Indeed, the Catholic Church was the largest landowner in Montreal. Cameron quickly became aware of another aspect of the Catholic presence, which he noted in an early paper. Cameron had come from the Albany Hospital and commented on the differences between the psychiatric patients he had treated in New York and those who came from all over Quebec to the newly opened Allan Memorial. In Albany, the hospital had admitted proportionately more patients with depressive and manic reactions; at the Allan they encountered great numbers of anxious, guilt-ridden and hostile patients.

He concluded that the reason for this difference was that in Quebec, "a moralistic evaluation of living is much more dominant than in the Albany area; 'good' and 'evil,' 'sin' and 'conscience' are considerably more active issues than they are in most other parts of the continent." Cameron correctly perceived what was happening in Quebec. Rural Catholics, who had been taught to take baths in a shirt and pants to avoid sinful exposure of their own flesh, had migrated to Montreal, attracted by the employment opportunities. Once in the big city, they were exposed to situations that conflicted with their moralistic upbringing. For some, the anxiety produced by the clash of their religious education and the temptations of Montreal proved to be crippling. Significant numbers found themselves at the Allan seeking treatment.

The Allan had no religious affiliation; it was part of an academic institution and, as such, Cameron felt, should be on the cutting edge of psychiatric innovation. Church institutions were largely custodial, and they lacked the funds to attract top professionals. Those they did attract rarely had the time or initiative for research after personally dealing with hundreds of patients. Research was confined to administering another shipment of the latest barbiturate and watching to see which patients would quieten down. But at the Allan Memorial, Cameron wanted to push the frontiers of science forward, and to do that certain old beliefs and stale traditions would have to be ploughed under.

*   *   *

Cameron subscribed to his former teacher Adolf Meyer's belief that the "individual is not an entity complete in itself, but that it has functions meaningless save in interaction with others." In the 1940s, there was a growing awareness in psychiatry that various social groups — family, friends, church, peers — with whom an individual is associated, help to shape his personality. In 1947, Cameron wrote:

> We see that a group set up in one way will produce a preponderance of personalities which are definitely hostile; another arrangement will produce individuals whose trend is toward conformity with tradition and who bitterly resist all innovation; still another arrangement of a group will produce an excess of sexually deviated personalities.

Cameron hoped that by understanding the ways in which individuals were shaped by social structures, it would be possible to alter or influence those structures to "exercise a positive control." Meyer had argued the need to study the patient as part of his environment. Cameron took this concept one step further by suggesting the environment should also be changed.

Cameron felt that society often rewarded behaviour that was, in fact, symptomatic of psychiatric problems. In a 1947 speech to the Canadian Dietetic Association, he broached the topic of the "nice girl."

> Let me talk about a type which has not been found out by society, and which is comprised of damaged and potentially harmful personalities, to which, however, society still gives approval and prestige. This type is the "nice girl." Now she is still so highly regarded that it is necessary for me to hurry and say that I mean "nice" in the worst sense of the word. She is the sort of girl who is so nice that she can never do

anything that her mother would not want her to do. She is so nice that there are many people with whom she cannot deal, there are many aspects of living which she cannot think about, much less talk about. She prides herself on keeping herself to herself and will not discuss with anyone what she considers to be her own affairs. She is the sort of person that mother's describe as "such a sweet girl" and from whom these mother's sons back away with disrespectful unanimity. If her mother does succeed in getting her married, she is just as sexually frigid as you would expect.

Cameron suggested that:

We go boldly up to the "nice girl" and despite her outraged cries and those of all the other "nice girls" — of whatever age or sex — push her around a bit, pull off some of those wrappings of nicety and propriety, and quite dispassionately look her over and see what she is like.

Cameron further stated that what he found under the wrappings was "extremely unsound, unhealthy and curiously reminiscent of the stuffy, unventilated and often downright smelly and fetid bedrooms of the Victorian period."

A year later, in 1948, in his book *Life is for Living*, Cameron accurately predicted the nature and the date of the sexual revolution of the 1960s. His enlightened views were not unique among his colleagues in the medical profession. They were, however, provocative to much of the general population in Quebec. Not everyone was ready to see the "nice girl" exposed.

In 1949, Cameron presented a paper to the Bronx Society of Neurology and Psychiatry in New York in which he focussed on the cultural barriers to successful psychotherapy. He stated that belief systems that had strongly influenced an individual were deeply rooted and posed problems for psychiatric treatment. He invoked the comparison he had made three years earlier between Quebec patients and those he had treated in Albany, stressing that in Montreal there was a conflict between behaviour and exacting religious mores that produced guilt and resulted in anxiety. Where psychotherapy was used in treatment, the therapist was hindered by what Cameron termed "the patient's moralism." Many of the Quebec patients had been conditioned to seek moral solutions to what Cameron felt were behavioural problems. Within the Church there were well-marked areas of "good behaviour" and "bad behaviour." If members behaved badly — sinned — they atoned. Cameron was frustrated by the fact that psychiatric problems could so easily be dismissed as moral problems that were considered outside his jurisdiction.

Cameron told the Bronx Society that:

> Although in our society, the rights of physical torture are now denied to the exponents of the religious systems, the rights of threat and intimidation, the right to terrify and misinform the young are still conceded to them.

A colleague said of Cameron:

> Cameron insisted he was an atheist. I don't think he was, though. He screamed about it all the time. It was the one subject he couldn't discuss without losing his temper. One day we had a meeting at the Allan regarding fees. One doctor said, "What do we do about charging the clergy?" Cameron responded immediately. "Charge them double." He was a missionary about atheism. I don't think he had gotten religion out of his system; he was still battling out his religious stance. My guess is that he had God and his father mixed up and I don't think he had a lot of use for either one.

Outside the medical community, Cameron at first tempered his criticism of religious beliefs and practices. He spoke of outdated traditions but he didn't necessarily name religion as a culprit. In 1948, he addressed a parent's meeting at St. George's School:

> In particular, we have to be especially critical of those systems of belief, those social institutions, which make excessive use of anxiety and guilt to control people. We are beginning to recognize that our social institutions, our systems of belief, are our inventions. If we invented them once then we can certainly invent and build up better ones.

Through the 1940s and early 1950s, Cameron developed this theme in dozens of papers and speeches, becoming increasingly specific about where the problem lay — the Church — and where the solutions could be found — psychiatry. "Cameron firmly believed, and he was not alone, that psychiatry had *the* answer to moral problems," Dr. Brian Robertson commented.

Given the religious influences in Montreal and the widening circle of Cameron's psychiatric evangelism, it was just a matter of time before his views became public knowledge. On April 24, 1951, he delivered a speech to the Rotary Club of Montreal that sparked a bitter public controversy. Overestimating the vision and tolerance of the local chapter, Cameron proposed to the Rotarians that the "moralistic system" was responsible for many of society's current problems, including the growing threat of communism. "In the thinking of some of our groups who are particularly indoctrinated with this moralistic viewpoint," he told his audience, "one actually finds the belief that evil is an integral part of man's nature and hence, being by nature evil, he must inevitably fall into evil ways." He went on to develop the theme of guilt being used as a control by the Church, which in turn produced anxiety, a point he had made in earlier speeches. He expanded his philosophy with the Rotarians, however, to cite conversion to communism as a possible result of that anxiety:

> It would be idle to say that communism spreads only by means of naked force or because, in contrast to ourselves, Communists are ruthless, unscrupulous, unresting in their hatred, to do so would be to fall into the trap of our own moralism. Vast numbers of men . . . have turned willingly to communism. They have found in its collectivism, an escape from anxiety. They have turned from freedom to authority. In their deep-down insecurity they have been glad to trade personal direction for the reassurance of being told what to do, for the warm comfort of head-down unity in the huddling herd. The solution to frustration, anxiety and other problems lays not in communism, but in an insistent demand that we be concerned with what is and not with what some system claims should be, in regard to human behaviour.

Nineteen fifty-one was a banner year for anti-Communist sentiment; the Korean War was being fought and the activities of American Senator Joe McCarthy were well-publicized. A year earlier, McCarthy had publicly stated that there were fifty-seven card-carrying Communists working in the U.S. state department. Although his charges proved to be unfounded, his campaign to drag domestic Communists out from under every bed in America helped fuel a national paranoia about the perceived Communist threat.

In Montreal, religion had always held the potential for emotional debate. Cameron had taken both issues, wrapped them up together, and delivered them to the staid enclave of the local Rotary Club. They weren't too interested in hearing that the Church of the Ascension's eleven o'clock service was turning the congregation into Communists.

The next day, the Montreal *Gazette* reported the speech under the headline "Moralistic attitude in behaviour makes us red, says psychiatrist." The speech quickly prompted hostile reactions. The Anglican Church interpreted Cameron's views as a direct attack and responded angrily in the April 25th edition of *The Gazette*. Canon W. H. Davison labelled Cameron's speech "frightful heresy" and said it struck at the very basis of the Christian religion. The Anglican Bishop of Montreal, John Dixon, called Cameron's views "fundamentally atheistic, a denial of the existence and the grace of God." Cameron had stated in his speech that "man was limitlessly capable, through his own powers, of changing his habits and ways in the direction of more effective and socially effective living." Dixon branded him a secular humanist and was quoted in *The Gazette* as saying, "purely secular humanism [is] the expression of man's basic sickness, the disease of pride and self-sufficiency . . . Secular humanism dethrones God and enthrones man. But man has never made a success of being his own god."

The issues raised by Cameron did not disappear quickly from the public eye. Public criticism of Cameron continued to make the news for a few weeks, unfortunately coinciding with a fund-raising campaign of the Royal Victoria Hospital, which administered the Allan. Some Church leaders asked how, in good conscience, they could urge Christian congregations to support the campaign, given Cameron's atheism. Bishop Dixon, however, cautioned that the two shouldn't be tied together and that the hospital should not be made to suffer. Senator A. K. Hugessen joined Dixon in a plea to separate the two issues; refusing to fund the hospital would only hurt the infirm, he reasoned.

Cameron's views were first presented in the media as essentially an argument between science and religion. Yet the scientific community offered no public support of Cameron's position. After all, there was the delicate situation of the Royal Victoria Hospital's fund-raising efforts to be considered. Any further comment from the scientific community would only exacerbate an emotional issue. But there were other reasons. Cameron had alienated some of the prominent scientists who might have come to his defence. Both Wilder Penfield and Dr. Donald Hebb, a McGill psychologist, were respected scientists, and both had running feuds with Cameron, or had at least clashed egos with him. Hebb refused to attend psychiatric meetings chaired by Cameron and would later publicly criticize Cameron's work. Aside from personal differences, there were those in the McGill scientific community who felt that Cameron was not necessarily representing the views of science.

Karl Stern, an Allan psychiatrist, had recently published his autobiography, *Pillar of Fire*, which dealt with his own religious experience. He was a Jew who had converted to Catholicism. The book, which was selling briskly, was the source of some ire to Cameron, according to a colleague. In his book, Stern had outlined a distinction between science and "scientism," writing that science was present knowledge, held in a spirit of responsible caution, while "scientism" was unproven dogma asserted with arrogance. Cameron felt the book was a personal attack and his relationship with Stern became strained. A few years later, Stern protested what he felt to be Cameron's "scientism." In a rare foray for a doctor, Stern approached Health and Welfare minister Paul Martin with his complaint and suggested that the Allan was not deserving of government support. Stern was a distinguished doctor and scholar and Martin gave his opinions some weight, concluding that "there may have been grounds for his complaints [but] I didn't feel they were one hundred percent substantial."

A Montreal *Gazette* editorial appearing on April 28 quoted from Stern's book and added that "Dr. Cameron does not necessarily speak with the voice of science. He may not even be regarded as speaking necessarily with the voice of psychiatry. What he is really doing is expressing the views of Dr. Cameron." Cameron was censured not just for his views but for the spirit in which they had been advanced. "This spirit seems to have the spirit of 'scientism' in a particularly extravagant form," read the editorial. "It has neither the responsible caution of science, nor the mellowed maturity of humanism. Scientific views expressed in this spirit are not only departures from moralism or religion. They are, even more, a departure from science."

The academic community also failed to rally to Cameron's cause. Herbert Quinn, a professor of political science at Sir George Williams College, submitted an article to *The Gazette* on May 2, entitled "The Philosophy of Dr. Cameron." Quinn dissected Cameron's remarks and suggested that "A careful reading of [Cameron's] address indicates quite clearly that in rejecting traditional morality, what he wants to do is substitute his own moral code." Quinn's wife was a social worker at the Allan at the time, working with the families of patients. After the Rotary Club speech, Quinn always referred to his wife's place of employment as "that pagan place."

In today's cultural climate, Cameron's speech would attract little attention, but in the Montreal of 1951 it created a heated controversy that enjoyed a long run on the cocktail circuit. A year later, the issue was still of sufficient interest that Paul Martin opened a National Health Department Advisory Committee meeting with the dictate that psychiatrists leave theology to the theologians and refrain from attacks on religion. He urged a spirit of co-operation and suggested that Cameron "work through the problems of mental health with religious leaders rather than make statements conflicting with the consciences of Roman Catholics, Protestants and Jews who believe in God."

The debate about moralism, communism, science, and religion railed on without Cameron's input. While Montreal's intellectuals and clerical spokesmen dissected his views, he walked back up the mountain to the Allan, obdurate and disappointed that so few were ready to discard the old ways. The board of directors of the Royal Victoria may have wanted to haul Cameron onto the carpet for almost scuttling their fund-raising campaign, but they didn't. He wasn't the type of man who could be summoned to the office like a schoolboy and given a good dressing down. He was the kind of man that a colleague would complain about privately to his wife, worrying that one day that grandiose son-of-a-bitch would get everyone into trouble. But they were careful who they confided in at work.

*   *   *

As a younger man, Cameron had used science to square off against religion but as *The Gazette* editorialist had pointed out, Cameron's views were not necessarily representative of science. Although Cameron had earlier supported the need for a scientific method in psychiatry, by 1951 his views had altered significantly. In 1931, he had argued that psychiatry needed to establish more exact methods of examination and measurement. Subjective descriptions and intuition were of little use if they did not withstand the rigors of experimentation and could not be used to predict further results. Cameron felt that psychiatry could benefit from a solid set of precepts; of classification, terminology, measurement and diagnosis. It was a problem he examined in greater detail in his book, *Objective and Experimental Psychiatry*. He described how the "hard" sciences, such as chemistry and physics, had grown through an expanding set of verifiable truths that could be used in further experimentation and proposed that psychiatry do the same.

By 1948, Cameron had revised this opinion. He felt that the objective methodology of the "hard" sciences was, in fact, restricting when applied to psychiatry. Chemistry and mathematics dealt with absolute truths and Cameron had come to feel there were few absolute truths in matters concerning the human organism. In his paper "The Current Transition in the Conception of Science" (1948), Cameron advocated an "open system . . . one in which there are no final facts, no unchanging truths, where everything is relative and conditional . . . " He pointed out that "in the laboratory, the world, with all its contaminations, its uncontrollable variables, its uncertainties which simply would not submit themselves and be qualified, was shut out."

Cameron concluded that psychiatry ultimately fell between the medical and social sciences. He wrote:

> Psychiatrists have a special responsibility to act as leaders and guides in entering and opening up new territory. We have the responsibility not only to create the new tools and the new concepts, but we also have the most serious duty to assist in finding means to destroy the old and obstructionist. It is one of the graver lessons of our times that the new, the more liberal, the more effective, does not immediately succeed without our active assistance in driving out the old, the harmful and the entrenched.

Cameron seemed often to oppose prevailing opinion. In 1931, his argument for scientific experimental methods in psychiatry was a new one, and not readily accepted by everyone. By 1951, however, there was a strong movement in psychiatry towards the principles of scientific method. There was increasing support for pursuing research to discover an organic cause for certain mental illnesses, and a growing body of experimental techniques to test the organic theory. But Cameron had abandoned his stance on the scientific method. He saw psychiatry as a science, but also as the main force for social change.

"It seems reasonable," he wrote, "that psychiatrists, together with their colleagues in the other sciences, will increasingly concern themselves with the planning of the kind of social organization — the goals, the rewards, the sanctions in which all men will live and in which they will seek expression of their needs."

*   *   *

An increasing number of schizophrenics and depressives were referred to the Allan for treatment. Cameron wanted a treatment that would get patients well, and get them well fast. As a researcher and a clinician,

Cameron was a pragmatist. He did what he thought would work. There were few effective treatments for these illnesses in the early 1950s, and the lines between research and treatment were blurred.

"Cameron was a 'do something' kind of person." said Dr. Robin Hunter, a former colleague, now at the Clarke Institute in Toronto. As the awareness of mental illness became more wide-spread, an awareness that Cameron had done much to excite, more government money was directed at the problem and more pressure was put on the psychiatric community to produce results. A January 18, 1949, memorandum from departmental officials to Paul Martin, the minister of health, outlined the scope of the problem:

> One person in eighteen to twenty will spend some part of his lifetime in a mental hospital. One person in ten of the general population will be incapacitated by some variety of mental disease at some time during his life.

Cameron had focussed money and attention on the problem of mental illness, and now he had to produce some results. "He felt the pressure of the time," said Hunter. "He was looking for a huge breakthrough."

Cameron's pragmatic approach to treatment had precedents in two widespread treatments of the time. Both electroshock treatment and insulin coma treatment, were used to treat schizophrenia, because they seemed to work. There was no clear scientific rationale about how or why they worked.

The isolation of insulin by Banting, Best and MacLeod in 1922 had launched a biological approach to the treatment of schizophrenia. Small doses of insulin were sometimes used to stimulate the appetite in people with chronic illnesses, including mental illness, and psychiatrists noted the beneficial effects of these doses on the moods of psychotic patients. Manfred Sakel (1900-1957) experimented with insulin and found that high doses appeared to diminish overactive states in psychotic patients. He developed this further in 1933, giving schizophrenics doses that were high enough to induce coma. Sakel published his results and the treatment was used in Europe with some encouraging results. Labelled insulin-shock treatment, it was not without hazards, among which were irreversible coma, circulatory and respiratory collapse. Doctors had to be highly skilled and the nursing effort required was intensive.

Insulin shock was not universally accepted by the psychiatric world, partly because the theoretical underpinnings were elusive. No one could come up with a clear reason why it worked. Cameron was the first in North America to try the treatment, introducing it at the Worcester State Hospital in 1937. However, because of the dangers, unreliability, high cost, and administrative problems with insulin shock, it enjoyed a relatively brief utility, losing ground by the 1950s and disappearing by the beginning of the next decade. It was largely superceded by more reliable methods of shocking the nervous system, such as electroshock.

Electroshock is still in use and remains controversial. Although it is less hazardous and much easier to administer than insulin shock, it has the well-documented side effect of memory loss, the permanence of which is still the subject of debate. Fifty years after Italian psychiatrist Ugo Cerletti introduced electroshock, there is still no firm consensus on why or how it works.

Both treatments appealed to Cameron's pragmatism. He was prepared to forego the scientific explanations of a treatment if it produced results. Cameron asked only that treatment would result in a patient who could function outside the institute. He didn't care if the methods withstood scientific testing. He wrote, "The experimenter is capable on the basis of his natural facilities of a far more subtle range of responses than any battery of tests." The experimental method had a sterilizing effect, he argued. Human behaviour was a messy business, you couldn't expect to make any sense of it by wading in there with a slide rule.

Cameron's practical approach, however, occasionally reached extremes that troubled his co-workers. A former resident recalled an incident that revealed the flaws in Cameron's approach. At the Allan there was a schizophrenic patient who was the son of a prominent Montreal family. One day he left the Allan, returned to the family home, closed the garage door, sat in the family car and turned on the engine. Overcome by the carbon monoxide, he slumped down in the seat, unconscious. He was rescued however and re-admitted to the Allan. Cameron examined him and noticed that his schizophrenic symptoms had disappeared. He remarked on this curious series of events to one of his residents.

"Get me a cylinder of carbon monoxide," Cameron told the man.

"You can't be serious. That stuff is lethal," the resident replied.

"I know about that. I've been reading up on it."

The resident was sceptical. It was a pretty tenuous connection. "Where would I get the carbon monoxide?" he asked.

"Canadian Liquid Air Limited," Cameron said, giving him the address on Sherbrooke Street.

The resident went down to Canadian Liquid Air and asked the clerk for a cylinder of carbon monoxide.

"What do you want it for?" the clerk asked suspiciously.

"Treating schizophrenics."

"You better talk to the manager."

The manager pointed out that carbon monoxide was extremely toxic and if they had a problem, it wouldn't be just the Allan Memorial's ass that was on the line, it would be his own. Moreover, the cylinders they had on the premises were industrial grade and he would need a purer concentration for whatever he was going to do with it.

"The industrial grade is one hundred dollars a cylinder but the good stuff is five hundred dollars," the manager said.

The resident returned to Cameron. "It doesn't look good," he said. "We can get the industrial grade for one hundred dollars but it's no good for experimental purposes. A purified cylinder will cost twenty-five hundred dollars."

"Twenty-five hundred dollars? We don't have twenty-five hundred bucks for one cylinder of carbon monoxide," Cameron said, dejected.

Relieved to be off the hook, the resident kept his exaggeration to himself. "I knew we could afford five hundred dollars but I was pretty sure he couldn't go as high as twenty-five hundred dollars," he recalled later. It was a cheeky manoeuvre for a resident and underlined the doubtful climate surrounding Cameron's experimental acumen.

Cameron's move away from a scientific method in psychiatry began in the 1940s and grew more pronounced as his career progressed. By 1963, a year before he left the Allan, Cameron's methods had become more of a departure from accepted methods and funding was no longer as readily available. Cameron became increasingly critical of scientific method, writing:

Using these experimental methods in studies of human behaviour prevent really crucial and vital problems from

— 43 —

being brought forward for study both because the experimenter himself shrinks from breaking with accepted methods and unless he conforms with a design in accordance with experimental methodology of the basic sciences, he can expect relatively little financial support.

Dr. Robert Cleghorn wrote in his memoirs:

It is tragic that [Cameron] did not follow the concept of object and experimental psychiatry which he early espoused with great rigour. Had he acquired some depth of scholarly and scientific learning, he might have created a synthesis of the scientific views to which he subscribed, but this would have meant subscribing to the wisdom of the authority of those great pioneers in psychiatry such as Kraepelin, Meyer and Freud, that is, to father figures, a thing he could not do. His life was too hurried and diffuse to pause long enough to determine what he was escaping.

Psychiatry was the new religion of the 1950s," said Dr. Humphrey Osmond, a psychiatrist now teaching in the U.S., "and Cameron wanted to become a part of it. He wanted to make his patients his own." If psychiatry was the new religion, Cameron had appointed himself High Priest. It was his aim to direct the future of the profession from his political vantage point.

CHAPTER FOUR

PSYCHIC DRIVING

A new wing was added to Ravenscrag in 1953, doubling the bed capacity of the Allan. The new rooms were bright, comfortable and each had a large mirror covering one wall. Cameron wanted to create the atmosphere of a hotel rather than a psychiatric hospital. He had been advised against installing the mirrors; they would be the first casualties of patients in psychotic rages and could become a hazard. Only one was broken though, surprising almost everyone. "Treat people like people and they will act that way," Cameron told his residents. "Treat them like animals and you will get animal behaviour in return." In one of the new rooms was a woman who had undergone a lobotomy. Cameron asked resident Ed Levinson to go in and talk to her and to mark the experience. "Don't ever do anything to someone that you can't reverse," he told Levinson after his conversation with the unresponsive woman.

The Allan was like a travelling repertory company where everyone had to take on a variety of roles. Cameron asked that doctors teach as well as carry a patient load, and he pushed for research and published results. "Cameron would hound us like hell to get abstracts into the hands of psychiatric associations," recalled Dr. Dancey. Dr. Lloyd Hisey, a big man with a relaxed air, resisted Cameron's prodding:

> I remember having an argument with Cameron and saying, "No, I'm not going to give that paper at the American Psychiatric Association." And he said, "You're not? Don't you ever want to become a professor here?" And I said, "Not particularly. In view of the way you have to juggle hospital politics and university politics, you're out there having to beg for money all over the place." But Cameron was good at begging money.

Although Cameron had explored a number of research possibilities in Brandon, Worcester, and Albany, he had yet to consolidate his energies into a single viable line of scientific inquiry. Most of his published papers dealt with his administrative innovations, such as the open-door hospital, or presented his personal philosophies. His first sustained area of research came about in 1952 and asked the question: can psychoanalysis be automated? Cameron was cool towards analytic procedures primarily because of their slowness rather than their principles. Patients often underwent psychoanalysis for years before a significant effect was noted. If the technique could be speeded up, perhaps it would become a practical therapy.

In March of 1948, Cameron heard of a recent innovation called "sleep teaching," a technique that eventually supplied him with the technology to try to speed up the process of psychoanalysis. He asked Hisey, then in charge of the EEG laboratory at the Allan, to look into it. Hisey wrote to the Linguaphone Institute in New York and asked for information on their newly-patented Cerebrophone, a sleep-teaching device. He received a reply from Max Sherover, the president of the Linguaphone Institute, outlining the progress they had made to date with the machine.

Sherover was an entrepreneur who had acquired the American rights to the British-owned Linguaphone Company in the 1930s. At that time, the Linguaphone Company was involved in teaching foreign languages with phonograph records. Sherover wondered what would happen if the records were played while students were sleeping. Maybe they would wake up remembering everything on the record. If it worked, years could be cut from the educational system; people could learn a new language every month, actors could memorize their lines overnight, calculus would be painless.

Sherover designed a crude prototype to facilitate his sleep-teaching theory. It was a suitcase-sized phonograph with a clock that could be preset to activate the phonograph at any time during the night. In 1946, psychologist Charles Eliot conducted preliminary tests at the University of North Carolina using a modified version of Sherover's machine that were encouraging. He cautioned though that the results were inconclusive and it was too early to predict that "tomorrow's university would be an inner spring mattress."

A more sophisticated experiment was conducted with a group of twenty chronic nail biters at an upstate New York summer camp. While they slept, a record repeated the single sentence, "My fingernails taste terribly bitter," six hundred times during the night. Thirty-three nights and two hundred thousand repetitions later, the first returns came in; one boy quit biting his nails. Two more had ceased the following weekend, and by summer's end another five had quit.

The machine was modified slightly, christened the Cerebrophone and launched onto the market. Testimonials flooded in; Spanish opera singer Ramon Vinay used it to perfect his Italian before facing the daunting audience at Milan's La Scala Opera House. He reported all traces of his Spanish accent gone. A German woman working for an American magazine lost her accent through repeated playings of "The White Cliffs of Dover." In a 1950 issue of *Time* magazine — one which also announced that Senator McCarthy was ready to name names of card-carrying Communists in the State Department, the success of the Cerebrophone was demonstrated with a photograph of Miss Washington of 1949 learning French in her sleep.

Sherover marketed his Cerebrophone for one hundred and twenty dollars, stating that, among other things, it could be used to learn languages, music, and morse code. The package included an underpillow speaker so that the sleep-learner could pursue his studies without disturbing others.

Hisey passed the information along to Cameron, who did little with it for the next few years. The concept of repetition as a therapeutic treatment appeared in a 1953 paper of Cameron's, "Unorthodox Working Concepts for Psychotherapy," but was not dealt with in any detail. "We had a machine built at the Allan," Hisey said, "and tried a bit of this sleep learning but I gave it up." It didn't appear to have much therapeutic application.

By the early 1950s the Cerebrophone had given way to the Dormaphone, an improved version of its predecessor. Despite enthusiastic advertisements, the device didn't seem to be fulfilling its early commercial promise. Concrete educational results were few, testimonials dwindled, and impatient consumers looked elsewhere to spend the fruits of their new prosperity. The Dormaphone died amid the sunnily marketed products of American know-how. The DeSoto had just come out with a tip-toe shifter, Ford introduced its one hundred horsepower V-8, the engine that "whispered while it worked," and sleep-teaching quietly disappeared from the consumer lexicon.

Scientific interest in sleep-teaching also waned, but Cameron felt that it held some promise. In 1953, he took some of the traits of Max Sherover's sleep-teaching technique and adapted them to an experimental treatment he called "psychic driving," initially an attempt to automate and intensify psychoanalysis. Cameron taped a therapy session with a patient, isolated what he felt to be a key passage, then played that message back to the patient repeatedly. The premise was that the repetition might break down psychological barriers that had been erected by the patient, forcing him to confront the suspected source of his problem.

In 1953, Cameron tried his psychic driving technique on a forty-year-old French-Canadian woman who was suffering from depression, the result of rejection by both her husband and her mother. Cameron isolated a thirty-second passage from her session that described a childhood incident where the woman's mother had threatened to abandon her if she didn't keep quiet. Cameron played the tape back to the woman, noting her reactions. After nineteen repetitions, the woman said, "Does it go on all the time? I hate to hear that — it upsets me; look at me shaking." After thirty-nine repetitions, she yelled, "Stop it! Stop it!" and made threatening hand gestures. But after forty-five repetitions, the woman poured out a stream of pent-up frustration. She spoke of her lifelong envy of a more popular sister, her own awkwardness with men, and her inability to stand up for herself. It was the sort of cathartic realization that might have taken months of analysis. It occurred to Cameron that had he stopped at thirty-nine repetitions, when the patient was yelling for him to stop, he would have quit only minutes away from success.

The technique of using the patient's own voice — a treatment Cameron termed autopsychic driving — quickly presented a few problems. He observed that people rarely liked the sound of their own voices and were disappointed by the frequent pauses and awkward syntax in their conversations. The message itself often produced a defensive reaction from the patients, and some refused to acknowledge the voice as their own. Not every patient would sit still and listen to a traumatic episode of their life recited to them in a voice that was foreign-sounding though uncomfortably and undeniably their own. One of the ways Cameron tried to overcome this resistance was to play the message to the patients while they were asleep. He induced a chemical sleep with a combination of drugs — Thorazine, Nembutal, Seconal and Veronal — then repeatedly played a record that had been made from the patients' sessions. The results were mixed, and Cameron reported that the messages seemed to have more impact when the patients were awake.

As a researcher, Cameron was not an innovator. He was a scientific magpie who read and travelled widely and picked up whatever shiny piece of work looked promising, then took it back to the Allan to apply to his own research. Psychic driving was to become a twelve-year project for Cameron, and in that time he borrowed from a number of sources, expanding and redefining his research mandate. In its early incarnation, Cameron borrowed not just from Max Sherover, but from the increasingly topical area of brainwashing.

The concept of brainwashing first came to the attention of the western world during the Moscow show trials of August 1936. Fifty-four leading Bolsheviks abased themselves with grovelling confessions to crimes they could not have committed, and for which they were subsequently convicted of treason and shot in Lubianka prison. The question arose of how hardened party members could have been coerced into zealously denouncing their ideals at a public trial, the outcome of which was never in doubt. Incarcerated in Lubianka prison for months before the trial, they were tortured on "the conveyor," a disorientation technique, in which lack of food and sleep was alternated with interrogations to enhance suggestibility. The months that Stalin's prosecutors had to prepare for the case and the ruthlessness of the torturers resulted in a horrifying judicial sham. When Nicolai Bukharin, a leading Bolsehvik, deviated from the script prepared by the prosecution, his comrades denounced him. A group psychology had developed among the accused Bolsheviks, a dynamic so forceful, that it would last for the duration of the trials.

In 1949, the Hungarian government put Josef Cardinal Mindszenty on trial, and he confessed to crimes of treason that he apparently did not commit, recalling the tenor of the Moscow show trials. Mindszenty's zombie-like appearance caused concern among western intelligence agencies; a CIA security memorandum declared that "some unknown force" had controlled him. The CIA was sufficiently nervous about the unknown force to send the head of scientific intelligence to Europe to investigate the Soviets' interrogation methods.

The term *brainwashing* came into the language in 1950 when Edward Hunter, a CIA operator working as a journalist, wrote an article for the *Miami News* entitled, "Brainwashing tactics force Chinese into ranks of Communist Party." The word was taken from the Chinese *hsi-nao*, meaning "to cleanse the mind."

Brainwashing quickly became the subject of public paranoia, military concern, and scientific curiosity. Psychiatrists were compelled by the possibility that techniques to produce political conversion could perhaps be used therapeutically to effect a conversion from psychotic behaviour to normal behaviour. Cameron introduced the topic in his lectures and commented often to colleagues about brainwashing. "This brainwashing business, Doc," he said to one resident, "If we knew more about it, maybe we could use it to help some of these people." Not much was known about the actual techniques of the Communists, but it was suspected that they used a combination of isolation and indoctrination. The prisoner was kept isolated for an extended period, exposed to cold, hunger and fear, and eventually allowed to join his interrogator. In a state of vulnerability, the prisoner was susceptible to the demands of his interrogator, often the first human being with whom he had contact for weeks.

Brainwashing was a method of breaking down existing belief systems and replacing them with others. Cameron's psychic driving was designed to do the same thing by breaking down existing patterns of behaviour and replacing them with other, more productive patterns. In 1955, Cameron presented his psychic driving therapy to the one hundred and eleventh annual meeting of the American Psychiatric Association in Atlantic City. Ever aware of the power of publicity, he also presented the technique to the general public in a *Weekend Magazine* article entitled, "Psychiatrists Develop Beneficial Brainwashing."

Above the title was a photograph of an anguished looking woman wearing headphones. Beside her a psychiatrist looked on with detached scientific interest, his hand adjusting the knob on what looked like a transformer for a model train set. The caption read, "Patient listens to her own voice repeat its 'confession' over and over again as the psychiatrist notes her reaction." Psychic driving was described as a "daring idea designed to help neurotic patients rebuild their damaged personalities by using a modified form of brainwashing."

Discussing his new therapy in *Weekend*, Cameron said, "Any technique that can leave a persisting imprint on one's mind, even if it is only used in treatment, can certainly cast light on what we perceive is done under the heading of brainwashing." He said that he faced the same problem as "professional brainwashers" in that patients, like prisoners, tended to resist the treatment and tried to defend themselves against the unpleasant impact of their own words repeated to them. Despite these difficulties, Cameron reported that all of the patients who had undergone psychic driving had benefitted. In the optimistic prose of the day the article stated that "In the past two years, more than one hundred persons have thus been successfully brainwashed — Canadian style." The article ended by describing how the dynamic implant — the actual message being repeated — stayed with the patient until he had changed. Once the patient readjusted, the dynamic implant lost its force.

Cameron used the patient's own voice for the dynamic implant because he "found by experimentation that the patient's own hesitations and emphasis are much more potent to him than any anonymous recorded voice." That potency at times worked against Cameron, causing the patient to leave the room rather than listen to the message. Nor did every patient offer up a neat revelation to be used as the driving statement. In an effort to expand the flexibility of his treatment, Cameron produced a variation that he termed heteropsychic driving, where the therapist composed the driving statement and it was his voice or that of an assistant on tape. In his first published paper on the treatment, "Psychic Driving," he wrote that heteropsychic driving seemed to work best when extended over longer periods of time — up to twenty hours a day for fifteen days. He noted that heteropsychic driving often produced a longer-lasting effect. The impact of the driving message was still in evidence weeks after the treatment was discontinued. He concluded his paper by stating that further research would involve the "wearing down of defences in the sense that defences were maintained only by means of continual effort and if they are continuously overloaded, their breakdown is to be expected. Analogous to this is the breakdown of the individual under continuous interrogation."

Autopsychic driving was something that Cameron could easily carry out himself in the course of therapy with his patients. All it entailed was the operating of a tape for ten minutes at the end of a session and the noting of the patient's reactions. Heteropsychic driving, with its longer treatment periods, was much more labour-intensive and required more sophisticated technology. To produce the machinery necessary for the technique, Cameron relied on the talents of technician Leonard Rubenstein.

Rubenstein was described by a colleague as a "boffin," a British slang term for the type of unkempt, absent-minded scientist who walked around scratching hypotheses in the air with a finger. Rubenstein had no medical training and had been hired for his electronic wizardry, a skill he had learned in the Royal Signals Corps. He was a tall man who walked with a Groucho Marx lope and had the basso voice of Paul Robeson. He kept to himself, working mostly in the behavioural laboratory in the stables behind the main building. Dr. Robert Cleghorn, remembers Rubenstein as "a technician given a great deal more authority than a technician should have. He wasn't in a very sound academic position." Rubenstein's commerce with staff members was minimal, confined usually to occasional housecalls to fix the broken television sets of Allan doctors. Nurses remember Rubenstein as shy and possessing a unique sense of humour.

Rubenstein developed a looped tape that continuously played the same thirty-second message endlessly. He also designed a floor-to-ceiling central unit that accomodated eight separate tapes, the messages of which were routed to speakers in separate rooms. One of the early methods of delivering the signal was through speakers installed in modified football helmets that were worn by the patients. Cameron hoped the message would have a greater impact if it sounded as if it were coming from the patient's own head. The helmets proved uncomfortable and, coupled with the often irritating effects of the repetition, resulted in a lot of helmets being thrown across the rooms. Cameron tried headphones, which were more comfortable, but unco-operative patients simply took them off. Rubenstein installed ceiling speakers, out of reach of the patients, but the doors were open and many patients simply left their rooms.

Clearly, the problem was how to get the patients to stay put while listening to the tapes. One way was simply to tell them to do so. Doctors enjoyed a greater infallibility thirty years ago than they do now, and Cameron often presented patients with the choice, "Do you want to get well or not?" He had an impressive reputation and a bedside presence that combined clinical concern with the charismatic touch of touring royalty. A former patient recalled his presence on the wards, "Here was this very important man and when he came to talk to you, his biggest concern was that you get well. He made you want to get better." As with his staff, Cameron could push his patients to get the best from them.

Not everyone was impressed enough to stay in the room and listen to the tape for twelve hours, however. Cameron tried a variety of drugs to make the patients more receptive to the taped statements, chiefly Desoxyn, Sodium Amytal, Largactil, and LSD. The drugs helped lessen patients' resistance, allowing the driving message to make the desired impression.

Cameron also used heteropsychic driving while the patients were asleep, extending the period of sleep to up to sixty days. Sleeping between twenty and twenty-two hours a day, the patients were wakened only for meals and calls of nature. Groggy from the sedatives, they were rarely truly awake and had to be attended to like babies. The message played through a pillow speaker while they slept.

Cameron also experimented with sensory isolation to prepare patients for psychic driving. Donald Hebb, an eminent scientist from McGill's psychology department, had conducted a series of experiments between 1951 and 1955 to test the effect of sensory isolation. Using volunteer medical students as subjects, he had cut off any undesirable variable stimulation by isolating them in cubicles and fitting them with translucent goggles. The longest stay in the cubicle was six days, but at that time, Hebb reported that profound changes had occurred. Students emerged disorganized, and some reported that they had experienced hallucinations. Cameron adopted a variation of Hebb's model, but few of his patients were inclined to stay in the cubicle for long. Cameron reported that some left immediately upon entering.

One of the possible pitfalls of psychic driving was the selection of the driving statement. Cameron cautioned that there could be setbacks if the message selected for repetition was inappropriate. One woman became so angered by a message outlining her sexual longings for her father that she bolted from the institute. She was later admitted as an in-patient, quite deeply disturbed. Cameron cited the incident as proof of the potency of psychic driving. "Cameron was very meticulous in choosing the driving statement," said a resident, "though he had no real expertise."

Another minor hitch was the voice used on the tape. Rubenstein's assistant, Zielinski, often taped the statements after they had been composed by Cameron. Zielinski had a strong Polish accent and at times the message was unclear. Former patient Karralynn Shreck remembered her message, which had been taped by Zielinski, repeating, "You are veak and inadequate." She eventually came to feel that she was thinking with a Polish accent and asked Cameron to change the voice on the tape. Cameron complied, replacing it with his own comforting Scottish burr.

Beginning in 1951, Cameron also began exploring the use of multiple electroshocks, a technique that was eventually used in conjunction with psychic driving as a disorganizing agent for particularly disturbed and/or resistant patients. In a 1951 progress report to the Department of Health and Welfare for a grant given to him to set up the behavioural lab, Cameron noted that "disorganization accumulates with ECT."

The use of electroshock to cure schizophrenia was based on the findings of Ladislaus Joseph Von Meduna of the Royal State Mental Hospital in Budapest. In the late 1920s, Meduna had read of clinical studies purporting that schizophrenia and epilepsy rarely, if ever, occurred in the same patient, and that if a schizophrenic did develop epilepsy, his psychosis would be cured. Meduna observed in autopsies that the glial tissue, brain tissue that connects the cell structures of the cortex, had thickened in epileptic patients while schizophrenics showed a deficiency of glial structure. From these findings, he concluded that induced convulsions, emulating those of an epileptic attack, might cure schizophrenia.

An early method of producing a convulsion was the injection of Metrazol, a synthetic version of camphor. But there was an unpredictable time lapse between injection and convulsion, during which the patient was frightened and difficult to control. The convulsions it produced were often severe enough to fracture bones.

Insulin shock therapy followed, but it was dangerous, time-consuming and difficult to administer. Patients were injected with insulin until they were comatose and then slowly brought out of it by the injection of glucose. It was a high-risk procedure and could result in irreversible coma, and circulatory and respiratory collapse if not administered carefully.

On April 15, 1938, Ugo Cerletti, a professor of psychiatry at the University of Rome induced the first electrical convulsions in a schizophrenic patient. The patient was a thirty-nine-year-old engineer who had been found by the Italian police wandering around the train station exhibiting delusional symptoms. Cerletti had been experimenting with electroshock on dogs and felt the technique was sufficiently established to try on a human subject. He attached two electrodes to the frontoparietal regions of the engineer's skull and gave him eighty volts for one fifth of a second. The man reacted with a jolt, and his body stiffened. These were not exactly the results Cerletti had been hoping for. He concluded that he had used too low a voltage and proposed that the experiment be repeated the following day with increased current.

The engineer, who had been listening to the conversation between Cerletti and his assistant, solemnly said to them, "Not another one. It's deadly." Cerletti was shaken by the man's appeal but resolved to carry on with the experiment. The following day Cerletti applied one hundred and ten volts for one fifth of a second. The patient lost consciousness and appeared subdued after the treatment. There was a memory deficit but he was lucid. Such were the beginnings of a treatment that has been perhaps the most controversial tool of modern psychiatry and has become a gloomy reminder of its basement beginnings.

Electroshock is still being used widely, chiefly for treatment of depression rather than schizophrenia, and its supporters claim that it is often the last bulwark against suicide for a depressed patient. It's detractors argue that it is simply aversion therapy and rather than face another treatment, the patient "escapes into health." The reason for electroshock's apparent success with depressives remains uncertain. One explanation that has been offered is that the slight brain damage produced by the voltage erases the most recent memories that led to the patient's depression. This theoretical basis suffers from the possibility that when the patient's memory returns, his depression will return with it.

In 1948, two British doctors, L. G. Page and R. J. Russell, developed a method of intensifying the shocks. Instead of what had become standard — one hundred volts applied for three tenths of a second to the temples — they increased the voltage to one hundred and fifty and lengthened the duration to a full second. Four seconds after the initial shock, between five and nine additional shocks were given in rapid succession, each for one second. The result was a treatment twenty to forty times more potent than standard electroshock. Page and Russell tried their technique on schizophrenic patients, advocating daily administration of ECT until symptoms disappeared. They published their results, outlining the practical application of the Page-Russell method. Two attendants would hold the patient to minimize the bucking produced by the current, while a third inserted a wooden spatula between the patient's teeth and held his jaws shut. The impetus behind the Page-Russell procedure was the hope that it would accelerate the healing process and reduce the backlog of schizophrenics languishing on the wards of asylums.

Two American doctors, Doctors Kennedy and Ancell also experimented with the use of intensive ECT by administering multiple treatments, labelling their technique "regressive shock therapy." ECT destroys memory and tends to do so in reverse chronological order. A psychiatrist familiar with the technique described its effect on a patient, "We had a patient at the Allan who was given intensive ECT. He had four children and after a few days of treatment, he no longer remembered the youngest child's name. A few days later and he didn't recognize the youngest, though he still knew the two eldest. By the end of the week, his wife had become a stranger." Kennedy and Ancell reported that their patients were regressed to the level of four-year-old children. When their memory gradually returned to them, it was hoped that their schizophrenic symptoms would not.

Cameron began experimenting with a variation of Kennedy and Ancell's work in 1951. ECT was already in use at the Allan, as it was in almost every psychiatric facility on the continent. But Cameron felt that a more forceful application of it might produce more impressive results.

Cameron used Page-Russell's intensive shock treatments in conjunction with normal ECT, administering up to three treatments a day. He originally reasoned along the lines of Kennedy and Ancell, thinking that you could regress patients, particularly schizophrenics, back to their infancy and then retrain them. He later revised that opinion, stating that "regressive shock therapy" was a misleading term. He felt that intensive ECT produced a disorganizing effect rather than an easily plotted regression. Cameron called his own application of intensive ECT "depatterning." When a patient was completely depatterned, after thirty to one hundred and fifty electroshocks, he was unable to walk or feed himself, and would likely be incontinent. Reduced to this infantile state, his schizophrenic patterns were gone and he could subsequently be "repatterned" through psychic driving, psychotherapy and occupational therapy.

"It was an aggressive treatment," a colleague said, "but Cameron was impatient of timidity . . . He had enormous faith in normalization; you could scramble the eggs and later they will come back as whole eggs."

Dr. Brian Robertson, current director of the Allan, was a medical student in New Zealand when he heard about Cameron's treatments:

> I heard about the "McGill" treatment — depatterning, when I was a student. The irony and, to some extent, the tragedy was that it was all based on a carefully worked out theory of brain functioning that, of course, was all wrong, but it was a coherent theory . . . it was a mix, Cameron's own mix of learning theory and some psychoanalytic theory that, in fact, you could create a sort of clean slate in the mind then you could build them up again away from the old pattern. That was a preoccupation with Cameron. He used massive amounts of ECT and induced, in effect, a transitory brain sickness, stopped the brain from working to its full capacity. Then you began to build them up again; put them to sleep and built them up with psychic driving.

One former resident who administered the depatterning treatments for Cameron felt it was worth trying and was often the only hope for extremely disturbed people:

> It seemed to work. The patients were hopeless, nobody could help them. The relatives were desperate. We gave two shocks a day for up to seventy-five days, along with Largactil and

Seconal. We had a portable box and we could do twenty patients in an hour. There was a big ward with twenty beds in it and we just went from bed to bed with the box and hooked them up. Their delusions disappeared.

In a few cases, the intensity of the shock would collapse a patient's vertabrae. "They were a little shorter," the resident admitted, "but that was the worst thing about it, really."

Most residents didn't like the treatment, however. "Residents on call hated the ECT ward," a former resident remembered. "We hated getting a call that someone was having respiratory difficulties after being given ten ECTs that day. The problem with depatterning was that there was never enough money to set up a proper rehabilitation program. That would also interfere with Cameron's 'quick fix' solution." It would be less of a breakthrough in the treatment of schizophrenia if the patients required six months of nursing and therapy before they could function outside the institution.

Cameron's colleagues weren't quick to embrace the treatment either. "None of us used it," Dr. Dancey said. "One of the problems was, when he got the slate clean, what did he replace it with. His own ideas? Well, some of us felt his ideas weren't too hot." Another doctor referred to depatterning as "electrical lobotomy."

One doctor who did try depatterning had his patient whisked out of the institute when her parents came to visit. They would have found a daughter who was incontinent and didn't recognize them. In retrospect, the doctor wondered how Cameron dealt with that aspect of the treatment. Cameron addressed the problem in a 1962 paper, "The Depatterning Treatment of Schizophrenia:"

> The social worker has the responsibility, sometimes reinforced by the physician, of advising the family of the treatment procedure and the fact that he will have a considerable memory blank when he recovers; that he should not be visited during the actual period of treatment.

Cameron reported enthusiastically on both psychic driving and depatterning to colleagues and to the press. Under the headline, "Two-month sleep, shock, new schizophrenic cure" in the Montreal *Gazette*, September 7, 1957, Cameron outlined his depatterning treatment, reporting only a few minor relapses in a sample group of twenty-six schizophrenic patients he had treated. As in *Weekend Magazine*, he reported virtually one hundred percent success with the treatment. Those who had suffered a relapse were given follow-up ECT and their schizophrenic symptoms again disappeared.

His optimism was just as evident in his scientific papers. In analyzing a group of six patients who had undergone psychic driving and depatterning, Cameron described how one became so disturbed and antagonistic towards the driving message that driving had to be stopped. He wrote that none gave full, conscious acceptance to the driving statement, and that five of them felt it was a voice in the basement or several people arguing rather than a doctor's voice. Yet in summing up his studies, he pointed to an increase in warmth in the patients and concluded that the treatment showed promise. Unable to concede anything to mental illness, Cameron took his victories where he could find them.

Some of the psychologists from the McGill psychology department who came to work at the Allan were not as optimistic as Cameron. The psychologists were employed largely to administer various psychological tests designed to measure a patient's condition or progress. One psychologist tested a twenty-four-year-old patient who had been depatterned and noticed that he had lost twenty points of IQ. She criticized Cameron's therapy at a meeting, citing the loss of IQ. Cameron listened to her complaint and commented that it was an interesting observation. "He welcomed the view of others," said a colleague, "but his attitude was, 'if you don't like it, give me something better, don't just complain!' "

The psychologist who criticized Cameron's depatterning therapy recently recalled their basic philosophical difference: "I'd rather have a guy with crazy ideas and alive, than a vegetable who goes to the corner to get his milk and gets home again without tripping or saying anything nasty to someone. It's a question of what you consider quality of life."

On rounds one day, Cameron ushered his entourage into the sleep room and woke up one of the psychic driving patients to demonstrate the effectiveness of the dynamic implant. The patient was a woman who was having trouble achieving intimacy with her husband and the dynamic implant was a positive one — "Jane, you are at ease with your husband." Cameron woke her up and asked her what the driving message was. She replied, "Jane, you are a tease with your husband." This anecdote made the rounds at cocktail parties leaving people to speculate on just what kind of effect two hundred thousand repetitions were going to have on her sex life.

Cameron's research abilities were generally not held in high esteem at the Allan, either by his colleagues or by residents, but Cameron kept attention focussed on his goals rather than his methods. He was a clinician, a teacher and primarily a leader. "He was a leader in the best sense," said former chief resident Dr. Eddie Kingstone. "He was unselfish, he gave people an opportunity to learn and he helped careers." Cameron's research was only one aspect of his career and not a particularly visible part. It was published and discussed, but it was not an important part of most of the residents' lives. "Cameron's work did not dominate the Allan," Kingston said. "He had his own little team for psychic driving, he wasn't dragging people into the mainstream. He wasn't trying to get people to be like him in any way. He wasn't trying to start a cult, and he couldn't tolerate sycophants."

Cameron created a mood of optimism at the Allan. There was a feeling that a major psychiatric breakthrough was just around the corner. "We all believed that there were cures on the horizon," Kingstone remembered. "I don't think anybody believes that now." Residents were galvanized by Cameron's enthusiasm, and most were prepared to accept his research despite reservations. At any rate, they weren't in a very strong position to criticize the work of a man of Cameron's stature. A psychiatrist who was trained at another institution in the 1930s explained the residents' dilemma. Early in his own residency he was ordered by a superior to insert an icicle in a woman's vagina. She was being treated for anxiety and the senior psychiatrist suggested that this treatment would calm her down. "I didn't want to do it, you know, but I was just starting out and didn't know if perhaps it was some kind of therapy that worked." The residents who trained at the Allan may not have liked depatternings but they were rarely sure that the treatment was wrong. The results were published in psychiatric journals, heralded in local newspapers and Cameron had an international reputation.

Cameron's peers were not always in agreement with his methods either, and a number of them voiced their opinion. But as Clifford Scott, a former analyst at the Allan suggested:

> In the medical world, you have to be tolerant of what people do unless it is something illegal. The history of medicine is full of people doing all sorts of things that later doctors disapprove of. I wasn't asked to approve of Cameron's work . . . He was a law unto himself. People often become a law unto themselves. Later the laws change and they are prosecuted for what they did.

The members of the McGill psychology department were not as susceptible to Cameron's charisma as were employees at the Allan itself, and they were not as dependant on his political largesse for career advancement. Many in the department felt his work was simplistic. "We used to laugh about it," one psychologist remembered. Donald Hebb, the leading scientist in the department and no fan of Cameron's, was more pointed, "If you look at what he actually wrote, it would make you laugh. If I had a graduate student like that, I'd throw him out. Cameron was no good as a researcher . . . He was eminent because of politics."

CHAPTER FIVE

BRAINWASHING AND ISOLATION RESEARCH

Josef Cardinal Mindszenty's blank confession in 1949 had triggered a nervousness among western powers and the search for a "truth drug" again found its way onto intelligence agencies' agendas. In the summer of 1949, the CIA's head of scientific intelligence travelled to Europe to investigate Soviet interrogation techniques and "to apply special methods of interrogation for the purpose of evaluation of Russian practices." The CIA's specific concern was that drugs or hypnosis were being used on prisoners during interrogation.

Communist paranoia was intensified by the outbreak of the Korean War in June 1950, pitting the North, aided by Communist China, against the South, shored up by a United Nations peace-keeping force that included Canadian and American troops. On the American home front, freshman Senator Joseph McCarthy, ex-marine and bull-goose loony of the Republican fringe, accused the State Department of harbouring fifty-seven, card-carrying Communists. His domestic hunt uncovered few Communist infiltrators, but it kept the public eye centred on the spectre of communism.

Canadian military authorities were sufficiently concerned by the threat of communism and the suspected threat of Communist brainwashing that on June 1, 1951, a meeting between scientists and representatives from Canada's Defence Research Board (DRB) was held at the Ritz-Carlton Hotel in Montreal to discuss "the general phenomena indicated by such terms as 'confession,' 'menticide,' 'intervention in the individual mind' — together with methods concerned in psychological coercion, change of opinions and attitude."

Sir Henry Tizard of the U.K. Defense Research Policy Committee was visiting Canada at the time, touring research facilities and Canada's DRB seized the occasion as a chance for the western powers to sit down and discuss the pressing topic of behaviour control. The U.S. Central Intelligence Agency, which had been interested in behaviour control since its inception in 1947, was invited to attend. Dr. Caryl Haskins and Commander R.J. Williams of the CIA attended as representatives. Unbeknownst to the others present, Haskins and Williams were members of the Agency's BLUEBIRD program. BLUEBIRD was the code name for the CIA's first organized foray into the area of behaviour control. Conceived in 1950, it was classified top secret and initially addressed the possible operational uses of hypnosis. An internal CIA memo defined the goal as "controlling an individual to the point where he will do our bidding against his will and even against such fundamental laws of nature as self-preservation." BLUEBIRD was also concerned with investigating Soviet means of brainwashing, as well as any western research that was being done in that field. Canadian representatives at the meeting were N. W. "Whit" Morton and Dr. Omond Solandt of the DRB, and Dr. T.E. Dancey, a psychiatrist who worked with the Department of Veteran Affairs and who held a post at the Allan Memorial Institute. Also present were Dr. James Tyhurst, a psychiatrist, and Dr. Donald Hebb.

The spirit of the meeting was one of co-operation. The Second World War had brought the Allied powers together in a brotherhood that the Cold War was maintaining. Many scientists, including Dancey, had been claimed by the government war effort, in 1939, in some capacity. The purpose of the meeting was to discuss possible avenues of research into methods of Communist brainwashing techniques with the aim of "determining means for combatting communism and selling democracy." Tizard announced at the onset of the meeting that there had been nothing new in the brainwashing business since the Inquisition and there was little hope of achieving any profound results through research. The Communists' apparent success in extracting confessions had more to do with ruthlessness than any remarkable new developments. Tizard was more concerned with the dissemination of Communist propaganda and the infiltration of labour unions by Communist agitators. He suggested they focus their energies in those areas rather than invest in research on the subject of individual conversion.

It was agreed by all that there was no evidence that the Soviets were doing anything new in the field of interrogation; neither Communist activities nor western research had indicated the existance of a "truth drug." Nonetheless, both the Canadians and the Americans felt that incremental gains in knowledge that might be achieved through research would be worth the money and effort.

A general discussion followed on the subject of brainwashing. Dr. Dancey produced some scientific articles on the topic and it was suggested that interviews with prisoners who had been brainwashed might be of interest. Questions on the use of drugs and the permanency of changes achieved with brainwashing were raised, and historical references of forced confession, such as the Salem witch trials were cited.

Most of these ideas had already been explored by the CIA through the BLUEBIRD program. In July 1950, a BLUEBIRD team went to Tokyo to interrogate North Korean prisoners of war. They administered combinations of the depressant Sodium Amytal and the stimulant Benzedrine, and also tried to induce amnesia in the POWs. They reported back that their interrogation had met with some success. This first BLUEBIRD operation had been concealed even from U.S. authorities, and neither Haskins or Williams, if they knew of the Japanese trip, volunteered any information to the Canadian scientists in Montreal. The BLUEBIRD program existed as a bureaucratic cell within the CIA. The Agency's minutes of the Montreal meeting stated that the CIA had "two separate but compatible research programs underway." One was through the standard channels, such as the discussion in Montreal, co-operation with U.S. and foreign defense authorities, and the other was the covert activity of BLUEBIRD. Neither Haskins nor Williams mentioned the existence of the BLUEBIRD program to those assembled in Montreal.

Dr. Omand Solandt, chairman of the DRB, remembers the meeting of 1951. "I suspected that perhaps they [CIA] had done some work on brainwashing which they weren't sharing, but we didn't necessarily want to know about it. It was, presumably, clandestine activity and we weren't an intelligence agency. Spying wasn't our business."

The CIA's minutes of the meeting state that they would continue to deal through the DRB for routine Agency activities, but "Should the need for co-ordination with foreign intelligence agencies develop, this will necessarily be laid on through intelligence channels rather than [the regular research branch] one." This meant, presumably, that should it be necessary for BLUEBIRD to conduct activity in Canada, they would go through the CIA's intelligence liason, which was the RCMP, rather than the DRB.

Dr. Hebb suggested to the assembly that research into the effects of sensory isolation might yield some clues to Soviet brainwashing techniques. A slight man who walked with a limp, Hebb had become a force in the field of psychology with the 1949 publication of his book, *The Organisation of Behaviour: A Neurological Theory*. Hebb had begun his career as a budding novelist rather than a psychologist. It was while labouring with a first novel that he became interested in Freud's work and went on to study psychology. He came to McGill in 1948 where he quickly established himself as the resident heavyweight in the psychology department and became an advisor to the Defense Research Board. Hebb had done some work related to sensory isolation and at the time of the meeting, was anticipating a grant to experiment with animals. The grant didn't permit experimentation with human subjects, but Hebb felt that further work could be done with humans if the animal experiments looked promising.

Hebb briefly outlined an experimental model for his isolation work, and it was agreed by all present that it would be worthwhile research. Even Tizard, who had resolutely rejected the notion of research through most of the meeting, was impressed by the proposal and agreed that it was worth proceeding with. The DRB tentatively committed itself to the financing of Hebb's work and it was hoped that his published results would attract the interest and comments of other experts throughout the three countries.

No mention was made of any operational use of Hebb's results, should they prove to be of value. But the CIA representatives hoped that the connections they had made at the meeting would lead to BLUEBIRD research in Canada. Their account of the meeting stated that " [Hebb] [1] in particular, indicated a keen understanding of the BLUEBIRD program, and was obviously interested in conducting research programs in connection with it. With the backing of [Hebb, McGill] should provide a centre of interest and activity which will be of the utmost value in the testing of various hypothesis as to control of the human mind."

Hebb's experiment was called X-38 "Experimental Studies in Change of Attitude," and received twenty-one thousand, two hundred and fifty dollars from the DRB for the first two years of research. None of the money went towards Hebb's salary, but was spent on materials, subjects and research assistants.

To facilitate the experiment, Hebb constructed a semi-soundproof cubicle (eight by four by six feet) with an observation window so that researchers could monitor the subject inside. The cubicle contained only a bed, a pillow and an air conditioning unit. Subjects were outfitted with

---

[1] The bracketed names are blanks in the CIA documents, but given the limited choices and the context provided, the inserted words are reasonable assumptions.

translucent goggles to prevent any visual stimulation. Cardboard tubes that extended from their elbow to past their fingertips prevented tactile stimulation (as well as masturbation, an early concern of the experimenters). The subjects were all volunteers — male students from McGill who were paid twenty dollars a day to participate.

Hebb designed the experiment, but much of the actual work was carried out by a team of psychologists who were using the model to test aspects other than the "change in attitude" goals of the Defense Research Board. Psychologists T. H. Scott, Harold Bexton, Woodburn Heron, and B. K. Doane used the cubicle to test such effects as the intellectual and cognitive changes that sensory isolation induced. Although Hebb's X-38 work was classified, much of the other work wasn't, and little attempt was made to keep the project secret.

Hebb had an impeccable reputation as a scientist and his experiment was conducted with a number of safeguards. No student would be urged to be a subject; the inducement would be monetary; the subject would be physically comfortable; he could terminate the experiment at any time. The subject would remain in the cubicle without any variable stimulation except the use of the bathroom and eating meals. He maintained contact with the experimenters through a two-way speaker system, but was discouraged from using it except for pertinent communication (i.e., he was hungry or had to use the bathroom). The most dangerous part of the experiment, one psychologist joked, was the cooking of experimenter Woodburn Heron's; Heron was the designated and inconsistent chef for the subjects.

Preliminary experiments weren't too promising. Six subjects refused to go on with the experiment as soon as they were told what it entailed. A few others dropped out almost immediately for reasons that seemed suspect; one complained of a fever that eluded detection by thermometer, and another remembered a pressing engagement. Despite the incentive of twenty dollars a day, the subject who stayed longest from among the first group remained for only three hours. He complained on leaving that the hum of the air conditioning unit was too loud.

A later subject lasted for twenty-four hours, sleeping for thirteen of them and spending another two-and-a-half eating and using the bathroom. Three recordings, selected for their unwavering ability to bore, were made available to him while he was in the cubicle. By signalling with a buzzer, the subject could choose from: four repetitions of "Home on the Range;"

a monotone reading of the stock market report; or a religious message for six-year-olds describing how they could attain purity of the soul. To the surprise of the experimenters, he signalled to listen to this entertainment forty-two times, eventually developing a preference for "Home on the Range." During bathroom breaks he became increasingly garrulous, putting off going back into the cubicle as long as possible. At one point he snappishly mentioned that if a neurotic person were to try it, he would crack up and it was a damn good thing he was used to being alone or *he* would crack up. An examination after his experience determined that he was unaffected by it other than a failure to appreciate the folksy charm of "Home on the Range."

Further experimentation established that if given the opportunity, the subject would listen to repetitions of a boring message rather than nothing at all. The next step in Hebb's X-38 experiment was to ascertain the effect of material that attempted to influence the subject. Hebb replaced the short, neutral messages with a series of lectures that argued for the existence of poltergeists. Subjects were questioned on their beliefs in psychic phenomena prior to the experiment and then questioned again upon termination to see if any conversions had taken place. Ideally, lectures on political subjects would have been the most effective, since that was the crux of the brain-washing issue, but Hebb rejected their use as potentially dangerous.

Both the subject and one of the researchers who wanted to witness the effects first-hand, managed to stay in the cubicle for six days. It was a relatively short period of time compared to what a prisoner might be subjected to, yet it proved sufficiently long to produce some changes. With the lack of any external stimulus, some of the subjects reported that they had been dreaming while they were awake — hallucinating. One described dots of light and geometric patterns that evolved into more complex images such as rows of little yellow men in black hats with their mouths open. Surrealistic images were recalled by some subjects; a procession of squirrels with sacks over their shoulders marching off to work, dinosaurs roaming a jungle, a parade of cat's eye glasses walking down a street. Some also experienced auditory hallucinations, songs or symphonies that played for them, and one felt the imaginary prick of darts that were fired at him by an imagined gun. Subjects reported that at first the hallucinations were entertaining, but that they eventually became disturbing and often prevented sleep.

The option of listening to the poltergeist lectures was offered to subjects who had been in the cubicle for more than eighteen hours. There were nine records, all arguing for a belief in psychic phenomena — specifically ghosts, poltergeists, telepathy, and clairvoyance. After all nine had been played, the subject could request them in any order of preference.

Hebb also tested the records on a control group who were not isolated. They were students who came and listened to the records in a room at their own leisure, over a period of days. When a control subject had declared definitely that he didn't want to hear any more records, he filled out a questionnaire to see if he registered any change in his attitude towards the material.

Both the control group and the experimental group showed a significant change in attitude after listening to the propaganda, but the change was much greater in the experimental subjects. After the experiment had ended, some of the experimental subjects repaired to the McGill library to search for information on poltergeists. In many cases, weeks after the experience, the change in attitude towards psychic phenomena provoked by the isolation experiment remained firm. The work, which extended through to 1955, proved that sensory isolation was a powerful tool in effecting change in attitude of an individual. It remains the most exhaustive study done on the subject.

By 1953, Hebb had demonstrated significant results and he wanted to present them at professional conferences. On January 1, 1953, Hebb wrote to Whit Morton at the DRB requesting permission to present some of his findings that were still classified. He suggested that he could present the "change of attitude" elements in such a way that they would be meaningful to psychologists but of little interest to reporters. Hebb cautioned that they should present their work before someone else leaked it, warning, "Don't forget that [Ewen] Cameron is also undertaking some work with this method and he'll talk about it freely."

Cameron had begun to investigate possible therapeutic uses of sensory isolation shortly after Hebb had designed his experiment. In a 1952 annual report to the Department of Health and Welfare, Cameron mentioned that he had begun work in that field, though a progress report from 1953 demonstrates that he was unable to get patients to co-operate in the experiment. Although Hebb and Cameron had as little contact as possible, Cameron was aware of Hebb's work, and that Hebb's experiment had produced some interesting results, Cameron adopted it in the hope that it would be of some use in the treatment of psychotics. But he had little, if any, success with sensory isolation alone. Later, after 1953, he used it regularly in conjunction with his psychic driving program.

Although Cameron had yet to develop a coherent use for sensory isolation, Hebb distrusted Cameron's instinct for publicity and worried that Cameron would take what he had to the press. Hebb felt that the DRB should make his research findings public first, to prevent any misconceptions. "Word is beginning to get around," he wrote to Morton, "and if we don't make a public statement, the psychologists are going to wonder why we don't — one of my reasons for reporting this is to keep it quiet, if you see what I mean." Morton felt it was still too delicate an issue and denied Hebb clearance to present his work.

In November 1953, Hebb tried again, this time seeking permission to present his paper, "The Effect of Isolation Upon Attitude, Motivation and Thought," which had been classified as secret, at Ewen Cameron's regional research conference at the Allan in December. In Hebb's correspondence with the DRB, he displayed a growing impatience with the cloak-and-dagger aspect of his work. Although, it had been established at the 1951 meetings at the Ritz-Carlton that his work could eventually be published, the bureaucrats at the DRB kept postponing the decision. Hebb warned that former subjects from the X-38 work had been talking and if one of them talked to a reporter, it would likely end in a distorted description of the research. "I think it immoral to keep scientific results secret unless really necessary," Hebb wrote in a final plea to Morton. "And it would be useful to me for the furtherance of our work and for getting financed, to be able to talk freely about it." Hebb signed his letter with a quick sketch of himself on bended knee.

Once more Morton turned him down citing the same argument Hebb was using to argue for publication; it might end up in the press in a distorted and unfavourable light. Hebb was vindicated in January 1954, when a *Toronto Telegram* headline appeared, announcing, "Human guinea pigs tell crash secrets." The article was about the isolation experiments, the "crash" referring to a cover story that had been given to some of the subjects. It had been explained to them that they were participating in an experiment to determine the effect of monotony on pilots and long-haul truckers, in an attempt to fathom unexplained vehicle crashes. The article didn't mention the "change of attitude" aspects and wasn't pursued by the press. It wasn't until 1956, that another leak, this one in *The New York Times*, created controversy over Hebb's work.

The story surfaced when two American doctors, Dr. Lilly and Dr. Felix of the Institute of Mental Health at Bethesda, Maryland, described their own isolation work to a U.S. congressional committee. They also mentioned Hebb's work, stating that "some of the important results [of Hebb's work] are still kept secret by the Canada Board of Defense." The quote appeared in the April 17, 1956, edition of *The New York Times* and the item was picked up by Canadian newspapers. a Montreal *Gazette* editorial (April 25, 1959) described Hebb's experiments as "gruesome" and students consequently protested on the McGill campus.

The public controversy surrounding Hebb's work prompted him to defend it in *The Gazette* (April 26) under the front-page headline "Brainwashing defence." Hebb declared that the rumours were exaggerated and the misgivings unfounded. "The purpose of the experiments," Hebb said, "was to find a means of defence against an enemy weapon. We were not trying to find bigger and better ways of torturing others, but to find out how to protect our own men." Hebb explained that in 1951 defense authorities in both Canada and the U.S. had been concerned about confessions being extracted from prisoners in enemy hands. Hebb had been approached to find a solution and he seized the opportunity to explore other scientific interests. He stressed in *The Gazette* that the isolation experiments had value beyond the brainwashing aspects that the DRB was interested in.

In retrospect, it appears that Hebb was right in suggesting that open publication of his work would defuse a news leak. When Cameron's psychic driving treatment had been reported only a year earlier the article was bursting with enthusiasm for Cameron's work. Cameron's ability to make people believe he was on the edge of a medical breakthrough encompassed colleagues, patients, and the media. The truth was, however, that at the time the "Beneficial brainwashing" article on Cameron's work appeared, few colleagues endorsed psychic driving, and the one-hundred-percent success rate cited was a fiction. Dr. Omand Solandt, chairman of the DRB, had made it known that the Defense Research Board would not fund Cameron's work because it involved ethically dubious procedures. Solandt was especially disturbed by depatterning and stated that "It was my view at the time and continues to be that Cameron was not possessed of the necessary sense of humanity to be regarded as a good doctor." But Cameron's unflagging optimism was a powerful PR tool. The press, for the most part, felt they were witnessing first-hand important psychiatric discoveries. It was rumoured that Cameron had a *Montreal Star* newspaperman on retainer to keep the Allan, mental illness and himself in the public eye. While there is no proof that this allegation was true, Cameron certainly enjoyed a good relationship with the press.

In Hebb's case, the isolation experiments were leaked out over a period of months, and media outrage is often measured in direct proportion to the degree of secrecy surrounding the information. When *The New York Times* article appeared, the issue was further exacerbated by the fact that Canadian Defence Minister Ralph Campney was unaware of Hebb's work. Campney stopped short of denouncing the experiment, but he achieved a degree of political distance from it. No politician wanted to be associated with a story that gave the impression that vaguely sinister experiments were being conducted at McGill University for the military at the expense of naive "guinea pigs." It was the manner in which the news of Hebb's work leaked out that gave it uncomfortable connotations. Cameron's work, by contrast, though it employed Hebb's isolation research, appeared as a sunny advertisement for a future free of mental illness. In modern political jargon, this is known as "putting a right spin on things." In matters of spin control, Cameron was something of an authority.

Hebb's disclosure on the front page of *The Gazette* effectively reduced the outcry to nitpicking editorials declaring that the subjects were not volunteers, that they had in fact been paid twenty dollars a day to participate in the experiment. If there was no lasting damage to its reputation, there was a slight tarnish on McGill's image.

Hebb's work also drew criticism from the scientific community. One colleague said, "I was scared of the isolation experiment. I stayed away from it." Despite the criticism, Hebb's experiment utilized strict scientific guidelines and employed safeguards for the subjects. Furthermore, it withstands the scrutiny of modern medical ethics. But the combination of science, politics, the media, and a pressing case of the Cold War willies created a minor sideshow at McGill.

CHAPTER SIX

THE SOCIETY FOR THE INVESTIGATION OF HUMAN ECOLOGY

President Franklin D. Roosevelt created the Office of Strategic Services (OSS) in 1942 to conduct clandestine wartime activities. One of the first orders of business for the OSS was to find or develop a "truth drug" for interrogation purposes. A truth drug committee was set up under Dr. Winfred Overholser, head of St. Elizabeth's Hospital in Washington. The OSS explored the uses of marijuana as a disinhibiting agent, trying several marijuana-laced cigarettes on August Del Gracio, a New York gangster. In the course of conversation, a mollified Del Gracio gave the OSS a detailed description of the New York drug trade, a disclosure they felt was induced by the marijuana. Although further testing claimed some success with marijuana, it was never exposed to rigorous clinical experimentation and it quickly faded from the OSS's short list of possible truth drugs.

In October 1945, a team of OSS men interrogated Walter Neff, a Nazi researcher who had worked with SS doctor Kurt Plotner at the Dachau concentration camp. Plotner had been instructed by the SS to develop a truth drug to facilitate the interrogation of stubborn Polish prisoners. He experimented with mescaline, a powerful hallucinogen, giving it to Dachau inmates and noting the effects. Neff told his OSS interrogators that the purpose of Plotner's work had been to "eliminate the will of the person examined," but the actual results — anger, disorientation, depression — had been chaotic and of little operational value.

President Harry Truman dismantled the OSS in 1945, but some bureaucratic elements survived and were incorporated into the Central Intelligence Agency, created in 1947. One of the surviving interests of the OSS was the continued concern about a truth drug. The CIA's hopes for the operational use of drugs and hypnosis were intensified by Mindszenty's 1949 confession. The idea that the Russians had developed successful brainwashing techniques pushed the CIA's truth drug efforts to the limit.

In 1950, BLUEBIRD — the program that sent Haskins and Williams to Montreal in 1951 — was christened, with a mandate to develop and investigate brainwashing techniques. BLUEBIRD underwent some departmental shifting within the CIA between 1950-52, going from the security division to the scientific intelligence branch, back to security, before arriving at the doorstep of technical services staff where it was renamed MKULTRA. MKULTRA was proposed by Richard Helms, a future CIA director, and was launched with a budget of three hundred thousand dollars, which was exempt from the normal CIA financial controls and protocol. MKULTRA would go farther afield than BLUEBIRD and the bypassing of routine Agency checks and balances was to expedite "ultra-sensitive work" in the field of behaviour control. Inaugurated in April 1953, one of the first priorities of MKULTRA was to investigate the operational possibilities of d-lysergic acid diethylamide (LSD) an hallucinogen that had properties similar to those of mescaline.

LSD was discovered in 1943 by Albert Hofmann, a Swiss chemist working for the Sandoz Pharmaceutical Company. Working in his laboratory in Basel, Hofmann accidently absorbed some of the chemical through his skin. Unaware of the accident, he began to experience the effects of the drug and thought he was going crazy. "I had the idea I was out of my body. I thought I had died. I did not know how it would finish. If you know you will come back from this very strange world, only then can you enjoy it." Taken in very small doses, LSD was able to induce a powerful and prolonged hallucinatory experience of between six and twelve hours.

Sidney Gottlieb, a CIA chemist and project director of MKULTRA, was quick to recognize the potency of this new drug. His interest in the offensive applications of LSD was underscored by the need to develop a defence against it. The possibility that the Russians had used LSD on Mindszenty couldn't be ruled out. A field report, never verified, claimed that the Russians had bought the world supply of LSD. LSD is extremely concentrated — a suitcase full would be sufficient to drug every person in America — and the rumour that the Russians had this capability was taken seriously by an edgy intelligence community.

Gottlieb was an obdurate CIA career man who was able, according to a colleague, to do "the tough things that had to be done." One of those tough things involved carrying anthrax poison to the Congo in an aborted attempt to assassinate Patrice Lumumba. When asked in deposition for the pending CIA lawsuit (Orlikow *et al* vs. the United States of America), if he had in fact personally transported the poison, Gottlieb replied, "Yes." Gottlieb's lawyer, sensing the delicacy of this admission quickly objected and conferred with his client, causing him to reconsider. "I am not at liberty to answer that question," Gottlieb stated. When asked if he had not just said yes, Gottlieb replied, "I never said yes."

An Agency oddball, Gottlieb lived in a former slave cabin and raised goats, rising at five-thirty in the morning to milk them. He had a stammer that became more pronounced when he was under stress. Despite the handicap of a clubfoot, he was an avid and expert folk dancer, taking time to learn new steps when his work took him abroad. He would become the driving force behind MKULTRA's search for effective methods of behaviour control.

When military intelligence reports arrived in 1953 stating that Sandoz was looking to sell ten kilos of LSD (one hundred million doses) on the open market, the CIA moved quickly. Two representatives were dispatched to Switzerland with two hundred and forty thousand dollars, only to be told by baffled officials at Sandoz that production to date of the drug had only been forty grams. It was later discovered that the U.S. military attaché in Switzerland had confused a milligram (one thousandth of a gram) with a kilogram (one thousand grams) skewing his calculations by a factor of one million. However, because the CIA men were there with a suitcase full of money, the business interests of both parties were piqued and Sandoz offered to provide the U.S. government with LSD at a fair price.

Fearful that the Russians had harnessed LSD's unpredictable qualities, Gottlieb began testing LSD himself. In 1953, he went overseas with a supply of hallucinogens and arranged for some to be slipped to a speaker at a political rally, hoping its effects would discredit his views. Later experiments garnered little in terms of research. The CIA began testing LSD on their most readily available supply of subjects: each other. They took it at their offices and observed one another's alternately sullen and giggling behaviour, and often unwitting subjects would run pell-mell through philosophical half-truths that refused to crystallize into articulate thought. They analyzed and interrogated one another, exploring LSD as a potential interrogating tool and noted that it produced a vulnerability that could indeed be effective in interrogation.

While the CIA was pursuing the intelligence uses of LSD in Washington, psychiatric researchers were exploring its therapeutic possibilities.

LSD was introduced to North American academics in 1949 when Viennese doctor Otto Kauders discussed the drug at a conference at Boston Psychiatric Hospital. Kauder's talk prompted a number of inquiries to the Sandoz Pharmaceutical Company and arrangements were made to ship quantities of the drug to North America. In 1949, there were no governmental bodies that monitored the sale and use of experimental drugs in medical research. The onus was on the manufacturers to use discretion in selling their products. If a researcher wanted to try a new drug, he simply wrote to the manufacturer and arranged for shipment.

LSD was originally thought by psychiatrists to induce a temporary psychotic state resembling schizophrenia. What later experimenters, such as Harvard professor and counter-culture guru Dr. Timothy Leary (turn on, tune in, drop out), described as a "trip," psychiatrists in 1949 termed a "model psychosis." One theory was that if research could produce an antidote to LSD, it might have a similar effect on schizophrenia.

But psychiatric investigations with LSD were not confined to finding a cure for schizophrenia. It quickly became the Great White Hope of psychiatric research in hospitals throughout North America and Europe. In 1950, Dr. A. K. Busch and Dr. W. C. Johnson of the St. Louis State Hospital experimented with LSD in an effort to make patients talk more freely during psychotherapy. Dr. Charles Savage tried LSD as an antidepressant in 1952. A year earlier, Dr. G. Benedetti used LSD on alcoholics, a possibility explored in greater depth by Dr. Humphry Osmond and Dr. Abram Hoffer at the University of Saskatchewan in 1957. Dr. Harold Abramson reported success with the drug in treating homosexual anxiety. LSD's disorienting "psychedelic" (a term coined by Humphry Osmond to describe the experience of LSD) effects were applied to the treatment of manic depressives, mental defectives, neurotics, alcoholics, drug addicts, and schizophrenics. Dosages varied widely. In 1957, Osmond advocated "a single overwhelming experience" created by two hundred to four hundred micrograms in treating alcoholics. To facilitate pychotherapy with neurotics, Abramson suggested small doses of twenty-five to one hundred micrograms be given over a number of sessions. LSD was tested on mental patients, normal volunteers, psychiatrists, mice, Siamese fighting fish, and snails, among other things. One psychiatrist at the Allan Memorial remembers: "Everyone was trying it. It was the Next Big Thing." By 1962, fourteen hundred medical papers had been published on the experimental and/or therapeutic effects of LSD.

A consensus on the effectiveness and best application of LSD was never achieved by the medical community. Hoffer and Osmond reported that thirty of sixty alcoholics given LSD remained dry for five years after treatment, yet it was not widely adopted as a cure for alcoholism. Mixed results were reported in almost all different categories of test subjects.

Many felt that LSD's greatest strength lay in using its abreacting qualities in conjunction with psychotherapy. The insights induced in the patient by the drug aided the therapist in extracting information on the traumatic episodes in the patient's life. It was suggested in a 1962 summary of scientific literature on LSD that the drug "activates the patient's unconsious so as to bring forth fantasies and emotional phenomena that may be handled by the therapist as dreams." Dr. H. LeFever likened the LSD experience to "the puberty rituals of primitive tribes, the object of which is to help the individual in the struggle to find just who and what he is."

LSD was found, ultimately, to be of little use in treating schizophrenia. It showed unfavourable results in testing and was considered dangerous because it could provoke prolonged psychotic reactions. The American Psychiatric Association concluded in 1962 that it was a potent drug "capable of inducing in a patient the single most powerful emotional experience of his life," and that it should be used selectively. It was also recommended that the experimenter take it himself before administering it to patients.

It was used at the Allan Memorial Institute on a number of different disorders, but without much success. "We used quite a bit of LSD," said Dr. Eddie Kingstone, former chief resident (1959-60) at the Allan, "and we never found it to be very useful. It seemed like a good way to hurry people out of the hospital because they didn't like the effects."

By May of 1962, the Sandoz Company had developed misgivings about the drug and polled a number of researchers on its value as a therapeutic tool. Precipitated partly by the ambiguous findings presented to the American Psychiatric Association earlier that month, Sandoz sent letters to various psychiatrists, including Ewen Cameron, stating: "We at Sandoz are faced with a considerable moral and practical problem in relation to the use and possible abuse of Delysid (LSD)." Replies varied widely concerning its effectiveness, but most doctors agreed that it was a potent drug and should be administered under strictly controlled conditions and by experienced staff. Cameron agreed that it should be administered by experienced staff, but stated that both the "effects and dangers of LSD were considerably overrated," although there is no evidence in his papers that he ever tried the drug himself.

Because there was no clear consensus from the scientific community, the expressed concern of LSD's manufacturer, and reports that it was being used "for kicks" outside of research institutions, the Canadian Food and Drug Directorate announced in October of 1962 that LSD was being withdrawn from distribution. Bill C4 was introduced in the legislature to ban its sale in Canada, but the move failed to entirely staunch research with LSD. However, it gradually disappeared from medical journals, having exhausted most therapeutic hopes, and by the late sixties LSD had been effectively co-opted by the counter-culture and Humphry Osmond's label "psychedelic" was being used to describe drug experiences, music and ill-fated fashions.

*   *   *

The CIA's MKULTRA program, having depleted the experimental subjects available within their own offices, decided to field-test LSD. On November 18th, 1953, a group of three scientists from the CIA, and seven from the Army Chemical Corps Special Operations Division (SOD), met in a cabin in Deep Creek, Maryland, for a three-day semi-annual review conference. Sidney Gottlieb saw the occasion as a perfect opportunity to covertly adminster LSD to the conference participants. He instructed his deputy, Robert Lashbrook, to put LSD in a bottle of Cointreau that was offered around the table after dinner. Two of the SOD men declined, one being a non-drinker and the other citing a heart condition. Twenty minutes after the post prandial liqueur, Gottlieb inquired if the scientists noticed anything amiss. They did, but analysis of exactly what was amiss deteriorated during the drug reverie that is peculiar to LSD.

Not everyone was enjoying himself. Lieutenant Colonel Vincent Ruwet later described it as "the most frightening experience I ever had or hope to have." Another unwitting participant was Frank Olson, a branch chief at SOD. Olson became paranoid under the influence of LSD and felt a trick was being played on him. Because of the duration of LSD experience, users often become edgy in the later stages when the euphoria wears off but the effect has yet to subside sufficiently to allow for sleep. There is an awkward twilight period in most LSD trips that can be very disturbing.

Olson had trouble getting to sleep when the meeting broke up at one a.m. and he appeared at breakfast the next morning tired and agitated. He remained that way throughout the day and, upon returning home, he told his wife that his colleagues had laughed at him and humiliated him. He was uncommunicative over the weekend, and at work on Monday he told his superior, Lieutenant Colonel Ruwet, that he wanted to either quit or be fired. Olson's depression deepened over the next few days and when news of his condition reached Gottlieb, he arranged to send Olson to see a psychiatrist.

Gottlieb contacted Dr. Harold Abramson in New York, a doctor who had worked with LSD under contract for the Agency and who had a top secret security clearance. Abramson agreed to see Olson. On the trip to New York, Olson's mood fluctuated, improving briefly while in the company of his escorts, Ruwet and Lashbrook. At other times, his mood moved towards extreme paranoia. Settled in a New York hotel, Olson crept out of his bed one night and wandered the streets of Manhattan, tearing up all his paper money and throwing his wallet away.

Abramson described Olson as psychotic and recommended hospitalization. It was arranged for Olson to be admitted to Chestnut Lodge, a Rockville, Maryland, sanitarium that had CIA-cleared psychiatrists on staff. Unable to get plane reservations that day, they spent another night in New York, where Olson shared a room with Lashbrook on the tenth floor of the Statler Hotel. They relaxed by watching television, then went down to the lounge where they each drank two martinis. Olson was cheerful and seemed to be enjoying the evening. After dinner they went back to their room to watch more television before turning in. Olson declared that he felt more relaxed and contented than he had since his arrival in New York. He left a call with the hotel operator to wake them in the morning and at eleven p.m. they went to sleep. At two-thirty a.m. Lashbrook was woken up by the sound of breaking glass. Olson had run through the window.

As a crowd gathered around Olson's body below, Lashbrook phoned Gottlieb with the bad news. When the police arrived at the hotel to question Lashbrook, they ran into a cement wall of Agency obfuscation. Lashbrook said he worked for the Defence Department and couldn't think of any reason why Olson would have killed himself. The only information he yielded was that Olson was believed to be suffering from ulcers.

Olson's widow, Alice, was informed that her husband had fallen or jumped through the window, but was not told any of the details concerning LSD or the reason for his visit to New York. The truth did not emerge until 1975, when a Rockefeller Commission studying illegal CIA domestic activities reported that a man fitting Olson's description had jumped from a New York hotel window in 1953 after the CIA had secretly given him LSD. Alice Olson went on national television with a statement describing her family's reaction to the news and launched a lawsuit against the CIA. President Ford subsequently apologized to the Olson family and Congress passed a bill in 1976 which awarded the Olsons seven hundred and fifty thousand dollars in compensation (though severing payment of Frank Olson's pension in the process).

Frank Olson's death was neither a setback for the LSD program nor for Sid Gottlieb's career. The Agency was now acutely aware of the risks involved with LSD and unwitting testing, but they felt its importance as an operational weapon was too great to abandon. The Olson case had come close to leaking out in 1953, and it emphasized the need for a more effective method of testing.

At the height of Cold War paranoia in 1953, the search for information on mind control intensified among the CIA's inner circle. CIA Director Allen Dulles discussed the subject with Dr. Harold Wolff, an eminent neurologist who was testing Dulles's son for brain damage incurred in the Korean War. At Dulles's request, Wolff and his colleague at Cornell Univerisity, Lawrence Hinkle, commenced an investigation into Communist brainwashing techniques. The report, which became the definitive government document on the subject, stated that neither the Chinese nor the Russians possessed any undiscovered, mysterious means to alter human behaviour, echoing the 1951 assessment made in Montreal by Sir Henry Tizard. What both countries had was the time and the disposition to carry out time-honoured totalitarian methods. Brutal, psychologically astute, and unrelenting, their techniques were grounded in primitive interrogation methods rather than esoteric drugs or machinery. This simple unattractive truth accounted for the fact that of the seven thousand one hundred and ninety U.S. prisoners held in China at the end of the Korean War, seventy percent had either made confessions or signed petitions calling for an end to the American presence in Asia. The Chinese used the "confessions" to wage an effective propaganda campaign by broadcasting tapes of captured Americans admitting to horrific war crimes.

Soviet and Chinese methods to some extent mirrored their respective cultural idiosyncrasies. The Soviet technique was blunt, oppressive and clumsily effective. Prisoners were cut off from all external stimuli for a period of weeks before they were allowed to meet their interrogators. By that time they were often glad of any human contact, and they joined forces with the initially sympathetic interrogator to examine their pitiful lives and pinpoint just where they went wrong. Hebb had demonstrated that six days of sensory isolation could effect a significant change. Six weeks of it left the prisoner weak, addled, and poorly equipped to handle the rush of sensory signals.

The Chinese were more subtle, their techniques consisting of a multi-layered application of basic psychological tactics. They used isolation to the same calculated end, but combined it with an involved re-education program, the aim of which was to produce the sort of servile zeal that George Orwell profiled in the character of Parson in his book 1984 ("Of course I'm guilty! . . . Thank you for saving me before it was too late").

Wolff's brainwashing study program for the CIA was incorporated into the Society for the Investigation of Human Ecology (SIHE) in 1955 with Wolff as president. Originally associated with Cornell University, where Wolff was on staff, SIHE financed Wolff's attempts to find out how "a man can be made to think, feel, and behave according to the wishes of other men, and, conversely, how a man can avoid being influenced in this manner." SIHE was backed by CIA funds and allowed the Agency to fund research in the field of behavioural science without making its presence known. Although the CIA had yet to be caught interfering with human rights or the democratic process, there were scientists who baulked at doing work for it. Sid Gottlieb described the purpose of SIHE: "The Society was to act as a funding mechanism so that involvement of CIA's organizational entity would not be apparent in projects we were funding."

By 1957, The Society for the Investigation of Human Ecology had become a primary funding conduit for Gottlieb's MKULTRA projects, and scientific and intelligence aims were sufficiently polarized for Cornell to question their role in the union. The CIA, which had used Cornell's prestige primarily to launch SIHE as a funding agency, also reviewed the partnership and decided that Cornell had served its purpose. The association was dissolved in 1957, to the relief of both parties.

Wolff remained president of SIHE, warming to his clandestine role, and SIHE increased its funding activity. Although Wolff was president, much of the administration of the Society fell to its executive secretary, Colonel James Monroe. Monroe was a former U.S. Air Force project officer in the psychological warfare division of the USAF and had a background in brainwashing investigation. As Gottlieb described Monroe, "He had something to do with the interrogation of returned Korean prisoners. I wouldn't use the term 'brainwashing expert' but he had some experience in that area." Sam Lyerly and Walter Pasternak, both CIA psychologists from the behavioural activities branch, also moved over to the Society as consultants.

Pasternak had had some experience with drug testing on unwitting subjects. He experimented with the delivery of LSD from an aerosol can. He had rented a house in Marin County and spent the week cruising the local bars and inviting strangers to a party. There was no shortage of Marin County partygoers, but hot weather forced them to open the windows in the house and most of the LSD that Pasternak had liberally sprayed around the rooms simply drifted outside amid the smoke and heat of the revellers. The effect of the aerosol-administered LSD was seriously diluted and didn't seem to have any impact. An associate of Pasternak's, John Gittinger, improvised by locking himself in the bathroom and spraying the LSD vigourously. For twenty minutes he sat quietly, insulated from the party din and calculated the effect of the aerosol. There didn't seem to be any.

LSD experiments sponsored by the CIA did not always possess the laughable results of the Marin County fiasco. Dr. Harris Isbell, director of the Addiction Research Center in Lexington, Kentucky, received Agency funds to administer LSD daily to seven inmates for seventy-seven consecutive days. The subjects, mostly black drug addicts, had been induced to volunteer by the offer of time off their sentences or quantities of the drug of their choice, usually heroin. After forty-two days, Isbell reported that it was "the most amazing demonstration of drug tolerance I have ever seen," and subsequently increased the dosage.

Research into LSD was an Agency priority, but their quest for behaviour control methods extended to other areas. The sensory isolation research that Hebb had pioneered with Canadian Defense Research Board money was of interest to the CIA. They contacted Dr. Maitland Baldwin (a former McGill professor) in 1955 to continue investigations in that area. Baldwin had done some isolation work for the army that lacked the guidelines of Hebb's model. Baldwin proposed to go further, offering to do "terminal type" experiments for the Agency. A CIA medical officer vetoed the proposal, calling it "immoral and inhuman," and suggesting that Agency officials in favour of the work volunteer as subjects.

The CIA's behaviour control program, which had arisen from justifiable Cold War fears in 1949, evolved into a bureaucratic force within the CIA that, by the mid-1950s stretched the limits of ethical experimentation.

Not all of the researchers funded by the Society for the Investigation of Human Ecology were ignorant of CIA involvement. Many of them acted in the role of Agency consultants. LSD research in particular was carried out at a variety of American universities at the bequest of the CIA and financed through SIHE. It was not an unusual relationship considering the political climate and the fact that LSD research was proliferating throughout the academic world.

The Society for the Investigation of Human Ecology also funded activities that were unrelated to the behaviour control program. Two University of Oklahoma psychologists were given five thousand five hundred and seventy dollars to finance a study of teenage gangs. Colonel James Monroe told them that the SIHE money came from New York doctors and Texas millionaires who contributed for tax purposes. H. J. Eysenck, a high-profile University of London psychologist received twenty-six thousand from SIHE for studies on motivation. A CIA document revealed that the work had "no immediate relevance for Agency needs," but that Eysenck's name would "lend prestige" to the Society.

Other grants were dispensed for cover purposes that garnered neither prestige nor viable information for the CIA. Among them: an analysis of the Central Mongolian skull (seven hundred dollars) a look at foreign-policy views of people who owned fall-out shelters (twenty-five hundred dollars); the effects of circumcision on Turkish boys (five hundred dollars). These projects were financed simply to diversify SIHE's funding record, moving away from work that dealt strictly with behaviour control.

The MKULTRA program took a shotgun approach to behavioural investigation, and a few areas of research were too peripheral to merit their attention. They were aware that much of what they financed would fail to deliver anything of value to the Agency, but a combination of Cold War tension and budgetary *laissez-faire* enabled them to fund long-shots. One of the long-shots they funded was MKULTRA sub-project 121, a study of Yoruba cult healers in Nigeria conducted by psychiatrist Raymond Prince of the Allan Memorial Institute. In 1960, Prince was given seventeen thousand, seven hundred and eighty-one dollars and fifty cents to carry out an eighteen-month study of the ways in which the Yoruba dealt with mental illness. He had been to Nigeria before and felt there was something to be learned from their indigenous tribal psychiatry, but until MKULTRA no one would fund his return to study the situation in detail.

Prince is still at the Allan, occupying an office in the McGill Research Building. He could easily be cast in a film role playing the British scientist in Africa. It is not hard to picture him in the withering humidity of the wet season, pinkish and shining in a stained linen suit, jotting his observations in a damp notebook. Prince was an associate of Eric Wittkower, an Allan psychiatrist who had taken up transcultural psychiatry partly at Cameron's request. Prince was glad of the SIHE money and is unperturbed that the funding originated from the CIA. His view is one shared by many scientists: it doesn't matter where the money comes from if the work is ethical. He adds, "The CIA weren't necessarily the bad guys then."

Prince's work was seminal in the field of non-western psychiatric practices and produced an article, "Indigenous Yoruba Psychiatry." He was unaware of the CIA's presence and never met anyone from the Society, though he offered to show them a film of his work at their offices in New York.

What the CIA expected from Prince's research was outlined in an Agency document. "This study will add somewhat to our understanding of native [Yoruba] psychiatry including the use of drugs, many of which are unknown or not much used by western practitioners. It will also assist in the identification of promising young [deleted] who may be of direct interest to the Agency. [Prince] will be located in [Nigeria] thus carrying out the plan of developing [The Human Ecology Fund.[1]] as a world-wide organization. Since [Prince] will learn the [Yoruba] language, this project offers a potential facility for [deleted] project 95."

In retrospect, the unrealistic cloak-and-dagger aims of the Agency seem to be equal parts of bureaucratic rationalization and inflated expectation. By 1963, the MKULTRA program had spent twelve years studying the problem of behaviour control using top-level researchers and almost unlimited funds, and had turned up virtually nothing that hadn't been known in 1951. There was nothing new in the brainwashing business.

In 1963, the CIA Inspector General mapped the down side of the MKULTRA program in his "Report of Inspection MKULTRA/TSD" (Technical Services Division). He concluded that:

> The sensitive aspects of the program as it has evolved over
> the ensuing ten years are the following:
> a) research and manipulation of human behaviour is con-
>   sidered by many authorities in medical and related fields
>   to be professionally unethical, therefore the reputation

[1] The Society for the Investigation of Human Ecology changed its name to The Human Ecology Fund in 1961.

    of professional researchers in the MKULTRA program are
    on occasion in jeopardy.

b)some MKULTRA activities raise questions of legality.

c) a final phase of the testing of MKULTRA products places
    the rights of U.S. citizens in jeopardy.

d)disclosure of some aspects of MKULTRA activity could
    induce serious adverse reaction in U.S. public opinion as
    well as stimulate offensive and defensive actions in the
    field on the part of foreign intelligence services.

Sidney Gottlieb ignored the expressed concerns of the Inspector General and continued to advocate unwitting drug testing. Richard Helms, who was then the director of the CIA, agreed in an August 19th, 1963, memo that stated:

> Our judgement on the basis of the past eight years is that this kind of test [unwitting drug tests] is essential to carrying out our assigned responsibility and that the risks which are certainly real, are commensurate with the information acquired. This activity is not one that we relish or enjoy, but we believe it is necessary.

In 1964, MKULTRA became MKSEARCH, incorporating all remaining MKULTRA projects. The Human Ecology Fund had quietly disappeared by 1965. MKSEARCH limped on with the behaviour control concerns of the CIA until June, 1972, when Gottlieb finally dismantled it, giving the reason that "In addition to moral and ethical considerations, the extreme sensitivity and security constraints of such operations effectively rule them out." Finally, even Gottlieb had to admit that the program had yielded virtually nothing of value after twenty-two years.

When Richard Nixon was re-elected in 1972 amid the murmurings of Watergate, Richard Helms was purged as CIA director and shipped to Iran as the American ambassador. Sid Gottlieb decided to retire in the wake of his patron's exit and he advised Helms to have all MKULTRA documents shredded. On January 31st, 1973, Helms ordered that all documents pertaining to behaviour control research, specifically MKULTRA documents, were to be destroyed.

James Schlesinger became an interim director of the CIA before he was moved to the post of Secretary of Defence to help the beleaguered Nixon. In his brief role as CIA director, Schlesinger ordered a full disclosure of any illegal or improper Agency activities be made to his office. Some of the disclosures found their way onto the pages of *The New York Times*. When Gerald Ford became president, he appointed a commission headed by Vice-President Nelson Rockefeller to investigate possible CIA abuses. The circumstances surrounding Frank Olson's suicide finally came to light.

Olson's drug-induced suicide was framed in the context of a larger program of behaviour control through the use of "electric shock, psychology, psychiatry, sociology, and harrassment substances." John Marks, a journalist and former State Department official filed a Freedom of Information request asking for material pertaining to the behaviour control program. In June 1977, CIA officials notified Marks that they had found several boxes of MKULTRA documents that had survived Helms destruction order, apparently through misfiling.

A Senate select committee on Intelligence combined with Senator Edward Kennedy's sub-committee on health and scientific research held hearings to investigate the MKULTRA program. The discovery of the new documents brought the CIA's behavioural control program to light. Kennedy stated that:

> The Central Intelligence Agency drugged American citizens without their knowledge or consent. It used university facilities and personnel without their knowledge. These institutions and individuals have a right to know who they were and how and when they were used.

Admiral Stansfield Turner, director of the CIA, read from a prepared statement, declaring that the CIA had a moral obligation not to release the names of the researchers and institutions, both witting and unwitting, who had worked for the Agency. Turner cited his legal responsibility under the Privacy Act not to disclose publicly the names of researchers without their consent. However, Turner did agree to give the names to the joint committee on a classified basis.

The point was made by Senator Inouye that "there is an obligation on the part of this committee and the CIA to make every effort to help those individuals or institutions that may have been harmed by any of those improper or illegal activities."

CHAPTER SEVEN

EWEN CAMERON AND THE CIA

Cameron's immediate task as the new director of the Allan Memorial was to establish a program of psychiatric research; he knew it would be an expensive undertaking. Funding for research into mental disorders, however, was not a priority for the Canadian government in 1947. Indeed, Canada's National Research Council (NRC), the primary government funding agency for medical research, estimated that they had disbursed less than twenty-five thousand dollars in grant money for psychiatric research that year. But in addition to the limited NRC funds, Cameron had the Rockefeller Foundation's initial start-up grant of one hundred and fifty thousand dollars. This was to be distributed as an annual gift of thirty thousand dollars over a five-year period and was designated for the funding of teaching and research. The Quebec government matched the Rockefeller grant, giving the Allan an initial funding base of sixty thousand dollars per year.

Then in 1948, the federal government announced the creation of the Dominion Mental Health Grant Program. Under the program, federal money was made available to the provinces to improve mental-health facilities, hire personnel, and do research. By 1955, this program funded much of the research at the Allan. The Allan was the single largest beneficiary of the program, receiving one hundred thousand dollars in 1955 alone. Dr. Charles A. Roberts, head of the program, felt that it was perhaps a disproportionate amount and established that figure as the maximum amount available to any one institution, although he regarded this as a temporary measure.

At the time, Cameron was pursuing his psychic driving experiments under a scanty umbrella grant of seventeen thousand, eight hundred and seventy-five dollars that had been awarded by the Mental Health Grant Program to set up a behavioural laboratory. In a 1953 progress report, Cameron noted that he was having difficulty finding suitable staff to work with him on his project and was doing much of the research himself. His teaching, clinical, and administrative chores, combined with his political duties as president of the American Psychiatric Association, left him little time for the task. The solution was to find a research assistant and to find some money to pay him.

Having exhausted the limits of the Mental Health Grant Program, Cameron had applied for funding to the Defence Research Board. He thought that the DRB was the logical choice. They had funded Hebb's work and Cameron's psychic driving experiment explored some of the same possibilities and employed a variation of Hebb's isolation cubicle. But Omond Solandt, the chairman of the DRB was not kindly disposed towards Cameron's work, "My views of Cameron and the depatterning procedures were known to him, and I let it be known through Dr. Morton that I would not look favourably upon any application by Cameron to the Defence Research Board for psychiatric research." Solandt had consulted professionals and asked for their opinions of Cameron's work. "The feelings were mixed, the majority were against him."

Solandt's suspicions about the value of Cameron's research were confirmed when he witnessed the results of one of his depatterning treatments on the wife of a colleague. The woman had lived her life in the shadow of her mother. When she was married, the mother moved in, usurping the role of wife in all areas save the bedroom. When the mother died, the woman was incapable of directing her life and suffered a nervous breakdown. She was depatterned at the Allan with unhappy results. "She was treated by various people and finally sent to Cameron. She wasn't much to begin with and Cameron made her worse."

Solandt wasn't the only head of a funding agency who was critical of Cameron. Robert Morrison of the Rockefeller Foundation noted that Cameron's "lack of interest and effectiveness in psychotherapy and failure to establish warm relations with faculty members . . . were mentioned repeatedly when I visited Montreal." Another Rockefeller observer who visited the Allan reported that Cameron "appears to suffer from deep insecurity and has a need for power which he nourishes by maintaining an extra-ordinary aloofness from his associates."

In 1956, Cameron's "Psychic Driving" article appeared in the *American Journal of Psychiatry*, where it came to the attention of John Gittinger, a CIA psychologist who was working with Sid Gottlieb in the MKULTRA program. Gittinger was struck by the possible intelligence applications of psychic driving. In his paper, Cameron claimed that the repeated message would stay "implanted" in the patient for weeks after the treatment had stopped. He also cited the use of Hebb's isolation cubicle, drugs, and hypnosis to increase the patient's susceptibility to the message. These areas were of particular interest to the CIA. Gittinger instructed Colonel James Monroe of the Society for the Investigation of Human Ecology to contact Cameron and solicit a grant application from him. The Agency wanted to ensure that Cameron had the funds required to continue his work with psychic driving. In the spring of 1956, Monroe contacted Cameron and discussed the psychic driving treatment. Monroe reported back to Gittinger that it had been an interesting experiment and recommended that the Society fund Cameron.

Cameron didn't file an application with the Society until January 21, 1957, but the financial commitment was sufficiently firm for Cameron to offer Allan resident Ed Levinson a research appointment on the psychic driving project in June 1956. "He phoned me at home," Levinson remembers, "and offered me a post. He said he had seven thousand dollars for a one-year research appointment." Seven thousand dollars was the amount specified in the January 1957 SIHE application for a full-time research assistant, a figure that cannot be accounted for in any existing Allan financial records. It can be assumed then, that the January 1957 application was a formality and that Monroe had guaranteed Cameron the money before June 1956.

Cameron wanted to explore new methods of breaking down the patient's natural resistance to the dynamic implant. He suggested as possibilities the use of intensive electroshock, LSD — two methods he had already employed to a limited extent — as well as curare, a plant derivative that arrests the motor nerves, temporarily immobilizing the subject.

The proposed research appointment was a potent career opportunity for Levinson, and the seven thousand dollars a powerful incentive for the underpaid resident (a senior Allan psychiatrist made seventy-five hundred dollars a year in 1956). Levinson was, by his own accounting, one of Cameron's "fair-haired boys." Cameron had favourites among the residents, a group that tended to be bright, hard-working, and not always disposed to blindly following the "Great Man." Although Cameron sought power, often ruthlessly, he despised sycophants. "He would take a scunner to you," remembered a former resident, "and that was it. He wasn't likely to revise his opinion."

To Cameron's surprise Levinson refused the appointment; he baulked at one of the intended procedures to be used in the new research. Cameron had never completely resolved the problem of patients simply getting up and walking out of the room when their driving message was played over the speakers. In an effort to physically prevent the patients from moving, Cameron proposed to give them an intramuscular injection of up to one hundred and fifty micrograms of curare, effectively paralyzing them. Levinson considered it a dangerous procedure and didn't want the responsibility of administering the drug. He admired Cameron but felt that the proposed use of curare was "not within the bounds of reasonableness." Levinson said, "It wasn't a moral decision, I simply wasn't prepared to take the risk."

Cameron took his offer to another fair-haired boy, first-year resident Leonard Levy. Younger than Levinson and more ambitious, Levy accepted the appointment. "Cameron was a strong man in the eyes of a lot of people," Levinson said. "For a first-year resident like Levy, having the Chief smile on you was a potent thing. Cameron was very seductive because he was very powerful."

Prior to applying to the Society for the Investigation of Human Ecology, Cameron had already worked with sensory isolation, intensive electro-shock, LSD, and a variety of other drugs in conjunction with his psychic driving treatment. The application to the Society proposed little that was new other than the use of curare. It was mainly concerned with making psychic driving more efficient by breaking down "ongoing patterns of behaviour; more transitorily, more rapidly." The application revealed little qualitative change from the work Cameron had already done; what it did indicate was a quantitative change — longer periods of psychic driving, — and a willingness to intensify the treatment. In summing up the work he had done to date with psychic driving, Cameron wrote:

> By continued replaying of a cue communication, a persis-
> tant tendency to act in a way can be predetermined. . . .
> In other words, by driving a cue communication one can,
> without exception, set up in the patient a persisting tendency
> for that cue statement . . . to return to his awareness.

Richard Condon's book entitled *The Manchurian Candidate* was published in 1959. It was about a captured American soldier who was taken to a brainwashing centre in Manchuria and conditioned to become an assassin who would kill the President of the United States upon a predetermined verbal command. Condon's fiction echoed the original stated aims of the

BLUEBIRD project: "controlling an individual to the point where he will do our bidding against his will and even against such fundamental laws of nature as self-preservation." The CIA had been looking for an effective means of behaviour control for six years, and Cameron's custom-made independent project must have been a welcome piece of serendipity to Agency officials, who were under increasing pressure to produce results. If what Cameron claimed was true, the CIA had the means to produce a "Manchurian candidate."

Cameron's application was accepted by Monroe at the Society, then sent to Washington for Gottlieb's approval. Gottlieb approved it and it was designated MKULTRA sub-project 68, with John Gittinger as project officer. Between April, 1957 and June 30, 1960, the Society for the Investigation of Human Ecology provided Cameron with fifty-four thousand, four hundred and sixty-seven dollars and fifty-four cents for his psychic driving work, the second-largest grant administered among the one hundred and forty-nine MKULTRA projects outlined in the surviving CIA documents. Cameron's salary was not paid from the grant; most of the money went to purchasing equipment and paying the salaries of research psychiatrist Leonard Levy (twenty-four thousand, eighty-three dollars and twenty-six cents) and technician Leonard Rubenstein (six thousand and ninety-nine dollars, and ninety-six cents).

There were a number of casual workers on the project — psychologists, technicians, and assistants — none of whom were aware of the source of the funding. The information is not necessarily something that goes beyond the principal researcher who applied for the grant. Part-time assistants were aware that they were being paid from a grant as they received a cheque that was devoid of salaried staff benefits deductions, but there was no indication of the grant's origin. The cheques were issued by McGill University.

The first psychologist to do any work on the psychic driving project was Eve Libman, a staff psychologist then employed as a member of Cameron's service group. Cameron had set up interdisciplinary teams of psychiatrists, psychologists, nurses, and social workers to broaden the scope of patient care. Libman was a member of Cameron's team and administered various psychological evaluations; IQ tests, personality tests, Rorschach prints, and T.A.T. tests (thematic apperception tests).

Libman worked on many other projects as well as psychic driving and consequently tested only a few of these patients. She was more involved with Cameron's experiments with RNA (ribonucleic acid), research into memory and aging that was funded by Mental Health grants. This study was based on the theory that if you injected elderly people with RNA, their memories would improve. Libman said:

> We were doing memory testing. We tested these old people and I'd see them prior to them beginning their treatment and then afterward, and they typically improved. But there was one very notable thing about this, they were given the same test, so they got better at it. I mean obviously if you're going to administer something twice, they're going to remember a little bit more. And during one of the rounds, the clinical rounds, we were discussing this — at the time I was very young and inexperienced and really a junior member of the team — Cameron was talking about these interesting findings; that you just give them RNA and, lo and behold, their memories improve. And I suggested, rather timidly, shouldn't we be running a control group? Testing someone who wasn't given RNA. And there was dead silence. I was *very* aware that the Great Man was displeased. The issue was dropped.

The limits to Cameron's desire for input depended on who was supplying it and how large the audience was. Libman had an office in the basement of the Allan with two other psychologists. She felt that Cameron believed that the work of these two associates was of little consequence. All three psychologists had the same colour hair, and Libman jokingly suggested that most of the Allan psychiatrists thought is was only one person down there, that they were all the same dark-haired psychologist who would occasionally emerge from the basement to express a niggling doubt.

Libman only contributed a few hours to the psychic driving patients before Cameron brought in a full-time psychologist for the project in 1958. Laughlin Taylor, a young psychologist from McGill, was hired to do all the subsequent psychic driving testing. His job was to test the patient both prior to and after psychic driving, and to compare the results.

Taylor's initial meeting with Cameron went well. Cameron stated that he was willing to let Taylor use whatever tests and assessments he felt appropriate. British psychologist H. J. Eysenck had recently been trying to create tests that would quantify measures related to the emotional states of patients. The head of the clinical psychology program at McGill had been trained by Eysenck and suggested that some of his tests would be worth trying.

Taylor suggested it to Cameron, who told him to go ahead and do whatever he wanted.

Taylor maintained an office at McGill, but was on call for his work at the Allan Memorial. Cameron would call him up, often at odd hours, and tell Taylor that he had a candidate for psychic driving and that Taylor had twenty-four hours to administer the "before" tests. In the Allan corridors, Taylor heard rumours about Cameron's depatterning treatment. "This was the first whisper in terms of what happened in the past. This massive ECT was going on . . . patients had been given hundreds and were reduced to vegetables and were now in the Douglas [psychiatric hospital]. Everybody in the place talked about it." Taylor was given to understand that depatterning was no longer used as a treatment at the Allan and he never saw any depatterned patients during the course of his testing.

In fact, depatterning was still in use at the Allan in 1958 and continued to be used as a treatment until 1964, when Cameron left and his successor, Dr. Cleghorn, ordered a moratorium on its use. Taylor saw only a percentage of the pscyhic driving patients and none of these had been depatterned. One of the reasons was that ECT had moved out of the category of research and was considered a *bona fide* treatment and, as such, was not something that required the evaluation of a psychologist. Taylor only tested short-term cases. "I saw them, they went on the program — they were only on it for about two weeks — and then I saw them again." Many of the psychic driving patients were involved with the treatment for months; these long-term patients were not subject to Taylor's scrutiny. Cameron's research style involved a constant winnowing process so that those who reached Taylor were those whose chances at improvement were best.

Taylor's first disagreement with Cameron occurred when Taylor complained about the state of the patients he was to administer the "before" tests to. Many of them had recently received ECT, or were drugged, a condition that Taylor claimed was skewing his results. He stated that in order for the tests to have any value, patients should not have received ECT for a week prior to testing and to have been drug-free for forty-eight hours. Cameron eventually relented on this issue.

Cameron selected his psychic driving patients from the general patient population at the Allan. Although he reported that the best results were achieved with psycho-neurotics ("Effects of Repetition of Verbal Signals Upon Behaviour of Chronic Psychoneurotics," 1959), Laughlin Taylor also tested schizophrenics, depressives, neurotics, and alcoholics. " There was no systematic selection of patients. I couldn't see any. Somebody happened along and somebody said, "Well, what about trying psychic driving on them. What a good idea.' And on the project they went."

Taylor noted little change in patients after treatment; a few seemed better, some worse, the majority unchanged. "My general impression was that there was no change in these patients. I couldn't see a difference." In 1959, his misgivings about the efficacy of the treatment were compounded by ethical doubts. A psychic driving candidate, a Montreal woman, burst into tears one day when Taylor began his testing prior to treatment. When Taylor asked why she was crying, the woman said that she didn't want to participate in the research project but that she had to. Cameron had given her the choice of going into the psychic driving program or leaving the institute. She had suffered a "nervous breakdown" and felt that she couldn't cope at home. Faced with Cameron's alternative, she reluctantly submitted to the psychic driving. Informed consent, was often a luxury for the mentally-ill patient. They were in no position, practically or emotionally, to refuse.

Taylor was disturbed by the pressure that Cameron had exerted on the woman and became increasingly uncomfortable with the selection of psychic driving patients. "If a patient didn't show results," said Taylor, "Cameron dropped that patient out of the study and just didn't report him." He seemed to report only the successes. Another colleague describes Cameron's approach as a combination of unrealistic optimism and self-imposed pressure to produce a breakthrough. "Cameron was an impatient man. He had some pressure of time. He didn't want to stick with patients who weren't responding."

Taylor needed the work at the Allan to support his family, but because of his doubts about the nature of Cameron's research he decided to look for other work. A meeting with Cameron in 1960 hastened his departure. Taylor went to the Allan to discuss the evaluations that he had collected on the psychic driving patients. Cameron was preparing for an international conference where he was going to deliver another paper on psychic driving, and was in the process of selecting ten patients' histories for use as case studies.

"How can you report results on ten subjects?" Taylor asked. "What about all the others who didn't show any change?"
"That's only on your test results," Cameron replied.

Taylor suggested that if Cameron wanted to use the results of the psychological evaluations, he should use all of them, not simply those few that demonstrated improvement. Cameron replied that he conducted research in a controlled way before and had rejected it. His current method was to throw in as many variables as he could and use whatever came to the top. In treating mentally ill patients, virtually any treatment will produce some favourable results among a sample group. If you give them popcorn and show them films for three weeks, some percentage will show improvement. There is a formula doctors refer to, one third will get better, one third will get worse and a third remain unchanged. There are always good results to skim from the top.

"That is not scientific research," Taylor countered.

"That is the way we do research here, Mr. Taylor," Cameron said, "and if you don't want to be associated with it, you don't have to." Taylor left a few weeks later and was not replaced on the project.

*   *   *

With the help of the SIHE grant, Cameron was able to extend the driving sessions substantially. He was convinced that the message would have a therapeutic effect if the patient could be made to accept it. In each case, a negative message was initially given to the patient — "You have no confidence in yourself. You are weak and inadequate." It was designed to elicit an identification process in the patient and force him to confront his symptoms. The tape was eventually replaced with a positive message — "People like you and need you. You have confidence in yourself. People appreciate you and turn to you because of your value." This message would build-up the patient's sense of self-worth. In his 1956 paper, "Psychic Driving," Cameron wrote, "The practice has been to limit driving to ten to fifteen minutes on any given day as it is found that thereafter the patient usually succeeds in establishing defences or becomes so disturbed as to be unwilling to continue." By 1957, he had extended the driving period dramatically. "It was only common sense," he wrote, "to see what would happen if the repetition was increased tenfold, a hundredfold, or even more. And eventually our patients were listening to verbal signals we had set up ourselves on the basis of our knowledge of the patient, and listening from six in the morning until nine at night, day after day, and week after week." Negative driving went on for up to sixty days. Positive driving usually went on for longer, with one instance of one hundred and one days noted in Cameron's papers.

Cameron noted in a 1958 memo that, in an effort to break down the patient's defensive reaction to these extended driving sessions, "We have three methods of preparation of the patient: 1. prolonged sleep and ECT;

2. sleep used to reduce anxiety followed by sensory deprivation; 3. sensory deprivation." Cameron extended the use of these preparatory techniques to accord with the length of the driving period. He suggested that between thirty and thirty-five shock treatments were usually enough for depatterning; patient case histories note incidences of well over a hundred — many of them the Page-Russell type. He also recorded periods of sensory isolation of up to thirty-five days, noting that "Although the patient was prepared by both prolonged sensory isolation (thirty-five days) and by repeated depatterning, and although she received one hundred and one days of positive driving, no favourable results were obtained."

Cameron used the same isolation model that Hebb had developed, and employed the use of translucent goggles and cardboard tubes to cover the hands.

Other aspects of Cameron's isolation work differed from Hebb's. He wrote in a 1960 extract that:

> . . . our time structuring of sensory isolation is quite different from that of the Department of Psychology and all others since theirs was a self-imposed stay, whereas in ours the length of stay is imposed from outside and that we have also got two categories, namely, that we have got one in which some structuring is given in terms of staff saying 'Oh well, it won't be much longer,' or 'It will be a week or so,' or something of that kind, whereas with strict sensory isolation and the staff being forced to say nothing it was indefinite and therefore more disturbing.

Hebb was unhappy with what he felt was Cameron's wanton application of his work and he was critical of the whole course of Cameron's experimentation. In an interview with documentary film-maker Ronald Blumer, Hebb said:

> Cameron's experiments were done without the patient's consent. Cameron was irresponsible — criminally stupid — in that there was no reason to expect that he would get any results from the experiments. Anyone with any appreciation of the complexity of the human mind would not expect that you could erase an adult mind and then add things back with this stupid psychic driving. . . . The problem with

Cameron was that he didn't discard things when he was on
a bad wicket.

If Cameron ever thought he was on a bad wicket, there is no evidence
of it in his published results. In the first paper published during SIHE support, Cameron reported that while the type of change achieved, and the
durability of that change, fluctuated, "exposure to repetitions will produce
predetermined changes in all cases." As proof he cited the results of ten
psycho-neurotics (the disputed subjects that promoted Laughlin Taylor's exit
from the experiment). Cameron's belief in the success of his treatments came
partly from the conviction that the best evaluation of the patient's progress
was the opinion of the clinician. It was a view shared by a number of doctors at the time. He had earlier dismissed the patient's own evaluation of
his progress in a 1933 paper ("Mensuration in the Psychoses") as being the
least reliable. Laughlin Taylor's psychological tests followed close on the heels
of the patient's own judgement in terms of reliability:

> With regard to actual methods of assessment, we have found
> that psychological tests (which include the Rorschach, T.A.T.,
> figure drawings, and Carl Rogers Q-sort tests) are less suc-
> cessful than clinical assessment. Some of the tests are too
> susceptible to day-to-day changes.

Not all of the psychology department's tests were universally endorsed
in the medical quarter.

Cameron administered LSD to his patients using the same quantitative methodology he employed in his other methods of preparing a patient
for depatterning. A psychiatrist who treated one of Cameron's patients after
she was released from the Allan described Cameron's administration of the
drug:

> The first day, the patient was injected with one hundred
> micrograms of LSD, and there was no reaction. The second
> day, two hundred micrograms, again no reaction. On the
> third day, the patient received three hundred micrograms
> and the reaction was a panic produced by the buildup that
> stayed with her for two years.

Cameron's clinical persistance with large dosages of drugs and lengthy
duration of treatment stemmed partly from his belief that a crisis would
occasionally induce favourable change and that the mind had an almost

limitless capacity for normalization. Cameron's observation on the following incident is typical of this belief. He had observed a neurotic woman who was being treated at the Allan suddenly transform into an effective and functioning person when her son and daughter were kidnapped. She responded to the event with a purposefulness and resolve not seen in her previously. Cameron remarked to a resident that people were like boulders left from the ice-age that seemed rooted in one spot. Sometimes it was simply a matter of finding the right lever and exposing a face that has never been seen.

By all accounts, Cameron was not considered much of a scientist by his peers, and neither were some of his associates who worked on the psychic driving experiments. Leonard Levy, the research assistant, who did most of the actual work on the experiments, was described by a colleague as "less of a scientist than Cameron." Leonard Rubenstein, a technician, was also criticized for assuming medical responsibilities that were beyond his training. Cameron brought to the Allan a roster of important researchers, showing a keen eye for scientific talent, but he also had a blind spot that resulted in some peculiar appointments. Dr. R. A. Cleghorn wrote in his memoirs that Cameron showed:

> . . . impaired judgment by bringing in oddly assorted young men to assist in special projects. They proved to be indigestible people who, when the hypomanic flood ran out [Cameron's leaving], were a stranded nuisance. More than one proved to be a psychopathic character for which he had unhappily a blind eye.

It would seem that both Levy and Rubenstein fell into the "oddly assorted young men" category. Cameron's dubious theoretical basis for psychic driving was exacerbated by their lack of expertise and scientific rigor in administrating the treatments. Cameron received little constructive feedback on his work, and what little he did get — from the psychologists — he generally ignored.

The CIA was aware that in covertly financing MKULTRA work at a foreign university, they were entering into a delicate area, both legally and politically. At the time, an agreement existed between Canada and America regarding the protocol of funding research on one another's soil. It stipulated that any U.S. government support of research in Canada was to be channelled through the Canadian Defence Research Board. Any Canadian research done in the U.S. would also go through American government channels. By circumventing that established procedure, the CIA was, theoretically, violating

Canadian sovereignty. The need for secrecy was noted in an MKULTRA memorandum:

> In view of the fact that McGill University is in Canada, the following security considerations should be noted: 1) Dr. Cameron, the principal investigator and his staff will remain completely unwitting of U.S. government interest . . . ; 2) No Agency personnel will contact, visit or discuss this project with Dr. Cameron or his staff except under extreme circumstances.

Agency staff did visit Montreal, however, and contacted Cameron, but they were under the qualifying title of "staff agent." A staff agent, according to John Gittinger, is "a regular employee of the Central Intelligence Agency who is operating under cover and who could not admit that he worked for the CIA." The status of Sam Lyerly and Walter Pasternak, both of whom visited Cameron, was nominally that of SIHE psychologist, though Lyerly had come from the CIA and both would return to the Agency after the SIHE folded in 1965. Harold Wolff and James Monroe were more clearly defined as SIHE employees, but the status of all involved seemed to hang in the limbo of CIA terminology that distinguished between bureaucrats, consultants, active agents and staff agents.

All four men, Lyerly, Pasternack, Wolff and Monroe, visited Montreal to assess Cameron's progress with psychic driving. John Gittinger, project officer for MKULTRA sub-project 68, did not go himself, relying instead on the staff agent's reports like this one from Monroe. "[Monroe] was working fairly well with . . . the audio man [Leonard Rubenstein], who was working there," John Gittinger said. "I think Colonel Monroe spent a considerable amount of time with him."

Whether Cameron was aware of the CIA connection is the subject of conjecture. There is little in the Agency documents that survived Richard Helm's 1973 destruction order to prove that Cameron was aware of CIA involvement in SIHE. A recent polling of Cameron's colleagues revealed a roughly fifty-fifty split on this issue. "He probably knew about the CIA," said one colleague, "and he probably thought he was mounting an effort that would be of enormous benefit to mankind."

The threat of communism and the subject of brainwashing were of great interest to Cameron, the latter evidenced in the psychic driving project and the former topic appearing often in his papers. He described communism as the wholesale abdication of personal responsibility and considered it a societal aberration. A healthy society would not submit its will to the state. Cameron also felt that North America's next major military confrontation would be fought against Communists and he mentioned to his Allan colleagues the need for a bunker in the event of a nuclear attack. This attitude, however, was shared by many people during the Cold War years. In fact, teachers across the country conducted emergency drills; they herded students into school hallways and instructed them to put their heads into their laps and sit in a cross-legged sitting position. It was considered the first-line of defence against atom bombs.

Cameron posited that in the event of a war with the Communists, the West would need to be knowledgeable about brainwashing techniques. A former resident stated that "We were told that this [psychic driving] was to prepare for a potential war effort. He was involved in brainwashing, he made no bones about it."

It is quite likely that Cameron was aware of CIA involvement in the Society for the Investigation of Human Ecology. He had a vast number of reliable political and academic contacts who may have told him and it also goes a long way in explaining his immense interest in the military applications of brainwashing. Hebb considered his isolation research as a scientific pursuit which only happened to be of significant military interest as well. The CIA was thought by the public to be a reputable enough outfit in 1956. "If we thought of them at all," said one psychiatrist, "it was something like the Boy Scouts." Although the CIA had little in common with the Boy Scouts by the mid-1950s, it had yet to be caught doing anything wrong. It had already launched a number of illegal and unethical ventures, but its private deeds had yet to catch up with its public image.

The evidence confirming Cameron's knowledge of CIA involvement in his work is fragmented and circumstantial for the most part. One curiosity is a CIA trip report dated October 10-14, 1956, which records that: "Dr. [Maitland] Baldwin went to Montreal to discuss isolation techniques in reference to our most recent application."

Baldwin was the National Institute of Health researcher who had done research on the effects of isolation and who had offered to do "terminal type" experiments for the CIA. There are no records extant of Baldwin's meetings in Montreal. He could have been going to visit with Hebb, but Hebb's isolation research had been completed a year earlier to some acclaim. Cameron's MKULTRA application, however, had been solicited only earlier that year and involved the use of sensory isolation, an area of far greater interest to the CIA. The Baldwin trip, without any further documentation, remains a peripheral note that can be (and has been) picked up by either side in the Cameron debate as evidence either that: Cameron knew about the CIA; or that there is no hard information to lead to that conclusion.

There are those who would cast the CIA in the role of instigator of Cameron's excesses and the extremes he practiced in his psychic driving experiments were largely achieved during the years he was funded by the Society (1957-60). Yet the CIA did not direct his research. "Cameron was ruthless and he could be brutal," said a colleague, "but he was not corrupt. He had a streak of his father's presbyterianism in him." It could be argued that Cameron corrupted some of the scientific ideals he started out with in the course of his career, but he would not have lent himself to the grandiose schemes of another party, reducing himself to the role of bribed bureaucrat. If his judgment in research matters wavered, his ego was resolute.

Cameron's psychic driving technique resembled the brainwashing techniques of the Chinese more closely than any other MKULTRA sub-project. Dr. Robert Jay Lifton, a professor and psychiatrist who researched Chinese "thought reform" in the 1950s, stated in a 1986 affadavit that Cameron's procedures as outlined in his application to the Society were "non-therapeutic and potentially dangerous techniques of repetition and isolation which were extensions of the totalistic methods of 'thought reform' or brainwashing used in Chinese prisons and elsewhere."

Given the potential for the practical application of Cameron's work one has to question why the CIA ceased funding sub-project 68? Cameron not only claimed to effect a predetermined change in behaviour in every case, he also claimed that the depatterned subject would have absolutely no recollection of receiving treatment. From a strict intelligence point of view, this, theoretically, would mean that you could influence the subject through psychic driving and then erase any memory of being influenced with massive electroshock. In Richard Condon's *The Manchurian Candidate*, the brainwashing victims had no recollection of being brainwashed. As noted in John Marks book on the CIA, *The Search for the Manchurian Candidate*, Condon's novel may have been based on a 1953 CIA meeting where it was mentioned that "individuals who had come out of North Korea across the Soviet Union to freedom recently, apparently had a blank period of disorientation while passing through a special zone of Manchuria."

There was an expressed CIA interest in amnesia the year Cameron applied for his Society grant. John Gittinger recalled an Agency consultant, Dr. Cavenaugh, who "had an idea that there would be a certain advantage in certain people being able to forget certain things for a period of time . . . ," a theory with both defensive and offensive applications. Cameron had referred to his depatterning treatment as "differential amnesia," designating "the greater degree of amnesia which exists for pathological than for normal happenings produced by depatterning." On the surface, Cameron's therapeutic theories and the CIA's intelligence mandate seemed to dovetail perfectly on the issue of behavioural change.

Besides the coincidence of aims, the Society for the Investigation of Human Ecology had in Cameron a prominent figure who would lend prestige to their international profile. "Cameron was considered a 'status researcher' at that time," said Gittinger, "and it looked good, or it seemed to [to] the people around the Society."

The CIA lost interest in Cameron's work simply because the reality of his research results bore little resemblance to the successes described in his published papers. Two Agency observers and two Society representatives visited Montreal through the course of Cameron's funding and were thus in a position to measure the actual results against his claims. Sam Lyerly reported back to Gittinger that the concrete gains were marginal. "Sam was the technical research-oriented man," said Gittinger, "and he talked a good deal about what he was able to find out about the audio type of thing that [Cameron] was doing, and I talked to him considerably about that. And it was based largely on his recommendations that we lost most of our interest in [pyschic driving] after that time [1960]."

In fact, had an agency representative undertaken a first-hand examination of the psychic driving patients it would have revealed that not only did Cameron *not* produce a change in every case, patients who had listened to five hundred thousand repetitions of a single sentence were sometimes unable to repeat the sentence even once afterwards! The depatterned patients, while missing a period of weeks or years from their memory, including any recollection of their treatment, were very limited in their responses. Immediately after treatment, patients were often incontinent, disorganized, and unable to feed themselves. They were robotic, helpless, and under constant nursing care. In Montreal, the inflated espionage hopes of the CIA converged with the clinical realities of the mentally ill.

Sam Lyerly reported back to the Agency that Rubenstein's technology was primitive. Walter Pasternak concurred, telling Gittinger that "It didn't seem to really live up to the expectations that we had hoped might come from it."

By 1963, Cameron had arrived at the same conclusion. In a paper read that same year to a meeting of the American Psychopathological Association (of which Cameron was president), Cameron admitted the failure of the project:

> As so often happens in a long research, we took a wrong turn and continued to walk without a glint of success for a long, long time. I won't recount to you all the things we tried to stop the working of these defence mechanisms against repetition. Let me say that we vastly increased the number of repetitions to which the individual was exposed, that we continued driving while the individual was asleep, while he was in a chemical sleep, while he was awake but under hallucinogens, while he was under the influence of disinhibiting agents. We tried driving under hypnosis, immediately after electroshock, we tried innumerable combinations of voices, of timing and many other conditions, but we were unable to stop the [defence] mechanisms.
> I, Dr. Levy, Dr. Ban and Mr. Rubenstein found it was possible for the individual to be exposed to the repetition of verbal signals, such as I have described, a quarter to one-half million times and yet be unable to repeat these few short sentences at the end of this extraordinary large number of repetitions.

He concluded: "To these we gave the rather misleading term of 'dynamic implant.' Actually at the time we were implanting nothing."

This assessment of psychic driving was a denial of the enthusiastic conclusions offered in ten previously published papers on the subject. In 1955, he had reported that, "One hundred patients had been successfully brainwashed — Canadian style" in *Weekend* magazine. Two years later, Cameron wrote that "We can, without exception, set up in a patient a persisting tendency for the cue statement . . . to return to his awareness" (Psychic Driving: Dynamic Implant). In 1959, all ten of the case histories presented in "Effects of Repetition of Verbal Signals Upon the Behaviour of Chronic Psychoneurotic Patients" improved dramatically. In 1961, another ten selected case histories improved and Cameron concluded:

We should like to emphasize the value of this procedure as offering the possibility of replacing prolonged psychotherapy — both from the point of view that it can achieve results where prolonged psychotherapy is ineffectual and it is much more economical of time than psychotherapy ("A Further Report on the Effects of Repetition of Verbal Signals").

In "Repetition of Verbal Signals in Therapy," Cameron wrote, "It is now possible for us to state that exposure to repetition produces a change in every case." Another twenty-seven case studies showed marked improvement according to the paper.

In the canon of Cameron's published work with repetition, there is not a hint of doubt about the efficacy of the treatment. The single qualification made is the concession that psychic driving showed less success with chronic schizophrenics than with other patient groups.

The absence of any critical acuity over a twelve-year period in the face of what can charitably be described as poor results can be attributed to a number of factors. One of the factors is that some percentage of the psychic driving candidates had been labelled "untreatable;" any change in this group would have been interpreted as progress. On that score, Cameron's rampant optimism employed a flexible definition of *change* and an idiosyncratic reading of *progress*.

As his work progressed and was publicized as a runaway success, Cameron's investment in psychic driving became much greater. In terms of academic achievement, research is like a poker game; if you fold immediately you gain nothing and lose little. Once you are in for a substantial bet however, it becomes increasingly difficult to lay your cards down. By 1963, Cameron had ten years, ten published papers, and hundreds of patients invested in psychic driving. His scientific status, up until the early 1960s when his RNA work began to take priority, was hitched solely to the psychic driving work. Although his 1963 critique on psychic driving was a qualified statement — he suggested that the use of psychic driving on a considerably shortened voluntary basis would yield results and had done so — he did not continue his research with psychic driving and the paper that resulted from the speech, "Adventures in Repetition," served as the program's epitaph. The last years of his life were spent working in the RNA-memory field, an area, he remarked to Dr. Cleghorn, that had produced a number of Nobel candidates.

In 1960, Cameron's psychic driving was added to MKULTRA's growing list of projects that had failed to deliver anything of Agency interest. Both Colonel Monroe and Cameron negotiated with the U.S. Air Force to provide further funding for the work, apparently without success as there is no record of USAF sponsorship of Cameron's work. The Society granted Cameron a three-month funding extension to enable him to find support elsewhere and retreated from Montreal. "We never got any payload out of [Cameron's work]," Sid Gottlieb admitted.

The development of Ewen Cameron's research career and the growth of the CIA from an intelligence arm of the President to an all purpose espionage troupe short on accountability were parallel, rather than complementary events. In 1963, ten years after leaving office, Harry Truman reflected on the CIA, which had originally been created to co-ordinate, evaluate and disseminate foreign-intelligence information. Of their progress, Truman commented:

> I never had any thought that when I set up the CIA that it would be injected into peacetime cloak-and-dagger operations. For some time I have been disturbed by the way the CIA has been diverted from its original assignment. It had become an operational and at times a policy-making arm of the government. I, therefore, would like to see the CIA be restored to its original assignment as the intelligence arm of the President and whatever else it can properly perform in that special field — and that its operational duties be terminated or properly used elsewhere. We have grown up as a nation, respected for our ability to maintain a free and open society. There is something about the way the CIA has been functioning that is casting a shadow over our historic position and I feel that we need to correct it.

Truman later wrote:

> The CIA was set up by me for the sole purpose of getting all available information to the President. It was not intended to operate as an international agency engaged in strange activities.

By 1963, the CIA's Inspector General, Lyman Kirkpatrick, condemned some of the MKULTRA activities as "unethical and illegal" and an Agency medical officer rejected the proposed funding of Maitland Baldwin's "terminal type" isolation experiments as "immoral and inhuman." Sidney Gottlieb, project officer for the MKULTRA project and obdurate Agency hardballer, admitted in deposition that "It is true that many people both within and without the Agency considered these [concepts involved in manipulating human behaviour] to be distasteful and unethical."

The MKULTRA program had strayed from the CIA mandate outlined by Harry Truman and had existed outside many of the Agency's own internal accounting procedures. Dr. Edward Gunn, former chief of the CIA medical staff, testified in a 1975 Senate hearing that he had never been informed of the MKULTRA program to any extent and that his offer of medical advice was rebuffed by the technical services division, which administered MKULTRA. The behaviour control program was accountable only to Agency Director Richard Helms, who had helped conceive the program in 1953, and Sidney Gottlieb, head of the project. It was a program that was out of control, and, as Gottlieb admitted, it failed to deliver anything of operational value in more than two decades of existence.

Cameron also began with the best of intentions, but he gradually distanced himself from both his initial adherence to objective psychiatry and the humanist principles that he had espoused with such conviction. In 1963, he wrote that in the experiments with psychic driving ten years earlier, he had noted in all patients the same reaction — "discomfort, aversion, embarrassment and resentment. And indeed I noticed in myself a reluctance to do this — I felt I was being unkind, insensitive, unperceptive — that in a word, one simply didn't do this sort of thing to people. For these reasons, namely the patient's feelings and my own, I felt increasingly sure that there must be something of importance hidden." Cameron's conviction that the treatment would yield therapeutic results eventually overcame his distaste for the work. For ten years he was optimistic about his treatment despite his lack of success. Laughlin Taylor remembers Cameron as a:

> . . . bustling bundle of energy, directed with tremendous force. It may have been directed initially in the interest of scientific inquiry — to what makes people tick and what causes these abnormalities — but I think it got completely out of hand. To me he was a megalomaniac who was completely out of control. I really feel that in all my contacts with the man, that his main guiding influence was this ego drive — to push Cameron. I always felt that science, psychiatry, patients, everything, came second to Cameron's needs.

In 1963, one year away from leaving the Allan, he reviewed the psychic driving program with clarity, apparently for the first time.

Dr. Ewen Cameron

The Allan Memorial Institute

(L. to R.) Doctors K. G. Charron, Cyril F. James, and Ewen Cameron

The official opening of the Allan Memorial Institute
(L. to R.) G. Blair Gordon, Hospital President, Hon. Paul Martin,
minister of National Health and Welfare, Dr. Jean Grégoire, Deputy
Minister for Quebec, and Dr. Ewen Cameron.

A room — possibly a staff lounge — inside the Allan

A 1957 *Montreal Star* photo story about a patient's
typical stay at the Allan Memorial

1. Patient and wife arrive at door of Allan Memorial Institute, the
psychiatric department of Royal Victoria Hospital. Over door is Latin
motto: *Spero*: "I hope." Average stay in Allan Memorial is six weeks.
(Photo no longer in existence)

2. He is worried as he answers routine questions in admitting office.
Significant recent development in mental treatment is development of
departments in general hospitals, with Allan leading the way.

3. In his own room, nurse takes his hat and coat, reassures him. May is
Mental Health Month in Quebec, Provincial division of Canadian Mental
Health Association is out to raise $100,000 from May 13 to 27.

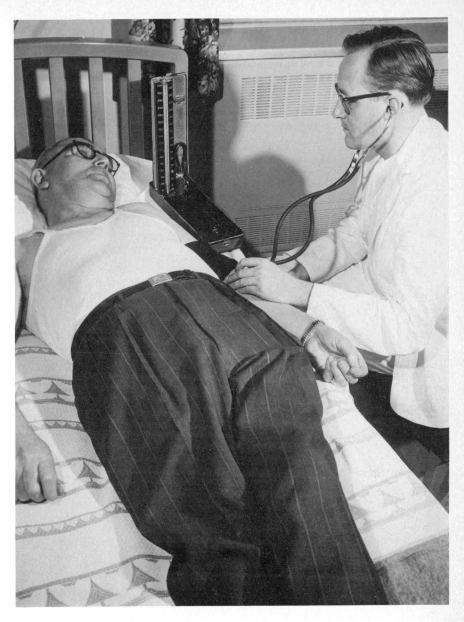

4. Doctor gives each patient entering the Allan a physical check. In Star photo series no real relatives or patients are shown. Institute staff members played roles of outsiders as well as those of doctor, nurse, etc.

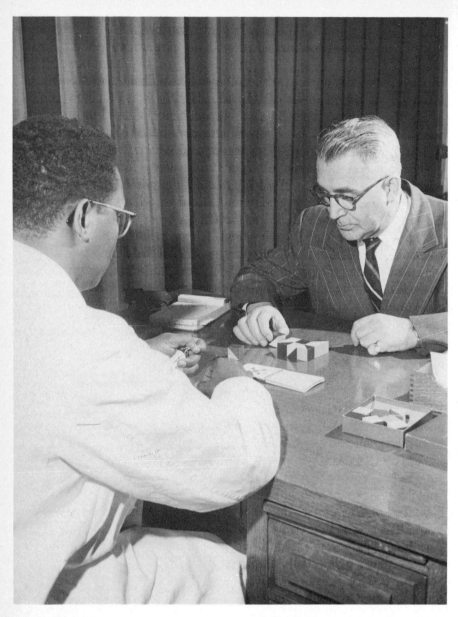

5. Arranging block is part of test given by psychologist. Old style mental hospital gave little treatment. Patients had to spend much of day sitting idle. Today the patients are active from morning to night.

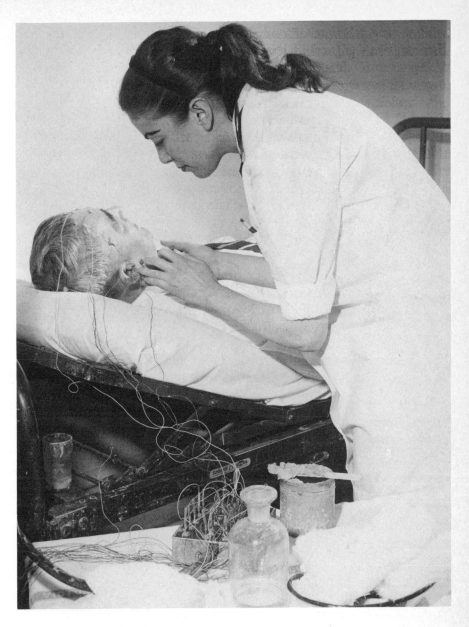

6. Fine electrode wires are attached to patient's head to prepare for EEG
— routine painless brain wave measurement which helps the doctors
decide what kind of treatment would be the best remedy for patient.

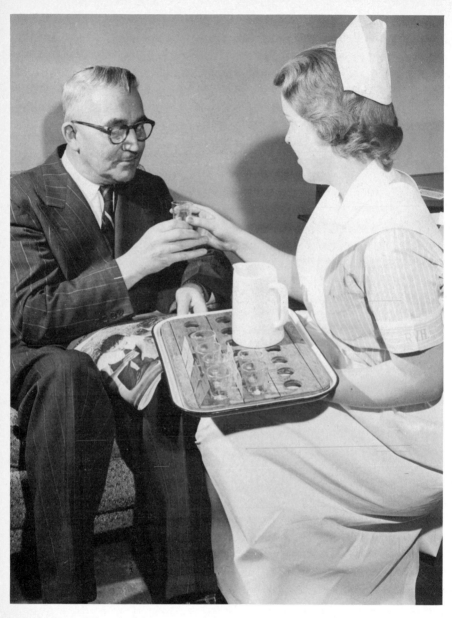

7. In the pleasant day ward, patient interrupts reading a magazine to
take medicine brought in to him by a nurse. Day may begin with
breakfast at 8 a.m., end with social evening. Lights are turned out after
10 p.m.

8. When indicated, physical treatment — like electroshock — is given in this therapy unit which serves day patients as well as those living in hospital. Day hospital system was invented at the Allan Memorial Institute.

9. Throughout patient's stay at Allan, social worker sees his wife often. During these meetings social worker helps her deal with her feelings about his treatment and problems when he comes back to home, neighbours and work.

10. Lunch with other patients is served by nurse. Canada's mental health problem is headlined by fact half of all hospital beds in country are occupied by mentally ill, too many still not getting active treatment.

11. Allan Memorial is housed in great former private residence, has spacious lawns, trees and flower beds. It is a voluntary treatment centre. Patients cannot be kept in the Institute against their will.

12. Main treatment emphasis at Allan is on psychotherapy, in which patient talks to psychiatrists, as here, at regular appointments. Group psychotherapy is also given which helps to speed patient's social adjustment.

13. Treatment team has valuable member in occupational therapist. Here she admires patient's finger-painting. Mornings tend to be for treatment, afternoons for other activity, but schedules vary, according to individuals needs.

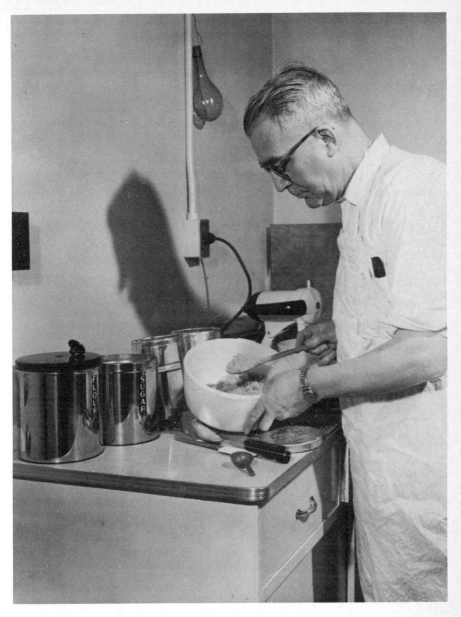

14. Men as well as women are welcome to use occupational therapy kitchen — or laundry with washing machine and irons. Nurses relished a peach cake made by a male disciple of Escoffier at the Allan last week.

15. Playing volleyball with nurses against other patients is part of the therapy. Treatment teams includes doctors, nurses, psychologists, occupational therapists, social workers, and all take part in social activity.

16. Relatives meet regularly with social worker to discuss their problems, help one another to solve them under her supervision. Here patient's wife, centre, raises a point during one of these most important meetings.

17. Patient plays ping pong. One measure of patient's improvement can be his eagerness to do things with other people. Hence the Allan Memorial emphasis, like that of other modern centres, is on social activity.

18. A keen pianist, patient plays for other patients and nurse in sing-song typical of social activities encouraged by nurses, social workers and other hospital staff. Patient at right is not yet ready to join in.

19. Receptionist shares in joy as patient, ready for discharge, meets his wife in lobby. Up to 70 per cent of new patients leave modern mental hospitals either well or considerably improved after active treatment.

20. Back at front door after six weeks, patient grins at view of city from upper Pine avenue as he waits for taxi to take him home. Like many other diseases mental illness can be successfully treated at modern hospitals.

Dr. Heinz Lehmann

CHAPTER EIGHT

JEAN-CHARLES PAGE
PORTRAIT OF A PLAINTIFF

Jean-Charles Pagé has had first hand experience with Quebec's evolving mental health system. A former alcoholic, he has dried out in L'Institute Albert Prévost, undergone psychic driving at the Allan Memorial, and has been incarcerated for eleven months in St-Jean de Dieu Hospital, then a six-thousand-patient asylum on the eastern edge of Montreal. He wrote a book about his experience in St-Jean de Dieu, *Les Fous Crient au Secours (The Mentally Ill Cry for Help)*, which became a bestseller in Quebec and was responsible for the creation of the 1961 Bedard Commission, a government-sponsored investigation of every mental health facility in the province. There is currently a prize awarded in his name, Prix Jean-Charles Pagé, for journalistic excellence in the field of mental illness. For the past six years, he has been a resolute non-drinker and is one of nine plaintiffs who are suing the CIA for negligence in it's funding of Ewen Cameron's psychic driving program.

*   *   *

On a bitter morning in the later winter of 1979, Jean-Charles Pagé got up early to watch "Canada A.M.," an early morning news program. It was still dark and the cold penetrated his small house outside St-André Est, a small town seventy kilometres west of Montreal. He and his companion, Jeanine, had hung a blanket across part of the west wall to keep the wind from whistling in but it didn't do much good. Pagé flipped on the large console television that dominated the cramped living room and sat down in his armchair.

John Marks, an American journalist, was being interviewed that morning. He had just written a book, *The Search for the Manchurian*

Candidate, a detailed exposé of the CIA's covert behaviour-control program in the 1950s and 60s.

The show's host was particularly interested in the Canadian angle: the work of Ewen Cameron at the Allan Memorial Institute in Montreal, that work had been funded by the CIA between 1957 and 1960 the Society for the Investigation of Human Ecology.

Pagé's interest was piqued; he had been a patient at the Allan in 1959. Marks talked specifically about psychic driving. As Marks described the treatment, Pagé recognized it as the one he had received. He wanted to know more about the CIA business and immediately called the show's research department in Toronto, hoping to speak to Marks.

Marks had already left the studio to continue his promotional circuit in Toronto, but he had left instructions for the switchboard to take the names and numbers of any callers. He would check in at the end of the day.

Marks called Pagé that night and gave him details on the connection between the Allan Memorial and CIA funding. Pagé contacted a Montreal lawyer to investigate the possibility of a lawsuit against the CIA. The lawyer said that Pagé had a good chance, but wanted a five-thousand dollar retainer. Pagé was on a disability pension and didn't have that kind of money. He barely met his monthly expenses as it was.

Pagé heard that another former Allan patient, Val Orlikow, had launched a suit in Washington, D.C., against the CIA. In February 1980, Pagé contacted Orlikow's lawyer, Joseph Rauh. Rauh accepted Pagé's case without a retainer, adding him to the existing Orlikow suit. They were asking for one million dollars per plaintiff in damages. Eventually, seven other Canadians joined the suit as the case received more publicity, and former patients identified themselves as victims. Pagé applied for his medical record and, after four-and-a-half months of requests, negotiations and bureaucratic error, he received it. He read it regularly, trying to recreate the events of his stay at the Allan. "You know it's funny," says Page's companion, Jeanine, "Since he found out about the Allan, he didn't touch a drop of liquor." The lawsuit is his new opiate.

Six years after the suit was initiated, it had still not come to trial. It made a big splash in the media in 1979-80, but it gradually died as an issue. Further media coverage was sporadic; an editorial by Allan Fotheringham; a mention on page seven of the Montreal *Gazette* that the lawsuit was on the agenda of External Affairs Minister Joe Clark's meeting with Secretary of State George Schultz; the sad news that one of the plaintiffs had died. "They are just waiting for us to die off," Pagé says of the CIA's stalling tactics. "And it's working." Florence Langleben, one of the plaintiffs, died in February 1986. Others in the case are frail and elderly, and Pagé wonders how many more will die before the case is resolved. There is no public pressure to bring the case to trial. As an issue it has quietly drifted away, having exhausted the public's tolerance for unresolved news items.

Pagé's house is an hour's drive west of Montreal, situated in a rural area between a small town and nearby farms, on the banks of the meandering North River. Beside Pagé's house, a blue tent is pitched; protection against the indigenous mosquito population. Inside the tent are two lawn chairs and a newspaper.

Pagé is fifty-four years old, a short French-Canadian man whose movements are animated by restless energy. He is smoking a cigarette and manages to look both hopeful and suspicious when he opens the door. His English is good and he speaks fluently, occasionally substituting a French word when he is stuck.

"What do you think of my house?" he asks. After a polite reply that focuses on the riverfront location, he presses, "Would you live here?" he asks accusingly.

He is reluctant to start his story; it tends to leave him upset afterwards. He is suspicious, too, unsure of who is on his side. Staring from across the kitchen table, he says, "I think you are from the CIA, that's what I think," and measures the reaction. After a quick call to his Washington attorney for reassurance, Pagé lights another cigarette. "I'm fifty-three but my brain is sixty-eight," he says. "How do you like that?" He explains that he has had some neurological tests done and that is what they told him.

He brings out his medical record, a well-thumbed document that charts his progress at the Allan. Reading from it, he comes upon items he is surprised to see, commenting that it is the first time he has noticed this or that particular point. The phone rings and after a brief conversation in French, Pagé returns to his case history, going back to the top of the page and working his way through with the enthusiasm of discovery, unaware that he went over the same page two minutes earlier. His short-term memory is ephemeral and regularly lets him down. When he reads he follows the print with his finger. Familiar passages take on the character of litany, an invocation of remembered wrongs and responses.

In 1954, Pagé was a budding twenty-one-year-old entrepreneur with a highly-developed taste for rye whiskey. "I had my own business manufacturing a material for sweeping floors. You remember Dustbane?" he asks. Dustbane was a green sawdust and oil combination that was used commercially to keep the dust down when sweeping floors. Pagé manufactured and sold a competing version that claimed to also wax the floor. He would make two tons of it in one day — Dust-O-Wax, he called it — then sell it out of his pick-up truck the next. He drove to schools, churches and stores around small-town Quebec and French Ontario, undercutting Dustbane's price. On a good day he made one hundred dollars, a lot of money for a twenty-one year old in 1954.

It wasn't his only job. His father had been the bailiff in Hawkesbury, a small Ontario town near the Quebec border, just across the bridge from Grenville, where the family lived. When he died, the job went to Pagé. Pagé's mother and sister were convinced that the job should be kept in the family, passed on like an heirloom. "It was a terrible job," he remembers. Turning people out of their homes with a table, four chairs and their winter clothes wasn't a popular occupation in a small town. He tried it for a while, but he didn't have the stomach for it and soon gave it up.

He also ran a string of betting pools in the areas around Grenville. He had nine men under him distributing what were called the "five-way pools," an illegal, but in Duplessis's Quebec, sanctified form of gambling that guaranteed two winners in every package of twenty. By the mid-1950s Pagé was going through more than a bottle of rye a day, but it didn't seem to be having any effect on his work. In the hotel bars of Grenville and Hawkesbury, he was always good for a touch. "Lend me a deuce, lend me a five," would be the chorus when he came into the lounge. He'd give them a slap on the back, tell a few jokes and shell out a few bucks. He had a lot to spare.

Pagé's knowledge of the area and general *bonhomie* were tapped by Maurice Duplessis's political machine in 1957. In the course of three provincial election campaigns, Duplessis had created an impressive political apparatus that generated votes through a combination of gerrymandered polling stations and widespread corruption. "You could buy a vote for five or ten dollars," Pagé says. In 1957, much of this system was lent to Diefenbaker for the Conservative party's bid for federal power. Pagé's job was to make sure all the Tories found their way to the polls.

Voting in Quebec in the 1950s was a cross between a cottage industry and a blood sport, and the electorate had become accustomed to receiving advice in making electoral decisions. A large family that delivered eleven votes to Duplessis's third provincial triumph had been given a refrigerator for their effort. They waited to see what the terms were going to be with this Diefenbaker deal. Television was the coming thing they had heard.

For every polling station, a car and two cases of whisky were assigned. Pagé ran one of the cars. He drove around the riding dispensing whisky and taking voters to the polls. It was a good way to earn a few hundred bucks.

At the age of twenty-four, Pagé experienced his first case of *delirium tremens* — the DTs. "I was making money but I was drinking real heavy," he explained. He went on an extended spree and woke up in L'Institute Albert Prévost, a private hospital where he found he was paying three nurses a dollar an hour to spell one another in a twenty-four-hour vigil. "God it was awful," he says. He recalls some of his hallucinations: "I saw a woman with her head cut off, blood running down . . ." The Albert Prévost experience put a temporary crimp in his drinking habits.

"But sometimes I'd get fed up with the small town and go on a spree in Montreal for a month, month-and-a-half," he says, "I was making the money for it."

Montreal had a vibrant nightlife; nightclubs were open until three a.m. and when they closed the crowd drifted to private clubs that served liquor until eight in the morning. "There were five women to one man," Pagé remembers. At eight a.m. Pagé went to a tavern that opened for the morning crowd. Taverns only served beer and for a rye man, that was bad news; beer tasted like stagnant pond water. But Pagé was fixed with the morning bartender and when he came in every morning, there was a ten-ounce bottle of rye hidden behind the toilet in the washroom. He'd walk in, go straight to the men's room, take a swig, then go back to the bar and nurse a couple of beers among the bleary day workers who were hurriedly sipping breakfast. At ten a.m., the lounge at the Casa Loma opened, and he could get some hard liquor. At night he went back to the clubs and started the cycle again. When the binge wound down, from a combination of fatigue, malnutrition, dwindling funds, and some atavistic survival mechanism, Pagé took the train home to Grenville.

He gave Alcoholics Anonymous a try for a month-and-a-half, but it didn't work out. AA had just started in Montreal and the meetings were attended mostly by skid-row drunks who had been recruited by social workers. As a young man with his own business, Pagé had little in common with the derelict crowd at the meetings, and he wasn't prepared to wait until membership trickled up into the middle-classes.

In 1959, Pagé was admitted to the Allan Memorial Institute as a paying patient. He was diagnosed as a chronic psycho-neurotic or schizophrenic personality. Dr. Kirby, his family doctor, had been an intern at the Royal Victoria Hospital, and had recommended Pagé's hospitalization. "Patient has depression of the agitated type," Pagé's medical record reads. "He is a fit candidate for continuous sleep and/or psychic driving."

Pagé was sent to South Two, the sleep ward that had twenty beds in it. He was kept asleep for thirty-six days with a combination of drugs — Largactil, Artane, Sodium Amytal, Nembutal, Seconal and Thorazine — administered two-to-four times a day. Pagé was roused to take the medication and to be fed. He remembers being spoon-fed by a kindly nurse and staring around the room at the other patients.

While he slept, Pagé received thirty-one days of psychic driving: eighteen days of negative driving, and thirteen days of positive driving. He remembers hearing the driving message coming from his pillow. "So I asked the orderly where it was coming from," Pagé says, "and he shows me this huge machine." (Rubenstein's state-of-the-art tape recorder loomed in the hallway.)

Pagé was woken up on four occasions to receive Page-Russell electroshocks. His case history notes that after the ECT he lost his ability to speak or understand English. Pagé was fluently bilingual; it was a common side effect noted by Cameron that multi-lingual patients often lost their ability to speak any language other than their mother tongue. Although Pagé was a francophone, the driving message had been in English. The Allan was essentially an anglophone institution and though it treated the francophone community, it had very few French-speaking staff members. After the Page-Russell, the driving message was switched to French.

After thirty-six days, Pagé was taken off the sleep therapy and psychic driving treatment and the abrupt end to his drug intake brought back his familiar post-binge shakes. His memories of the Allan are both pointed and disoriented. It was almost thirty years ago and the combination of time, drugs and the excesses of his alcoholic sprees have taken their toll.

He remembers being taken to another room after his psychic driving:

> There were five or six doctors in the room and a bed. I was lying on the bed and one doctor held some gas over my mouth. [The case history states that he received nitrous oxide at one point.] The others were gathered around the bed and there were pillows down at the end of the bed. While I had the gas, the doctors all yelled "kill him! kill him!" one after the other, left to right around the bed, then they'd start again and I'd kick the pillow. If you saw it in a horror movie, you wouldn't believe it. . . . I guess they were trying to get the shakes out.

The shakes obstinately remained and Pagé was put on twenty-eight days of sub-coma insulin treatment. Insulin coma had been dropped by most hospitals by 1959 as being too dangerous and of questionable therapeutic value, but sub-coma insulin treatment, a less drastic version, remained in use. Pagé was given insulin injections to lower his blood sugar, the insulin gradually burning the sugar out of his system and inducing a severe chill. "I had never been so cold," Pagé says. "I was freezing to death." Afterwards, he ate jam, and the sugar spread through his body like a thaw.

The insulin failed to get rid of his shakes. "I tried to make an ashtray but I couldn't sit still." He was too jumpy to stay in one place and moved around the ward anxiously, asking for his wife.

The case history notes a gradual improvement. He was able to concentrate long enough to produce some passable still-lifes in painting class, a source of surprise to Pagé. "I never painted in my whole damn life," he says, " I can't even draw," then continues to read from his history. "Patient is able to joke and became quite jocular about his behaviour last week when he left the Allan and, in a clearly defined bid for more attention, drank just enough beer so it would show up on his breath."

Pagé remembers the incident. "I left to find a drink to get rid of the shakes. It was the only thing that worked in the past. I couldn't find a club [that served liquor] so I had to settle for a tavern. I had a couple of beers but it didn't help. It got worse." When he got back he joked with the nurses and promised he wouldn't do it again. Bits of the old Pagé, the one most comfortable in hotel bars, were visible. He stayed at the Allan until the fall, restlessly wandering around the hospital, wound up tighter than a watchspring. The case history notes, "We still see him as being quite anxious. We are making very little headway." In November, a doctor gave him some sodium pentathol and his shakes finally went away. He was released on November 13th.

Upon his release, Pagé went to visit his wife, who was staying with her parents in Montreal North. His shakes were gone but he felt deflated from his stay at the Allan and ill at ease with himself. When he met with his wife in the awkward confines of her Catholic parents house, they fought. He left in a rage and hitchhiked to Grenville.

"My sister had a restaurant in Grenville and the restaurant had a pool room. So I'd take care of the pool room during the night." His Dust-O-Wax business had fallen by the wayside during his four-month stay at the Allan and there weren't any elections going on to tap his talents as a wheel man. He helped clean up around his sister's restaurant and watched the pool room. "Late at night she'd want to go to sleep and the guys still wanted to play pool, so I'd stay up and keep an eye on things." By the late winter of 1960, he still hadn't had a drink, carefully avoiding the hotel bar across the street.

By April, Pagé's mood improved. He decided to celebrate with a nightcap across the street. Before closing he went in and ordered a glass of Dubonnet, a civilized drink, he felt. One drink wouldn't hurt and he only had time for one anyway before the bar closed. He sipped his drink slowly, bid goodnight to everyone and left, returning to his sister's place. The next night he returned for another Dubonnet, lingering over it before returning to his sister's. On the third night, his new ritual exploded into the demonic excess that alcoholism inspires and the next day he woke up in the St-Jean de Dieu Mental Hospital.

When he opened his eyes, the first thing he saw were barred windows; he thought he was in jail. There was little relief accompanying the news that he was in St-Jean de Dieu. It wasn't high on anyone's list of places to wake up in. He wasn't a paying guest this time as he had been at the Allan. He had been committed by his exasperated relatives and this time the length of his stay was out of his hands.

St-Jean de Dieu was the largest mental facility in Quebec, housing six thousand patients, nine hundred workers and four hundred and fifty nuns. The nuns of Providence owned and operated St-Jean de Dieu, which at the time existed as the City of Gamelin, a walled fortress outside the eastern periphery of Montreal. It had its own fire department, railway system, and a labour force of several thousand inmates who were paid fifty cents a week by the enterprising nuns.

On the back wards were chronically disturbed and psychotic patients, most of whom would spend their lives in the beds they occupied, unclaimed by relatives. Many were violent or suicidal, and most of them were beyond the help of the limited treatments available. At the other end of the spectrum there was a lively group of binge alcoholics and general troublemakers; unwanted wives, superfluous business partners, and unfortunate rivals who had been railroaded into the institution on the signatures of various relatives and unscrupulous doctors. It was said of St-Jean de Dieu that it was too easy a place to get into and too hard a one to get out of. It was a convenient holding tank for people who were on the wrong end of scheming relationships. Once incarcerated, they could only be released with the approval of a committee of psychiatrists who pronounced them sane. Declared sane, they still had to prove that they had somewhere to go; they would not be released out into the street.

Early in his stay at St-Jean de Dieu, Pagé saw an orderly kick a strait-jacketed patient in the groin. "I saw a lot of things that were worse, believe me," he confides ominously. Beside the outbreaks of violence between psychotic patients and frustrated, underpaid staff, there were many inconveniences to endure. His clothes had been taken away and the ones they had given him didn't fit. Bathrooms were stocked with copies of *Le Devoir*, a Montreal newspaper, in place of toilet paper; the nuns sold tabacco at a one hundred percent mark-up, censored reading material, and paid only fifty cents for a forty-hour work week, and the food was terrible. The nuns had made arrangements to buy damaged tins of food at a discount and the menu relied heavily on fried luncheon meat.

"There was a guy there," Pagé remembers, "a reporter from *The Montreal Star*. He was a good guy. He used to tell everyone, 'When I get out of here, everybody's going to know what's going on in this goddamn prison. You'll read about it in the *Star*.' We never saw him again. He was put on one of the back wards with the psychotics and we never found out what happened to him. That made an impression on me. First get out, then talk."

Pagé got a job as a courier inside the institution, delivering mail, drugs in gallon pails, whatever was needed. It gave him access to areas that would otherwise have been restricted. He witnessed a number of ugly incidents as he made his rounds and thought of doing what *The Montreal Star* reporter had brashly threatened to do. He wanted to tell someone outside that patients lived in fear, that there was little treatment available, and that they were without decent clothes and food. "It was a question of dignity. We had no dignity. We were treated like animals. The people in there, the nurses and the orderlies, it's not that they're not human, but they're with sick people too long. They don't change them often enough."

Pagé didn't know when he was going to be released, so he devised a plan to be able to remember everything that he had witnessed. "My wife used to keep a diary so I decided I would phone her every day from St-Jean de Dieu. There was a pay phone that cost a nickel, and a nickel was a lot of money when you're making fifty cents a week. So I'd phone her and let it ring once and hang up. That was my signal for her to phone back. I'd tell her about something that happened and ask her to put it in her diary. She'd ask why and I'd say 'Just write it in,' and she would. She never imagined that I was going to write a book."

The only treatment Pagé received in St-Jean de Dieu was psychotherapy. Therapy was dispensed on a first-come-first-served basis, and the line outside the therapist's office formed early and was short on decorum. The interest in psychotherapy among the patients was partly due to the fact that the therapist decided if they were well enough to leave. Manoeuvering his way into his first session, Pagé was surprised to find both a nurse and a nun sitting expectantly alongside the doctor. As a Catholic, Pagé found the nun's presence a little oppressive in the context of the cathartic mood of the session. He started his confession cautiously, presenting an expurgated version of his life for the benefit of the Sister. Eventually he came to resent her presence and deliberately regaled his audience with the most shocking stories he could think of. It didn't do much to convince the doctor to release him but the nun gave in and didn't return. "If she was scandalized, that's her tough luck. It's supposed to be a private thing anyway."

After eleven months in St-Jean de Dieu, Pagé was granted a conditional release by a board of psychiatrists. Every morning he was given a day-pass and sent out to find work. If he could find a job, he would be released from the institute. "To get a job with a certificate marked 'St-Jean de Dieu' on it was hard. Employers would take one look at that and there was no job. Who wants a crazy person working for them?"

Frustrated by his futile attempts to find work, Pagé phoned *Le Devoir* and told them that he had a story for them. He gave the editor a brief description of his experience in St-Jean de Dieu and told them that he had kept a written record. The editor decided that it was too big a story for a newspaper article and put Pagé in touch with Jacques Hébert, a Montreal book publisher. Hébert was interested, but questioned Pagé's ability to write the book himself and asked him to submit a sample chapter. Using the notes from his wife's diary, Pagé wrote a chapter and Hébert decided that he could do the job. The result was *Les Fous crient au secours*. Priced at a dollar and distributed at newsstands, drugstores, and book stores, it quickly sold thirty-six thousand copies and prompted a public outcry.

Subsequently, the Bédard Commission discovered that the Nuns of Providence who ran St-Jean de Dieu had declared a profit of one million dollars the previous year. They received two dollars and seventy-five cents per patient per day from the government, the lowest amount granted by the government for hospital care, and yet from that *per diem* they were able to save fifty cents a day, resulting in a daily profit of three thousand dollars. It may have been management that the Harvard Business School might envy, but it was a conflict of interest between the nuns' desire for cheap labour, and a patient's right to proper hospital care. After the Bédard Report appeared in 1962, the patient population in St-Jean de Dieu was weeded out, and thousands were released.

In the wake of the Bédard Commissions' findings and the success of his book, Pagé was briefly the centre of attention. His relationship with his wife ended sourly and a succession of sales jobs and binges followed. His erratic memory and violent mood swings eventually rendered him unemployable. Since 1979, he has done little except soberly chart the progress of his lawsuit against the CIA. In six years his enthusiasm has been eroded. "In all this time, I always thought we'd win. Right now though, I don't know, I don't have that much hope. I'm tired."

CHAPTER NINE

KARRALYNN SCHRECK
A CLINICAL SUCCESS STORY

For the last several years Karralynn Schreck has been living in a small American town, out of range of the controversy over Cameron's work. In 1985, her family informed her of newspaper reports with headings like "Mad Scientist at Allan," and "CIA Doctor." Karralynn was shocked that Cameron's reputation was being called into question and was dismayed that no one had come forward to defend him. She wrote a letter to Dr. Brian Robertson, director of the Allan, commending Cameron and his work and also contacted Cameron's son, Duncan, now a Washington lawyer, in a gesture of support. She wanted the Cameron family to know that their father had saved her life.

Karralynn Schreck is a testament to the clinical strengths of Ewen Cameron. A pretty woman who smiled easily and conversed eagerly on the subject of her former psychiatrist. "He was the most special person in my life," Karralynn said of Cameron. "Until the day I die there will never be anyone like him. He made you respect yourself and care about yourself. He cared fiercely; there was a single-minded focus to it. You had to respond."

As a teenager in Moncton, New Brunswick, Karralynn had developed an anxiety disorder that kept her out of school after the ninth grade. By 1960, she had exhausted the efforts of the local doctors and was sent to the Institute of Living, a psychiatric facility in Hartford, Connecticut. It was a respected sanatorium for wealthy neurotics and, like most pscyhiatric institutions, it had its back wards where the chronically ill languished, often under restraint or in seclusion.

She was diagnosed "schizophrenic reaction chronic undifferentiated type" by the admitting doctor, and settled uneasily into her new home. Shortly after admission she began to suffer seizures — as many as twenty a day — which were diagnosed as epileptic. Medication failed to control them, and psychotherapy proved unsuccessful. She found her therapist cold and distant and was unable to communicate with him. She became severely depressed and began to burn the soles of her feet and the palms of her hands with cigarettes. She was placed in a locked room on the back ward which contained fifteen psychotic women. The other patients urinated on the floor, tore off their clothes, masturbated, and attacked one another on impulse. After a five-day stay with the lunatic element, Karralynn was taken off the back ward, but remained sullen and unresponsive.

By the 1950s it had become apparent that simply by moving patients from back wards to a more socially amenable atmosphere, a percentage of them would improve. Presumably, this axiom worked both ways. In the forced company of chronic psychotics, Karralynn regressed from anxious teenager to dangerously ill mental patient. Psychotherapy proved unsuccessful, and Dr. Francis Braceland, Director of the Institute, suggested she try the Allan Memorial. Braceland knew Cameron from a committee they both sat on and urged him to take Schreck as a patient.

By 1962, Cameron had a reputation for taking clinical "failures" off other doctors and into his care. "There was a tendency for psychiatrists in other provinces to send their patients to Cameron," said Dr. Peter Roper, a former Allan psychiatrist. "Some were sent from as far away as Europe. Cameron had served a number of years in a mental hospital and he knew what they were like. He tried to keep people out of them." Cameron considered himself to be the last bulwark against institutionalization in a state-run asylum.

Schreck was admitted to the Allan on August 2, 1962. She was depressed, anxious, uncommunicative, and still bore the scars from her attempts at self-mutilation. Cameron was her attending physician. "There was a sense of power about Dr. Cameron," Schreck said. "The sense that he was an extremely important shaker and mover. He walked like a whirlwind." He immediately rejected the diagnosis of schizophrenia, instead he pronounced that she was suffering from "extremely severe anxiety hysteria." His first order was for her to abandon the medication she was taking to control her seizures. She baulked, but Cameron pressed. "Do you want to be the kind of person who has to be helped across the street for the rest of your life?" he asked. Karralynn gave up the medication and the seizures stopped.

When Karralynn was admitted to the Allan in 1962, Cameron had already substantially abandoned his psychic driving treatment as it had existed in the late 1950s. As he announced to the American Psychopathological Association in 1963, the lengthy driving periods and intrusive preparatory techniques had proven ineffective. But a scaled-down version, similar to his earlier experiments in 1953, was still in use as therapy. Cameron retained the theoretical basis of psychic driving — a negative message would have an abreactive effect and a positive message would have a reinforcing effect — but the length of the sessions was reduced to two hours a day, three times a week. Under the influence of drugs — usually a combination of Desoxyn, a stimulant and Sodium Amytal, a depressant — patients listened to the driving tape and were asked to write their thoughts down as the tape played.

Karralynn remembers the experience as productive. "It was a catharsis for me. It was a way of being able to release all these feelings — pent-up feelings — and getting rid of them by writing them down. I thought it helped." This scaled-down version of psychic driving came closest to Cameron's initial intention. The patient's written response to the tape resembled a dialogue and, at the end of the day, the therapist would collect the written material and examine the patient's progress. The therapist, therefore, could treat far more people in a day than he would have been able to with psychoanalysis.

Tacked on to the end of Karralynn's driving message was the sentence, "When you see a piece of paper, you want to pick it up." This incongruity was initially the source of curiosity, then accepted simply as part of the text. The purpose of this sentence became clear some months later when a group of driving patients was taken to the Montreal Neurological Institute to watch a slide presentation. Among the slides was one of an empty gymnasium, and on its highly polished floor was a single piece of paper. "You could feel yourself react," Karralynn said. "You wanted to pick up the piece of paper." Cameron used this test in 1963 to demonstrate the intrinsic worth of psychic driving in its reduced form to the American Psychopathological Association.

Karralynn was transformed under Cameron's care. She became his star patient, her case history was trotted out for teaching situations. When her medical insurance benefits ran out, Cameron treated her free of charge for a year. In 1964, Cameron told her that he was leaving the Allan to take a post in Albany, New York, but that he would continue to treat her there if necessary. She left the Allan when Cameron did, and joined her parents who were living in England at the time.

Cameron kept in touch with Karralynn, writing letters to her in England. In them he cautioned Schreck against leaning too heavily on him. "With regard to your feelings about me," he wrote, "They are still as neurotic as all get out. When you say 'If I cannot crawl back to you with my tail thumping for a few kind words and a scratch behind the ears, then why bother making the effort at all,' I feel like giving that dog a resounding kick that distance below the tail which would do the most good." He implored her to quit thinking of herself as a patient and to start a life.

His quirky letter-writing style included a rare personal reverie. Describing England, Cameron wrote:

> Masses of appalling bones surround tiny islands of extremely able people and underground the sewers of London run through ruins of Roman villas. Where I grew up there was, a mile to the south, a line of low hills across which ran Hadrian's Wall and, a little bit over a mile to the north, was another range of slightly higher hills on which stood an old Pictish fort which, two thousand years earlier, kept watch on the enemy to the south.

The enemy to the south still existed, to an extent. The Maudsley Hospital in London was one of the few institutes more prominent than the Allan and it was run by Cameron's chief rival and one of his harshest critics, Sir Aubrey Lewis. Lewis and Cameron had been residents at Johns Hopkins together and had once been friends. As they grew up professionally, their inherent professional differences grew into barely-concealed hostility. Lewis, a prominent academician and scholar was contemptuous of what he held to be Cameron's half-baked experimental creations. He denounced depatterning as "barbaric."

In England, Karralynn Schreck suffered a minor relapse and medication was prescribed for her by a Liverpool doctor. She refused it, explaining that her Canadian doctor had advised against it. "When I told him it was Dr. Cameron, he didn't push. He had heard the name."

"Dr. Cameron was a warm, caring man," she said. "He looked at you as an individual and not in terms of someone else's evaluation of you. I know it sounds egocentric, but if I was the only one he helped, then he was a success."

Karralynn Schreck has since gone on to receive an honours degree in English and is currently working on an M.A. in psychology with the intention of becoming a therapist. "I want to work with people like myself who, but for the caring of a therapist who is truly interested in the welfare and progress of each patient, might fall through the cracks in the mental health system and end up a chronic mental patient."

Karralynn Schreck's successful recovery from mental illness is not a typical case. But her experience illustrates Cameron's clinical abilities, which are so vehemently championed by his nurses.

Alena Valdstyn, a former head nurse at the Allan, described his presence as electric:

> The patients adored him. Next to God there was Cameron. He was tall and very confident and he was a commander — when he walked into a room you felt that here is a person in charge, here is someone that will do something. He was a very strong father figure and he liked to keep his house in order. He had a patient on every ward so that when he made his rounds, he was able to inspect the whole hospital. He saw every patient every day, usually twice a day. On weekends he phoned from Lake Placid with questions: "Is Mrs. Jones responding to Largactil? How is Mrs. Smith's weight?" He really made an impression.

In a small sample of former Cameron patients there were a number of successes, though none as dramatic as Karralynn Schreck. The terms *success* and *failure* in psychiatric parlance are largely interpretive and open to debate by doctors, relatives, and increasingly, lawyers, but if a patient declares himself to be cured he is generally conceded to be such.

Failures are a trickier business. Cameron considered his depatterning treatment to be a successful one, though few relatives of depatterned patients would agree. His contention that much of a depatterned patient's memory eventually returns has been partly substantiated , but the detrimental effects of a permanent loss of ten-to-thirty percent of one's memory have not been sufficiently emphasized. Many relatives of patients depatterned by Cameron share the opinion that Dr. Solandt offered upon seeing a colleague's depatterned wife.

It is difficult to reconcile the polarized extremes of Cameron's clinical career. He was the healer who "fiercely cared" about Karralynn Schreck and she credits her complete recovery to him. But he was also the man who locked a depatterned woman in an isolation cell for thirty-five days and subjected her to more than half a million repetitions of a single message. When asked about the often violent dichotomies presented by Cameron's work, most colleagues simply shrug, "Cameron was Cameron."

Cameron wrote in the introduction of his 1933 book, *Objective and Experimental Psychiatry*, that "the influence which most strongly beat upon those of us who passed into psychiatry . . . was the humanitarian. Sympathy, patience, insight, rapport — these were the magic words." Commenting on this passage, Dr. Robert Cleghorn wrote, "Unhappily, [Cameron] was unable to bring these magic words to bear prominently on his dealings with disturbed people. He was seldom impatient but he seemed not to enter into the emotional vicissitudes of his patients, that is to say, to become a participant observer." Although Cameron's aloofness could extend to his patients, clearly in the case of Schreck, it didn't. It would also seem, though, that she didn't so much respond to therapy as she responded to Cameron.

Cleghorn testified to Cameron's considerable clinical power, but suggested that Cameron was not necessarily in control of that power:

> He did not decide how he could further capitalize on his considerable clinical abilities, for they were extensive, and his estimate of possible appropriate therapeutic measures were at times uncanny but these divinations remained both outside his ken and his appreciation.

Cameron's inability to capitalize on his clinical power is due to the fact that it was not built on a rigorous experimental foundation; it tended to be hit and miss. It came partly from his personal charisma; like the tribal shaman, it had been conferred upon him. He wrote in 1963, *"The experimenter is capable of on the basis of his natural facilities of a far more subtle range of responses than any battery of tests."* [the italics are Cameron's] Although his facilities were outside his understanding, they could be quite dramatic. "There was something of the Magi about Cameron," a colleague stated.

A former social worker related this incident:

> We were on rounds one morning and we heard this woman screaming. She had one of those screams that pierced

everything, you could hear her everywhere in the building. A resident came running up to Cameron in a panic because he didn't know what to do with her. Cameron prescribed an injection. Twenty minutes later she was still screaming. The same resident came back to Cameron still holding the needle. "We can't get close enough to give her the injection," he said. Cameron beckoned with his hand to a group of us to follow him. We all went into the room where the woman was. There was quite a big crowd in there, an audience actually. We were all waiting for the main event. Cameron didn't disappoint. He walked up to her and sat on the bed, talking quietly to her the whole time. She quit screaming and he slipped an injection to her so subtly that most of us didn't see it. It was like a magician's act. He had quite an effect.

The same qualities that gave Cameron his power as shaman — confidence, optimism — were often detrimental in his experimental work. The extremes he approached in his treatments were at least partly the result of his belief that he was on the right track and, despite the doubts of naysaying psychologists and sceptical peers, and that the patients *were* responding.

The shaman is traditionally both priest and doctor, his profession often a dictate from the spirit world rather than of his own choosing. Dr. Raymond Prince, a former colleague of Cameron's still at the Transcultural Psychiatry Division at McGill, observed the Yoruba Healers in Nigeria for eighteen months in the early 1960s. "Suggestion is the most important element in primitive therapies," he wrote in his paper, "Indigenous Yoruba Psychiatry." "In western science," he said, "there is a tendency to want to get rid of the placebo. Doctors want to think that their healing is based on science, not their personality. I don't know why. The personality can be a powerful tool."

Cameron was aware of the limits of western science in dealing with mental illness but had yet to define the limits of his own innate abilities. "Doctors have to recognize their limitations," said a former chief resident at the Allan, "Sometimes they just have to admit that they cannot cure that person. Cameron was unable to do that. It was both a strength and a weakness."

In Africa, Dr. Prince observed the progress of one hundred and one psychotics who were treated by village healers. Patients were washed with snail's water — a fluid found in the cone of the giant land snail — and sedated with rauwolfia, a root used to treat hypertension. When sorcery was perceived to be the source of the patient's psychosis, he was detoxicated by introducing medicine into the blood from razor cuts made in his shaved scalp. The medicine varied according to the illness, but could include various roots, the filings from a human tooth, and the fluid from a putrifying human corpse. To prevent relapses, the Yoruba employed elaborate discharge ceremonies often involving a blood sacrifice and incantation. Using these methods, the indigenous psychiatrists achieved a sixty percent success rate in treating psychotics, roughly the same figure posted by the Allan Memorial and, for a time, an enviable statistic.

The success of the Yoruba healers could be attributed largely to suggestion. As noted by Dr. Prince, the power of suggestion was derived from:

1) The omnipotence of the healer . . .
2) The healers impressive performance. During divination the patient does not even tell the diviner what the problem is; the diviner learns it through his spirit contacts; the diviner is often an intuitive psychologist and very much in tune with the peculiar stresses of his culture. He often makes impressive "blind" diagnoses
3) His use of sacred and magical formulae, gestures and paraphanalia
4) The anxiety of the patient, which is often deliberately increased by the healer, who may warn him of serious consequences should he fail to follow directions. The patient's anxiety is in marked contrast to the healer's confidence and optimism.

"Many of these factors occur in western healing," Prince wrote, "but while the suggestive element (when it is recognized) is criticized as unscientific in official western medicine, it is utilized to the fullest extent in Yoruba medicine." It could be fairly stated that suggestion was used to its fullest extent by Cameron as well, though, as noted by Cleghorn, not always consciously.

The parallel between Cameron's healing power and that of indigenous African healers is not a pejorative one. Cameron achieved impressive results, often using singularly unimpressive methods. Many of those who were treated successfully by Cameron speak of him in hyperbolic terms; *godlike, omnipotent.* His presence and power were inevitably part of any recovered patient's character profile of him. Prince had observed that the Yoruba healers often employed verbal commands as a therapeutic tool — "Don't listen to those voices! Stop behaving like a madman!" — relying on their status as a community sorcerer to enforce the commands. Cameron used the technique as well, often in the form of a rhetorical question — "Don't you *want* to get well?" — apparently to significant effect.

Doctors enjoyed a greater degree of infallibility in the 1950s and 60s than they do now. "The practice of medicine at this time was very paternalistic," said Dr. Frédéric Grunberg, president of the Canadian Psychiatric Association. "When you consulted a doctor there was a tacit consent that you were putting yourself into his hands and he did what was best for you."

By the early 1960s, Cameron was the president or past president of every major psychiatric association including the newly formed World Psychiatric Association, and could accurately be labelled the most prominent psychiatrist in the world. This status, buttressed by rumours on the ward of his importance and the frank adoration of his nurses, had a powerful effect on mentally ill patients whose sense of self-worth was already under assault. "Here was this important man," said one ex-patient, "and his main concern was that you get well." As both Schreck and Raymond Prince attested, he was able to focus his attention and energy with tremendous conviction. "He made you feel you were part of the team," Karralynn Schreck said. "Both of you working toward the same goal — to get you well."

Despite Cameron's claim to be an atheist, as a healer he was more akin to priest than scientist. But the same enthusiasm and confidence that could galvanize a patient like Karralynn Schreck could be a drawback when applied to research. Where patience was needed, enthusiasm was applied. "He wasn't a researcher," said Dr. Heinz Lehmann, a Montreal psychiatrist who pioneered the drug breakthrough in treating psychotics in 1954, "and he wouldn't want to learn either. A researcher soon learns to be patient, but his [Cameron's] temperament was very unsuitable. He was not a scientist or a researcher, neither by temperament nor by training or even by self-training. If he saw something looked good at first blush, that was it, he wouldn't want to test it a second time." The optimism apparent in his research papers supports Lehmann's opinion.

In the context of today's medical ethics, a number of Cameron's papers, most demonstrably those in which Laughlin Taylor was employed as a psychologist, would fall into the category of scientific fraud. He presented results out of context, rejected or distorted the analyses of co-workers, and neglected to qualify results or mention failures. The graphs submitted as evidence were often impressionistic: In "Effects of Repetition of Verbal Signals Upon the Behaviour of Chronic Psychoneurotic Patients" (1959), the three sets of bar graphs have no gradations marked. There is simply a large white bar representing the "after treatment towering over a small black bar, denoting the "before" treatment in such categories as "appropriate affect," "self-confidence," and "initiative." There is no indication of what these results are based on, who they represent, or how any of these qualities were measured. What they are is a collection of graphs representing Cameron's "natural facility" to measure a patient's response, presented in the language of objective experimental psychiatry.

Cameron's claim that his own "natural facilities" were better able to measure improvement than psychological tests was largely a defence of his shamanism. The corollary of his claim is that in the absence of objective tests, the experimenter is also capable of seeing a response that is a reflection of his own character — in this case unstinting optimism — rather than any real improvement. The wildly inflated results he reported in his papers were partly a function of his faith that the treatment *was* working, combined with the ambitions of a careerist scientist.

Hebb accused Cameron of not knowing when to leave a bad wicket, but Cameron was probably not aware that he was on a bad wicket. He believed that his treatments would show results, despite their questionable foundations. Commenting on the doubtful theoretical basis for depatterning, a colleague speculated that it had been designed to "exorcize the witchcraft-like spectre of schizophrenia." In a sense, it had.

CHAPTER TEN

DEPATTERNING
AND THE END OF AN ERA

*Physicians get neither name nor fame by pricking the wheals
or picking out thistles or by laying of plasters to the scratch
of a pin; . . . But if they would have a name and a fame,
if they will have it quickly, they must do some great and
desperate cures.*

John Bunyan

Dr. Lloyd Hisey, a former Allan psychiatrist recently touched on a point that has often been raised by former colleagues: if Cameron were alive, he would be able to answer most of the charges against him. "The most difficult thing for him to defend," said Hisey, "would be the use of electro-shock. He would have difficulty illustrating any good effects from it. The patients who were given electroshock three or four times a day complained about their memory, sometimes their memory never did seem to come back."

Cameron began to use repeated electroshock-depatterning in 1953 as a treatment for psychotics or severe obsessive-compulsives. There were three stages noted by Cameron in his depatterning treatment. In the first stage, after the initial ECT, the patient experienced some memory deficit but retained his orientation. In the second stage, after further ECT, the loss of memory became more acute. The patient lost what Cameron termed his "space/time image" — the sense of who and where he was — but he was aware of the loss. As a result, he suffered severe anxiety and was often difficult to control. Cameron often dealt with the anxiety by inducing a chemical sleep in the patient for between fifteen and sixty-five days.

In the third stage, after thirty or more ECTs, all anxiety disappeared. "He lives in the immediate present," Cameron wrote. "There is complete amnesia for all the events of his life." Patients were often incontinent, and some were unable to swallow solid food. In a 1960 memorandum, Cameron wrote, "Stage three of depatterning might be seen as protective. It puts the patient in an encysted system which is complete. In these circumstances sensory deprivation could be borne indefinitely."

The patient stayed in the depatterned state for five days, and was then "repatterned" through an intensive nursing effort and occupational therapy. One of the theoretical bases for depatterning was a condition termed "differential amnesia." Simply put, the patient would eventually remember or relearn normal traits and habits but not his psychotic symptoms. In his paper "Production of Differential Amnesia as a Factor in the Treatment of Schizophrenia" (1960), Cameron wrote, "In the years 1958 and 1959 we have treated fifty-three schizophrenic patients by means of depatterning and in all of those cases differential amnesia appeared."

Colleagues remained sceptical. "By the time I took over in 1964," Dr. Robert Cleghorn said, "there was a general consensus that this treatment was not as appropriate as he seemed to think." He later wrote, "It was therapy gone wild with scant criteria."

A former resident, Dr. B., remembers the Allan Memorial during the early 1960s as a place of great intellectual excitement. He said:

> I liked Cameron. I had great respect for the man. Overall he was a great benefactor. He gave the residents a chance to be exposed to a lot of theories and people and he produced people to occupy the chairs of psychiatry all over the country. His goals you could admire. But how he got there, my God, it was terrible. As a researcher, he was hopeless. He shot from the hip. He had lots of ideas but few were of any value.

Some of the residents were distressed at being involved in Cameron's work. "The residents were horrified by many of the things he did," said Dr. B. "Psychic driving and long-term curare were completely horrendous. Curare left them immobilized. They *had* to listen to the tape." But there was little that the residents could do. Dr. B. hesitantly drew the analogy of the Nazi system, uncomfortable with the force of its connotations:

> We were caught up in the system and couldn't do anything but conform. Put up and shut up. On a student visa, you were there if they found you suitable. And you were up

against the most powerful man in psychiatry. He had more or less dictatorial powers.

The foreign residents, more than half the resident population at the Allan, were in Canada on student visas. Cameron could ship them home if he wasn't happy with their work.

There was a growing feeling among the residents in the early 1960s that Cameron's depatterning would eventually end in tragedy. "Let me tell you about a patient we had at the Allan," said Dr. B:

> He was a little guy. The kind of guy you used to say was well over five feet tall. He could have been a jockey. He thought he was Superman, all braggadoccio and wild claims. He was at the Allan because he had a personality disorder. What he was was a damn nuisance. He wasn't under Cameron's care. He was under the care of a Turkish resident, a stupid policeman of a doctor who decided to depattern him. Some residents had a lot of control. The dolts often had more control — when you're a dolt, you sometimes have more freedom because no one wants to work with you. Well, the depatterning killed the little bugger.

The post mortem revealed that he had died of heart failure.

Like most doctors who knew Cameron, Dr. B. can successfully view Cameron, the man, separately from Cameron the researcher. Cameron's research could be laughable or horrendous, yet there was much to admire in the man. "He had a Scots Presbyterian streak in him," said Dr. B. "He was a fair man. He could be brutal and unscrupulous but he was not corrupt. He was his own arbiter of right and wrong. He stepped on a number of people but then, so do all powerful men."

In 1962, Cameron went on a trip to Japan, leaving Dr. Robert Cleghorn in charge of the wards. It was Cleghorn's first detailed contact with Cameron's depatterning results. "I saw one of the cases he was treating who happened to be a friend of one of my daughters. I was struck by her zombie-like, repetitious greeting. I saw how she was limited in her response and I was alerted."

Cleghorn was alerted but not shocked. His wartime experience and a life in medicine had inured him to some extent to the suffering that occurs in a mental institution. A thin man, almost frail now, Cleghorn is cast in the mold of the gentleman scientist: a vanishing breed. With scientific acumen he recognized that the theoretical basis for depatterning was "not only slim but dubious," and that as therapy it appeared to have little value. Yet, like Dr. B., he liked Cameron, recognized his achievements, admired his energy, and mourns his unfortunate public legacy. He still loyally refers to his former director as "chief."

In 1962, Cleghorn was asked by Cameron to chair a committee to limit the cases that were being recommended for depatterning. Cameron had begun to recognize that a few of his acolytes among the resident population were employing excessive zeal in choosing patients for the treatment. It had already demonstrated tragic results in the hands of the Turner resident. Cameron's optimism didn't always extend past his own work. Doubts were raised about the efficacy of the treatment.

Cameron's most sincere imitator, Dr. C., was a man who embraced depatterning with greater fervor than Cameron. According to Cleghorn, he was recommending "everything but the kitchen sink" for depatterning. Concerned with the man's excesses, Cameron asked a resident what made Dr. C. behave that way. "You do," the resident replied. Cameron's paternal gaze over the residents produced a kind of sibling-professional rivalry that had them vying for attention. "We were all little boys trying to please father," commented one resident.

"Because of Cameron's nature," a colleague said, "he hired people who were perhaps the worst elements of himself." They had his forceful qualities but lacked his clinical touch and humanistic philosophy. A nurse testified that Dr. C. used to tell patients that they were going for sleep therapy and then depatterned them. "Cameron would never lie like that," she said.

Dr. C. is remembered by colleagues as a sparkling, party-giving playboy with a leaden clinical manner and little concern for his patient's welfare. A significant few state unequivocally that he was a psychopath. "He should never have become a doctor."

Before Cameron left in 1964, it was established that Dr. C. was referring patients for depatterning who didn't warrant it. He was summoned into Cameron's office and stripped of his rank. In the exchange that followed, the fact emerged that Cameron was treating Dr. C.'s wife. She had sought Cameron's help in dealing with her increasingly difficult husband. Dr. C.

filed a suit against Cameron the next day, demanding damages from Cameron for meddling in his personal affairs.

When Cameron left, Cleghorn succeeded him as director and abolished the practice of depatterning entirely. "I had not objected to depatterning initially," Cleghorn said, "because I felt that if I was going to object about it, I was going to have to do an in-depth study of the theoretical background and I had other things to do." There was, by 1964, a growing feeling at the Allan that depatterning was not an effective treatment, a view supported by doctors outside the institution. "It seemed to me that the only thing was to get evidence. It's no use going on saying 'I don't like it. We won't do it. Other people won't do it.' There's no use in being wishy-washy like that; the thing to do is to find evidence. So I appointed a committee composed of Alex Schwartzmann, who was head psychologist, and he got Dr. Termansen and one other resident to collect data." Their job was to test the patients who had been depatterned and ascertain the efficacy of the treatment.

Schwartzmann and Termansen's brief report, presented to the Canadian Psychiatric Association in 1966, stated that the depatterning treatment had no advantages and many administrative disadvantages over similar forms of treatment. In a barrage of overlapping statistics, they declared that "seventy five percent of the sample tested demonstrated unsatisfactory or impoverished social adjustment and that a persisting amnesia retrograde to the depatterning and ranging in time from six months to ten years is reported by sixty percent of respondants."

Although the paper did not appear until 1966, Cleghorn had stopped the use of depatterning at the Allan immediately after becoming its director in 1964. Cameron was the main impetus behind depatterning and his departure ended most of its use. Dr. C was a notable exception. Although no longer a fan of Cameron's, he continued to embrace depatterning with enthusiasm. Cleghorn had declared that no one was to use more than ten electroshocks on a patient in any two week period. When it became evident that Dr. C. was continuing to exceed the maximum recommended and was in fact depatterning his patients, Cleghorn questioned him. Dr. C. denied that he was giving excessive electroshock and an argument ensued. Cleghorn told him that his appointment would not be renewed in the coming year and to make other arrangements. Dr. C. sued on the grounds of wrongful dismissal, appealing all the way to the Supreme Court. He lost his case. Dr. C.'s departure from the Allan was the denouement of Cameron's depatterning treatment and likely marked the last use of it in Canada. Although Dr. C.

still stands by its efficacy and would use it today if he were able, he is constricted by government regulations that stipulate that only six ECTs may be administered on a doctor's signature.

Cameron abandoned depatterning when he left the Allan and took a post as research professor at the Albany Medical School and Director of Research in Psychiatry and Aging at the Veteran's Administration Hospital. He had hoped that depatterning would prove to be the cure for schizophrenia but, by 1964, it had exhausted even Cameron's considerable optimism. "Cameron admired the Nobel winners greatly," said a former resident. "Had he found a cure for schizophrenia, he would certainly have been a candidate for the Nobel. He wanted the prize very much."

Cameron remarked on the work of Murphy, Minot and Whipple, who had won the Nobel prize for medicine in 1934 for their discovery of liver therapy for pernicious anemia. Pernicious anemia was a serious, often fatal disease at the time, and they effected a cure by feeding patients quantities of liver, up to several pounds a day. It was some years before the active agent, vitamin B-12, was isolated and sufferers could forego the unrelenting diet of liver. Cameron was taken with the persistance that Murphy *et al.* had exercised in their research. If one pound of liver helped, five pounds would help more. "That reasoning made an impression on him," said a colleague.

He adopted this approach in his psychic driving research: "If this thing worked after thirty repetitions," Cameron wrote, "it was only common sense to see what would happen if the repetition was increased tenfold, a hundredfold or even more." He applied this theory to his depatterning and sensory isolation experiments in much the same way. He took them past limits established by other researchers. Hebb had noted that six days of voluntary isolation had a profound effect, Cameron tested involuntary stays of up to thirty-five days. "He was impatient of timidity," said a colleague.

A cursory reading of Nobel winners in the field of medicine shows that a willingness to pursue extreme therapies sometimes results in success. Wagner von Jauregg was awarded the 1927 Nobel for discovering the "therapeutic value of malaria innoculation in the treatment of *dementia paralytica*." He achieved his breakthrough by infecting psychiatric patients with malaria, some of whom subsequently died.

In 1949, Portuguese neurologist Egas Moniz was given the Nobel for his pioneering work with leucotomy (lobotomy), first published in 1936.

The procedure involved cutting the nerve fibers in the brains of psychotic patients. A leucotome, a surgical instrument resembling an ice pick, was tapped through the bony orbit about the eyeball with a wooden mallet, then rotated so that the cutting edge destroyed fibers at the base of the frontal lobes. Moniz's first application of the technique, on a sixty-three-year-old former prostitute who was both psychotic and syphilitic, was pronounced a success. Others were encouraged by the results, and lobotomy was widely adopted as a treatment for severe psychosis throughout the psychiatric world.

"Cameron wanted the Nobel prize," said Dr. Frederick Lowy, a former Allan psychiatrist and current dean of the University of Toronto School of Medicine, "and he didn't care how he got it." Dr. Cleghorn wrote that Cameron "wistfully remarked to me on the number of investigators who had achieved the prize in the field of RNA (ribonucleic acid), which he was also exploring." It was his last research hope and the one he took with him in 1964 when he left the Allan to go to Albany.

In the fall of 1960, a committee was formed at the Allan to address the possibilities of erecting a research building on the grounds. The Allan had internationally established researchers, psychologists, such as Robert Malmo, Ted Sourkes and Eric Wittzower, but they had no room to work. "We were using every square inch of the Allan," remembered Dr. John Davis, a physician who was in charge of electroencephalography at the Institute:

> We had even dug out the corners of the unfinished base-
> ment and cemented that area to use the space. We were us-
> ing the basement of the greenhouse, the stable, the attic,
> and eventually, the tower, which wasn't heated. We had to
> bring electric heaters up.

The idea for the building was Cameron's and he set out to raise the necessary money. The initial design was gradually whittled down to meet the reality of the funding situation. One floor was removed, corridors were squeezed down to the minimum width allowed by the building code, and an auditorium was scrapped. Still, when it opened in 1964, it contained some of the most modern psychiatric research facilities in the world.

"The McGill Research Building was his proudest achievement," said Dr. Brian Unwin, a former resident. When the infrastructure was up, in the dead of winter, Cameron would conduct impromptu tours. The residents stood shivering in their hospital whites as Cameron, oblivious to the cold, pointed out where the computer cable conduits would run.

The research building also contributed to the growing tension between English and French factions in Quebec. The rise of French nationalism
had been given a voice in the Lésage government and there was a backlash
against the prominence of McGill. "French facilities were coming out of the
middle ages in terms of medical schools," said an Allan psychiatrist. "They
began lobbying like hell for funds." The Allan received a disproportionate
amount of funds as it was and the addition of the research building became
a sore point.

The provincial government stipulated that as a condition of their continued financial support for the building, Cameron would have to allocate
space to researchers from two French institutions; the University of Montreal and Laval University in Quebec City. "Laval didn't really care if they
had space there," said Dr. Rock Robertson, former principal of McGill, "they
were too far away anyway." It was more a political ploy than a practical
proposal.

Cameron's rapport with the provincial government was strained by
the early 1960s. Robertson remembers him coming back from his fund-raising
trips to Quebec frustrated. "I think Cameron pulled a few fast ones to keep
the research building as McGill's," said a colleague. "It probably exhausted
his influence in Quebec City. It really was Cameron's building, he was involved in every phase."

The building remained McGill's, but the French medical community
was sufficiently upset that members boycotted the opening ceremonies. At
the ceremony, one of the private donors approached Cameron and com-
plimented him on his achievement. "It's nice," Cameron replied, "But I
would give it all and more for one significant discovery."

In 1960, in the wake of Jean-Charles Pagé's book, the Bédard Commission was formed to investigate the state of Quebec's mental hospitals.
Initiated by the Minister of Health for Quebec, it gave Dr. Dominique
Bédard, Dr. Denis Lazure and Dr. C. A. Roberts the mandate to assess all
psychiatric facilities in the province. Dr. Robert Cleghorn reported that the
commission's visit to the Allan caused Cameron some concern and he became
irritable. He considered the visit an intrusion, feeling that the Allan was
the model of psychiatric enlightenment and above reproach.

The commission report, published in March 1962, noted that the
Allan used more electroshock than any other facility studied. In November
of 1960, seven hundred and sixty-six electroshock treatments were

administered to a patient population of one hundred. During 1961, twelve thousand ECTs were administered at the Allan among an approximate patient population of one thousand. More than fifty percent of the patients were treated with psychotherapy, the report noted.

The Commission also pointed out that the Allan received a disproportionate amount of funding from the Dominion Mental Health Grants, a fact that had been registered by Dr. C. A. Roberts seven years earlier. It was difficult to measure precisely how disproportionate the Allan's funds were, as Cameron refused to surrender the institute's financial statement for the commission's scrutiny.

Cameron's reluctance to give up the Allan's fiscal details was due partly to his resentment of the investigation and partly to the fact that the Allan's finances were in a state of disarray. The same optimism that invested Cameron's research was apparent in his financial management. He routinely hired staff when there was no money to pay them — a tactic he had initiated with Clifford Scott's appointment in 1954 — confident that money would turn up. It was a system based on faith rather than hard currency, and it worked as long as funding was easily available. By 1962, that was no longer the case.

In 1961, Cameron had irretrievably lost the financial support of the Society for the Investigation of Human Ecology and had been unsuccessful in wooing the United States Air Force as a benefactor for Allan research. These losses coincided with an alarming withdrawal of research funds from American foundations in general. In 1962, Dr. John Davis, returned from a visit to the National Institute of Mental Health (NIMH) in Bethesda, Maryland, with "some rather disquieting observations." The NIMH had made the decision to restrict research grants to Canadian institutions, afraid that they would be "accused of being in a position to unduly influence the direction and policies of medical research."

American money made up a significant percentage of the research funds at most Canadian institutions. When the American foundations withdrew their support, the shortfall was not made up by Ottawa, despite rigorous lobbying. "We felt at the time that the federal government should make up every dollar lost from the American foundations," said Davis. "They contributed some, but came nowhere near to what we were losing."

In December of 1961, Jean Gregoire, the deputy health minister for Quebec, effectively usurped most of Cameron's local power base with a proposal to create a psychiatric service within the Ministry of Health. Among its responsibilities would be the allotment of funds to all provincial psychiatric institutions. Until that time, all applications for funding for anglophone institutions in Quebec had gone through Cameron's office.

The Bédard Commission had already established that the Allan was getting more than its share of funds; Cameron's fund-raising trips to Quebec City were becoming increasingly unproductive. His arrogant manner and inability to speak French stymied his efforts to deal with the new government. When Cameron left the Allan in 1964, the fact that the Allan's financial structure was held together largely by Cameron's faith and unwarranted optimism became apparent and much of it collapsed into the lap of his successor, Robert Cleghorn.

In 1964, Cameron was sixty-three years old, two years away from McGill's mandatory retirement age for people holding top administrative posts. Professors could stay on past sixty-five on a yearly basis, but administrators had to step down. Cameron had attended a colleague's farewell party and had witnessed the man burst into tears. "They'll never get me to do that," he remarked to a colleague.

By 1964, two of his three areas of research were dead ends. Depatterning had suffered an ignominious end in the hands of irresponsible residents, and psychic driving, as Cameron stated in 1963, had for the most part been a ten-year trip down the wrong road. As well, his research methods were falling into increasing disfavour with government funding agencies. In 1963, he wrote:

> Using experimental methods in studies of human behaviour prevent really crucial and vital problems from being brought forward for study both because the experimenter himself shrinks from breaking with accepted methods and unless he conforms with experimental methodology of the basic sciences, he can expect relatively little financial support.

Medical research was coming under more stringent regulation. Former Quebec premier Maurice Duplessis's cavalier governing style was a thing of the past and the increasing bureaucratization of psychiatric services had reduced Cameron's dominance of Quebec's psychiatric world.

"Cameron was an achiever," said a colleague, "and he felt he couldn't achieve anything more in Montreal." He was increasingly hard-pressed to get funds for his own work and for others at the Allan. The French medical schools in the province were emerging as research centres and would certainly capture the lion's share of funding from a sympathetic government. Within eighteen months he would have to surrender his directorship of the Allan as well as his chairmanship of the psychiatry department at McGill. It was time to go.

"I remember my last conversation with him," said a staff member. "He was definitely not the robust, confident man he had been. Things weren't going his way and he was blaming it on the political changes that were happening at the time."

Cameron announced his decision to leave at a regular Thursday morning staff meeting, delivering a short terse message and offering no explanation. He didn't want a party in his honour. He later told a psychiatrist that Quebec was going through its adolescence and he didn't want to stay around to see it. He had predicted in 1948 that psychiatry would provide the sanctions and rewards that men would live by, ousting the Church from that role. With the rapid changes in Quebec in the 1960s, the Church's once pervasive influence had all but disappeared; but it wasn't psychiatry that had rushed in to fill the gap, it was bureaucracy.

By August, 1964, Cameron was gone and Robert Cleghorn had taken over as director. Cameron proved to be a difficult act to follow. "When Cameron left," said Alena Valdstyn, "there was no number two man. Cleghorn was well respected and a good scientist, but he wasn't Cameron. The mood had deflated. The greatest time for the Allan was when Cameron was there."

Cameron assumed his post in Albany at the Veteran's Administration Hospital where there was no mandatory retirement age and where he would have the space and funds to continue his research with ribonucleic acid.

Cameron became interested in RNA research after reading the results of an experiment with flatworms. The researchers had trained flatworms to execute a simple task — to move away from a source of light. After completing the task the worms were ground up and fed to other worms. The research question asked was: can knowledge be ingested? Would the worms who ingested the trained flatworms be better able to accomplish the assigned task. It was concluded that some knowledge was transmitted in this way as the former group appeared smarter.

Cameron accepted this premise and adapted it for use in his RNA research on memory. If ribonucleic acid was the substrata of memory and if it was administered to elderly people would their memories improve? Cameron was enthusiastic about his initial results, though Eve Libman, the psychologist on an earlier project, pointed out that the patients were given the same memory test and so naturally got better at it.

Cameron's last published paper was on RNA, entitled "RNA and Memory." It was based on work done at the Allan, although it wasn't published until 1966, the year before he died. A psychologist who worked on the project with Cameron commented on the article: "It was an enormously grandiose statement — almost bizarre in its grandiosity. It really attempts to say, 'I have done something, I have really done something with my life.' And yet it didn't really." Cameron continued his research on RNA in Albany but never published any of his results.

Cameron's death in 1967 marked the end of what he had termed the romantic-heroic era of psychiatry. Psychiatry was becoming more modest in its assessment of its abilities. Some of the swagger had been lost in the first manifestation of deinstitutionalization, and homeless lunatics were now shuffling around the major cities. Governments were curtailing the freedom of doctors to do as they saw fit. Drugs were regulated, ethics committees and hospital ombudsmen appointed. The new wave of researchers were better trained, less optimistic, and held more accountable. "Cameron was the last of the heroic freelancers," commented Heinz Lehmann.

CHAPTER ELEVEN

THE ALLAN MEMORIAL CONTROVERSY

Today the exterior of Ravenscrag has the sagging air of a private boys' school that is no longer attracting the right people. A series of modern additions has left it a small, antiquated part of the Allan complex, but it is still the flagship of the institution, its identifying symbol. A combination of inadequate funding and poor building maintenance, the original mansion is in a state of disrepair.

Inside, the faded elegance quickly gives way to outright dowdiness. Floor surfaces change from room to room, wall coverings are mismatched and the furniture has the asymmetry of donations from random sources. In the lobby are sombre portraits of Sir H. Montagu and Lady Allan; these face each other from opposite walls in ornate frames that have been painted hospital green.

Dr. Brian Robertson, the current director of the Allan, is tall, distinguished and authoritative. A native New Zealander, he speaks with a slight accent. He seems weary of the Cameron issue, but greets it with the calculated pluck of a politician. Robertson has inherited a worn structure and an institution that has had its reputation assaulted from a number of sides. Newspaper headlines like "Allan Memorial patients used as guinea pigs" and "Allan brainwashing was deliberate" haven't inspired confidence in a public that is inclined to take the press literally. Although he never met Cameron, Robertson's position has involved him in the controversy. He has acquainted himself thoroughly with Cameron's administrative legacy and the details of the research in question. He wrote an article defending Cameron which was published in the Montreal *Gazette*. In it, he cautioned that Cameron's work must be viewed from an historical perspective and should not be judged in the light of current ethical practices. "Cameron had a free hand," Robertson says;

He had a coherent vision of what was needed to construct a viable psychiatric network and he had the money available to do it. He recruited talent, attracted top people to make it happen. Having done that, Cameron occupied a very dominating role in the organization itself and at McGill. His power was much greater than mine could ever be.

Robertson's power as director has been diluted by the increasing bureaucratization of medical care:

What we have now is a very democratic, professional bureaucracy, you can't move one step forward without someone on the staff commenting on it. I have to be much more accountable to my peer group of psychiatrists. There are fewer residents. If I have an idea, a change I want to make, it has to go through a very extensive process of departmental, political consultations with everyone having their say.

For Cameron, there was only a short distance between whim and policy.

The status of the Allan in today's psychiatric world is a delicate topic for Robertson. Once a pre-eminent teaching hospital, it has fallen from the 'A' list. Where Cameron was able to recruit easily from all over the world, Robertson is limited. It is difficult to attract doctors to the Allan because Quebec has the lowest pay scale in Canada for psychiatrists.

*   *   *

"Cameron's research abilities were not great," Robertson says. "He was not a researcher of the first rank. He was too busy, he had too many things. He was in too much of a hurry. I think he was more of an organizer and a teacher. He was a very good teacher." Robertson points out that the complexity of the human brain wasn't entirely fathomed in Cameron's day. One could hold out hope for treatments that today seem horribly simplistic. "Cameron thought he could create a sort of clean slate of the mind," he says. "Then you could build somebody up again, away from the old pattern. It was a preoccupation with him. No one ever said there wasn't any opposition to it. There was. A lot of people didn't like his use of ECT. They felt that the efficacy of it was very much in doubt."

"But you see, it wasn't all Cameron's fault. He was the number-one psychiatrist in Canada. People sent him cases from all over. There was pressure on him from relatives to 'do *something* for God's sake.' Society doesn't like to face the mentally ill. There is a lot of pressure to do something for these people." Robertson raises the unsettling question that lurks beneath the surface of the Cameron issue: what if his treatments had worked?

He brings up the analogy of Heinz Lehmann:

Lehmann was at the Verdun Protestant Hospital [since renamed the Douglas Hospital] during the same era experimenting with drug therapy, but you see, the drugs worked. Cameron wasn't really a good scientist. What makes a good scientist is someone who is patient and is prepared to spend a lot of time on one thing. Lehmann was extraordinarily patient. He worked twenty hours a day, kept detailed notes. He was prepared to accept incremental increases in knowledge as opposed to a breakthrough. Cameron was impatient and looked for a short cut.

CHAPTER TWELVE

HEINZ LEHMANN
THE DISCOVERY OF DRUG
THERAPY

There are two people who made psychiatry in this country and they are Ewen Cameron and Heinz Lehmann.
Dr. Simon Ramesar
former chief resident at the Allan

Heinz Lehmann is an internationally-respected psychiatrist who made his reputation in 1954 when the results of his work with chlorpromazine (distributed under the pharmaceutical name Largactil) were published. Largactil had been developed during the Second World War by a pharmaceutical company that was looking for a drug to remedy sea sickness, which was rampant among soldiers aboard the Allied troop ships. Largactil failed to cure sea sickness, but anaesthesiologists discovered that it could be used to induce hypothermia and slow the heart rate. French psychiatrists began to experiment with it as a sedative.

Lehmann, who was fluent in French, learned of Largactil in the French literature that is routinely distributed by drug companies. He began to conduct research with Largactil at the Verdun Protestant Hospital, using volunteers from his small, trusting staff as the first subjects.

Dr. Koranyi, a volunteer, remembers the experience. "We went into his office at six a.m. and he gave us sixty milligrams. 'Just do your usual rounds,' Lehmann told us. I was asleep in ten minutes." Lehmann began to administer the drug to his patients as a sedative, but he soon realized that it had other properties. He noticed that schizophrenic patients stopped hallucinating while under the influence of the drug. Their symptoms seemed to go into remission. He tested this effect rigorously and, in 1954, published his findings.

It was the Tristan chord of twentieth-century psychiatry, separating modern treatment from its less attractive predecessors. The discovery of Largactil was the advent of effective drug therapy for mental illness. It was a substance that would eliminate, at least temporarily, the debilitating symptoms of schizophrenia — delusions, paranoia, and auditory hallucinations. Largactil heralded two concomitant discoveries: first, that there was a biological substrate to mental illness, it was not just a psychological maladjustment, and, second, that patients could now be treated with sufficient success to enable them to function outside the walls of an institution.

Located in Verdun, a satellite of Montreal, the Douglas Hospital is situated well back from the road. With its lush, spacious grounds and Georgian architecture, it resembles the *ante bellum* houses of the southern U.S. Between the hospital and the road is a large gracious house, the director's residence. In the 1950s, the hospital housed close to two thousand patients. It was a desperate, crowded, locked-door reservoir for every deeply disturbed Protestant in southern Quebec.

In the film archives at the Douglas there are sixteen-millimetre films made by Heinz Lehmann in the 1940s. In one of the films, a young Lehmann appears before the camera, a slight, dapper man in a double-breasted suit. He looks like the actor Adolfe Menjou. After a brief introduction, Lehmann talks to three catatonic men who are sitting on metal chairs. They look completely mad; they have insane smiles, skewed eyes, facial tics, and the lumpen faces of Bosch peasants. Lehmann addresses each individually, talking with a quiet persistance. "Hello Mr. Smith, how are you today?" There is no response from Smith; he doesn't acknowledge Lehmann's presence. "Are you feeling well? Can you lift your hand up for me?" Again there is no response. Lehmann takes the man's hand and guides it up. When he lets go, the arm doesn't move. It doesn't even drop the inch or so you might expect when support is withdrawn. It stays absolutely immobile as if it were a wire that had been twisted into position. None of the three men ever acknowledge Lehmann, the camera, or each other.

The film documents catatonia (once a relatively common disorder, now a rare occurence) and provides a rare glimpse of mental illness as it existed forty years ago. During this era the practice of psychiatry is often described by doctors as "frontier psychiatry."

Lehmann's scientific acumen is the result of innate curiosity and vast clinical experience rather than formal training. He is a self-taught researcher. Most of his energies are devoted to teaching now; he divides his time between the Douglas Hospital, the McGill Research Building and a post in Albany, New York, where he can be found from Wednesday afternoon to Friday evening.

The passing of forty years has had curiously little physical effect on Lehmann. He looks much as he did in his teaching films. He came to Montreal before the Second World War and started work at the Verdun Protestant Hospital as a junior psychiatrist. He had neither the time nor the money for post-graduate training.

> In the beginning, I worked from eight in the morning until about one or two in the morning. There were only four doctors at the hospital and sixteen hundred patients. I had all the male patients — seven hundred patients. Just to physically see them, to cover the ground, took three days. We didn't have any drugs and I had one registered nurse and some untrained attendants. There were a lot of restraints, a lot of seclusion. The only thing we had to treat them was barbiturates — heavy sedatives — and if you gave them too much for too long you intoxicated the patient.
> We were a warehouse of mental wrecks. They could not be left at home and we didn't have any treatment.

Despite the medieval conditions and rampant bedlam of the Verdun Protestant hospital, there was no shortage of customers.

> There is a whole different *weltanschauung* now about institutionalization. You are supposed to feel very guilty today about putting someone in a mental hospital. Exhaust every possible means. Not then. The first real crazy thing they did, they were put in an institution. The ethical thing was not to lock them up in the attic, but to put them in a hospital. Nobody felt guilty. They had done the right thing. When I started we had nothing to treat them with. It caused a big sensation when it was shown that if you injected Sodium Amytal in a stuporous patient, they would come out of their stupor for a few hours. We had a lot of stuporous patients. Now we don't see them at all. I had to go around and feed by stomach tube the stuporous patients. They couldn't even swallow. They would just be lying there like corpses. To bring them out even for an hour and hear them talk rationally

was a miracle. But you couldn't always have them on Sodium Amytal or you would kill them, they would become intoxicated. Then came insulin-coma treatment and ECT. That was even more miraculous because you could free patients for days, weeks and months from symptoms. And that was unheard of. I remember they sent me to the States to see how it was being done. We had an insulin-coma unit that could treat nine or ten patients. But the treatment would go on every day for several months, and so you couldn't treat many patients with insulin. With ECT, it was effective for depression but not so much for schizophrenia, and most of our patients were schizophrenic.

Schizophrenia had become the most pressing problem for psychiatrists in the 1950s, particularly in the large mental hospitals. Depressives were sometimes cured by simply leaving them alone for extended periods. Before ECT, they would linger on the wards until they were better or until they died. But with the introduction of electroshock treatment, depressives were able to function outside of the institution and their beds were increasingly taken up by schizophrenics, who were rarely released and gradually came to fill the institutions.

ECT and insulin-coma treatment relieved the symptoms of some mental patients but they didn't cure them, and there was no follow-up care of the patient to see if the symptoms were still in remission. "We didn't want to follow them up," says Lehmann:

> We knew when they left the hospital after insulin-coma, their relatives would say, "will this happen again?" and you'd say, "Oh no, don't worry, he's fine!" We worried. We knew he would likely come back. But we didn't want to know in the meantime. They would show up like a bad penny. Nine times out of ten they would come back. There was no other place for them to go. If they were still in Montreal, they would come back to you.

When I started, my salary was about fifteen dollars a month. And from that, I would buy chocolate bars every morning and take them with me. There were some patients who were so agitated that they screamed always and I could never talk to them. They would be restrained in bed and I would pop a piece of chocolate in their mouths. They would be surprised, then they would chew it and I could communicate with them for a few minutes. There was a lot of improvisation.

The stifling humidity of Montreal summers presented some serious problems to the patients at the Verdun hospital. There was no air conditioning and agitated patients restrained in their beds would develop high fevers and in some instances die. The top floors were like a sauna. Lehmann knew that trains were air conditioned. He went to the railyard to take a look at how it was done. There was an icebox under the cars and air was pumped over the ice and into the compartments. Back at the hospital, he rigged up vacuum cleaners and iceboxes and made a tent of the patients' bedsheets. With the vacuum cleaner blowing in reverse, he pumped air over the ice and into the makeshift pup-tents, cooling the patients.

At night Lehmann prepared the sedatives for the patient population. The hospital lacked the money to hire a pharmacist or to buy the drugs in capsules. They bought everything in bulk and Lehmann measured out the doses after his rounds. Occasionally he would read for an hour before going home, combing the psychiatric literature for new ideas. The nurse who married Lehmann was advised by co-workers to stay away from him. Only a drug addict could keep those kinds of hours, they warned.

Although Lehmann had no post-graduate training, he developed a clinical experience with psychotics that was matched by only a handful of people. He once applied for a job at the Allan Memorial. An appointment there would give him time for research and help him realize his academic ambitions. Cameron turned him down on the grounds that the Verdun hospital couldn't spare him, hiring Karl Stern for the position instead. Lehmann joked that perhaps he wasn't tall enough. Cameron, over six feet himself, seemed to lean towards tall men when recruiting staff. Lehmann decided that if he couldn't work at an internationally-renowned institute, he would put the Verdun Protestant Hospital on the map.

When he first experimented with Largactil, there were a few hitches. "When I tried it on the staff, it lowered their blood pressure. Some of them fainted. For all I knew they might have died from it. We didn't know how toxic it was." He bought a slide rule, learned statistics at home from a book, and continued his experimentation. Although short on help, time, money, and formal training, he had the freedom to do as he saw fit and an insatiable scientific curiosity.

After he had established that Largactil reduced the symptoms of acute schizophrenics, Lehmann pursued the use of the drug in a preventative role:

> It occurred to me that if you kept on giving small amounts of these drugs, smaller than what you gave for acute treatment, maybe you can prevent the breakdown again. When we tried smaller doses, it took about a year, but I knew I had something unique. We established what we called an out-care clinic where they got Largactil. And that was fantastic. Before, when they were out, you never saw them again until they arrived with relatives, sick again.

The significance of effective drug therapy opened up new territory in psychiatry:

> We had now demonstrated that there was a physical, biological substrate for mental illness. For fifty years we had been looking for a physical cause and hadn't found it, the only hope for mental patients was through psychotherapy, psychoanalytic oriented psychotherapy. The drugs showed indirectly that there was a physical substrate, otherwise how could a physical substance change it? That opened the door to what we call the neurosciences now — the whole biology and particularly the chemistry of the brain. We have learned an awful lot about neurophysiology and neurochemistry which we probably wouldn't have if we hadn't demonstrated first that there must be something there because these drugs worked. And we found out years later *how* the drugs worked. It frightens me now because everybody is fascinated by neuroscience and we're getting away from the personal element of psychiatry — of the actual patient. We are in danger of being seduced by the new instrumentation, of becoming intoxicated with technology.

After the Largactil breakthrough, Lehmann was quickly established as a major figure in psychiatry internationally. The National Institute of Mental Health (NIMH) in Washington, D.C., offered to support his research and gave him a seat on their selection committee to award grants. American psychiatrist Nathan Kline convinced the U.S. Congress that the new drugs would eventually eradicate all mental illness and that research money would be a wise investment. He argued that science was close to a cure for mental illness where upon most of the patients in state institutions could be released and the substantial financial burden they represented would be considerably lightened. Congress gave the NIMH two million dollars for psychopharmacology research grants. After disbursing only one million dollars, NIMH had exhausted possible recipients.

"It seems ludicrous now," Lehmann says, "but we had all this extra money. That doesn't happen nowadays." It was a time of great optimism but there was a grievous downside.

As one of the founders of drug treatment, Lehmann has done a lot of reflecting on its hasty spawn — deinstitutionalization:

> The politicians thought, "In ten years we can close all the hospitals. We have the drugs now and we'll have everybody out in the community." It became a catastrophe. The psychiatrists who sold the government on the new drugs were not the ones who knew all the details, the drawbacks, the side effects, the distance still to be covered. They didn't know how often these people would relapse. They oversold the drug.

Fueled by the optimism that can be endemic among elected officials, politicians bought the idea of deinstitutionalization in a big way. Emptying the hospitals would save millions and it was an issue that would appeal to the electorate. Drug therapy provided an opportunity to get people out of institutions and into society. "But society wasn't prepared for it," says Lehmann. "They didn't care. Instead of waiting until they had put a lot of money into producing agencies to support these people, they sent them out to fend for themselves. It was a disaster." Lehmann stares at his desk and absently plays with one of the objects on it. "If I had it to do again I wonder if I would make a big fuss about these new drugs, because you know, it did just about as much harm as good. The politicians took over. Deinstitutionalization was premature, precipitous, and motivated by enthusiasm, stupid over-enthusiasm and political greed."

Deinstitutionalization of the 1960s, especially in the United States, resulted in the release of great numbers of mental patients whose symptoms could be controlled by drugs but who actually could not cope on their own. There was little in the way of community support and these patients without families were simply added to the welfare rolls. Their abilities to cope were marginal, and significant numbers drifted from rooming house to rooming house, losing contact with any source of medication and becoming part of the growing ranks of the homeless.

The 1950s have been described as the romantic-heroic era of psychiatry by a number of doctors. Optimism was feverish and major discoveries were deemed imminent. "There was going to be a breakthrough," Lehmann says:

> Everybody was just feeling it. We didn't know where it would be or what it would be, but we knew we were close. Cameron was right to look for it but he was looking in the wrong corner. He had the conviction that a breakthrough would happen, but he didn't have the evidence. He wanted to produce the evidence, he very much wanted to be the pioneer who produced it.
>
> It's ironic that one of the reasons he didn't find what I found is that he didn't bother to learn French. [Lehmann is married to a French-Canadian woman and speaks French at home] These articles on Largactil, they had been published in France, in French only. The drug company producing Largactil brought me this literature in French — they leave it with every doctor and you never have time to read it — but I read it one Sunday morning.
>
> It struck me as something different, something worth experimenting with. Cameron got the same thing, but of course he couldn't read it, nobody there could read French. If he had been able to read French . . . , [Lehmann shrugs] It's ironic that his whole attitude, the hostile attitude toward the French, prevented him for making this discovery because he could have done it much easier than I did at the Douglas Hospital.
>
> Cameron was not a scientist. His temperament was very unsuitable. He was probably a very good clinician. But to be a scientist you have to learn an extra amount of honesty with yourself. You have to be very sceptical, particularly when you have good results. You have to say, "There must be something wrong, it couldn't be so good." With Cameron's temperament, it wasn't so. If he saw at first blush it looked good, okay, that was it. He didn't want to try a second time to see why it turned out that way. Most of his results, when you look at the methodology, were deceiving because he just hadn't followed through properly. The conclusions were wrong.

Although Lehmann has no respect for Cameron's research, he advises against hasty judgements:

> Only dull and irresponsible physicians would come in and do their eight-to-five and not care about trying anything else. There was practically no treatment, so unless you went into research and did something yourself, you were limited in your ability to help these people. For anyone who had any kind of a dynamic conscience it was an impossible situation; to see thousands, hundreds of thousands of people in mental hospitals and never getting out.

On Cameron's research Lehmann commented that:

> It wasn't a criminal experiment using people as guinea pigs. It was a heroic, very aggressive treatment based on a certain theory which proved to be wrong. As so often is the case, even with a wrong theory some of the treatments helped people, some were damaged by them.
>
> Today, it's unthinkable that anyone would do research without having informed consent from the patient first. But in those days they wouldn't have known what you were talking about. Of course your patients would agree. Of course they would be very glad you would do something because nothing could be done anyway. Of course the relatives would be every happy for any research, anything that could be done that wasn't just keeping them there. So I didn't ask the patients, I didn't ask the relatives, they were all very glad when they heard it was being done, that they were on the research drugs, and I certainly didn't have to ask the government, which I would have to do now. There was no agency where you had to ask whether you could use a new drug. I did what I thought was right.

Lehmann believes that Cameron had his patients' best interest at heart, but it did not always translate into beneficial treatment:

> I think that Cameron started off very well as a pioneer of the scientific method, but then he didn't grow. I didn't always like the new methodology either — control groups, double-blind experiments — but I realized that I had to go with it. He stayed with the scientific approach of the 30s and 40s

and that wasn't the scientific approach of the 50s and 60s. Scientifically, he was treading water.

"I didn't like Cameron personally," Lehmann says:

He turned me down for a job and I found him cold and distant, but I have no doubt he thought he was doing what was best for his patients. I didn't like his theories; I thought they were simplistic . . . it was nonsense what he was doing. What he was doing was experimental, but what I was doing was experimental. I just happened to be lucky. Mine turned out and his didn't.

If anyone would have dared to tell him, "Look Dr. Cameron, I think you ought to work carefully with some researchers and learn a bit about statistics," he would have said, "Now look, Doc, you don't tell me how to conduct research." He was so convinced that he knew as much as anyone else about research, it wouldn't have been possible to get him to take any training.

But this was not ivory-tower research, it was very practical, very pragmatic — too much so actually. Cameron would say, "Let's try this, let's try that." He was so impatient, you know, anything just to get them better. He never learned how to run a good experiment and I considered, as many others did, that his research was very simplistic.

Cameron congratulated Lehmann on the Largactil breakthrough. "He was very nice. I'm sure he must have been jealous as hell, but still, publicly, he would always compliment me." Asked whether Cameron used the results of Lehmann's drug research, he answered, "Well, he had to."

Cameron did use Largactil in his psychic driving therapy. Dr. Cleghorn notes in his memoirs that Cameron seemed to miss the significance of the drug breakthrough in 1954, preferring instead to stay with his depatterning program. Cameron continued to search for his own breakthrough, ignoring the tremendous opportunities presented by Lehmann's discovery.

CHAPTER THIRTEEN

THE AFTERMATH OF DISCLOSURE

On August 2, 1977, *The New York Times* article appeared headed: "Private Institutions Used in CIA Effort to Control Behaviour." It outlined the MKULTRA program and identified McGill University as the site of behaviour control experiments. On August 3, in response to these accusations, a Joint Hearing before the U.S. Senate Select Sub-committee on Intelligence and Sub-committee on Health and Scientific Research was held in Washington to examine the extent of the MKULTRA program. The stated purpose of the hearing was to "address the issues raised by any illegal or improper activities that have emerged from the [CIA] files and to prevent such improper activities from occurring again."

Senator Daniel Inouye concluded his opening remarks with the statement:

> There is an obligation on the part of both this committee and the CIA to make every effort to help those individuals or institutions that have been harmed by any of these illegal or improper activities.

Senator Edward Kennedy concurred:

> The Central Intelligence Agency drugged American citizens without their knowledge or consent. It used university facilities and personnel without their knowledge. It funded leading researchers, often without their knowledge. These institutes, these individuals, have a right to know who they are and how and when they were used.

All the senators and assorted CIA staff present condemned the "grandiose and sinister project." Senator Inouye asked CIA Director Stansfield Turner to report back to the committee in three month's time on the progress of the CIA in locating and notifying individuals who had been affected by MKULTRA at the eighty-six institutions involved. Turner replied that he would.

On August 4, the subject of CIA-sponsored behaviour control experiments at McGill was raised in the Canadian Parliament. Andrew Brewin, MP for Greenwood asked Secretary of State for External Affairs, Liberal Don Jamieson, if he had read *The New York Times* article on brainwashing at a Canadian university. "Is the minister aware," asked Brewin, "that persons who are subjected to this treatment lose the sense of sound, sight, smell and in some cases, touch and time also, and that the experience has some serious effects upon their personalities?" "Like the Liberals," called out a Tory backbencher.

"The only evidence I have about changes in people's personality," replied the Honourable Don Jamieson, "relates to this House and is usually the result of actions taken by the other side." Jamieson agreed to investigate the matter and said he would consider the possibility of registering a protest with the U.S. government regarding their intrusion into the affairs of Canadian citizens.

In late August, 1977, the first official account of the CIA's activities was given to the Canadian Embassy in Washington by U.S. officials. The Canadian government expressed concern that the MKULTRA project had been a violation of Canadian sovereignty.

What constituted a breach of Canadian sovereignty, particularly in reference to research funded by the American government on Canadian soil was not always clear. Until 1954, all U.S. military-sponsored research contracts at Canadian institutions contained this clause: "The contractor may disclose information relating to this contract to the Canadian government at any time regardless of the security classification placed thereon." A Canadian Defence Research Board memorandum noted that after December, 1954, "Without warning, the USAF began to offer contracts in which it [the clause] was omitted." The removal of the clause was the subject of debate at the Defense Research Board. They asked one another in the ensuing discussions, how far the DRB was prepared to go to enforce its will on the U.S. military.

The question was tempered by the fact that almost two thirds of the medical research in Canada at the time was financed by American sources. It was decided finally that scientists in Canada doing work for a foreign power without the knowledge of the Canadian government would be a violation of the Official Secrets Act. In searching for a solution, the spirit of compromise which invests Canadian/U.S. relations was evident; we don't want to lose their business but we don't want them running the store. It was decided that all American research contracts from military sources would be channelled through the Canadian Defence Research Board, and neither country would fund classified defence research on the other's soil. If the U.S. felt that a specific classified project could best be done at a Canadian institution, they would approach the DRB who would then fund the work themselves. The same arrangement would work should the DRB want to fund classified work in the U.S.

Occasional violations of this unwritten agreement were noted by Omond Solandt, chairman of the DRB from 1947 to 1956. When American agencies were discovered covertly funding classified research in Canada, the project was either terminated or taken over by the DRB. The MKULTRA program, which went through neither the DRB or the CIA's intelligence liaison in Canada, the Royal Canadian Mounted Police, was a violation of this agreement.

American authorities stated that they regretted the MKULTRA program's activities in Canada but stopped short of acknowledging that a violation of Canadian sovereignty had occurred. Instead an Executive Order was issued by President Jimmy Carter on January 24, 1978, which dictated that what had happened with MKULTRA could not happen again because of stringent new guidelines for American intelligence agencies. Carter's dictate, the culmination of investigations started under the Ford administration and galvanized by the Senate Sub-committee Hearings, ensured that the CIA would henceforth be more accountable, that it would operate in accordance with applicable laws and that a strong internal review procedure would be provided for. It was a document designed to protect the rights of American citizens. Although it did not address Canadian concerns it was perceived as a political signal that MKULTRA-style activities would not happen again in the future. The U.S. authorities assured External Affairs Minister Allan MacEachen "that such a thing would never occur again" and sent a copy of Carter's Executive Order. Though it didn't stipulate that such a thing *could* never happen again, the spirit of the document was accepted in lieu of formal guarantees. The whole situation was perceived as a political rather than a legal issue.

*　　　*　　　*

The CIA was working with the U.S. Justice Department to find former patients; their first step was to check the records at the Allan Memorial Institute. A memorandum from the office of the General Counsel for the CIA stated that, in the case of the Allan patients "long term after affects may have been involved" and that "it is doubtful that any meaningful form of consent was involved in their case." The possibility of a lawsuit against the U.S. government was raised in discussions between American and Canadian officials. Counsel recommended that contact with the Allan be initiated "with the goal of identifying the subjects of the described research."

The director of the Allan informed all parties that Cameron had taken his personal records with him when he retired in 1964, including patient lists. Exactly what had been taken was unclear because Cameron's son Duncan, a lawyer, had destroyed the records on the grounds that they represented a possible breach of doctor/patient confidentiality.

The CIA suggested that the names might be obtained by searching through the case histories; these, presumably, would have stayed at the hospital. Their suggestion was politely declined. Officials from External Affairs made inquiries at the Royal Victoria Hospital, where the Allan patient records were kept, but they were unable to uncover any names. However, former patients of Cameron's subsequently applied for their case histories; they received them, which suggests that the information is still in the Royal Victoria files.

While the U.S. Justice Department had taken the position that the CIA was under legal obligation to identify and notify anyone still suffering harmful after-effects as a result of participating in "research under the direction and control of the CIA," it was clear that the lack of evidence made it impossible to proceed. American authorities requested clarification of the following points; was the research conceived, designed, and managed by Cameron, or did the CIA influence the direction of the research in any way and; were there records of patients involved in Cameron's research. The answer to both was that it was difficult to be certain. The Royal Victoria was unwilling to produce names and the incomplete MKULTRA files made it impossible to determine whether the CIA had dictated or influenced Cameron's research.

*　　　*　　　*

On December 11, 1980, Velma Orlikow, a former patient of Cameron's and wife of Winnipeg member of Parliament, David Orlikow, brought suit against the CIA in a Washington D.C. district court. She solicited the services of Joseph Rauh, a prominent Washington lawyer and figurehead for the American civil rights movement. They were seeking one million dollars in damages on three separate causes of action:

1) That the CIA had placed control over funding of behaviour control experiments in the hands of employees known to have acted recklessly in earlier human experiments in which a non-consenting subject had died. (This referred specifically to MKULTRA Director Sidney Gottlieb and his deputy Robert Lashbrook who had administered LSD to Frank Olson who subsequently committed suicide.)
2) Those CIA employees negligently and recklessly failed to exercise due care and ensure that CIA-funded research would conform to established standards of care applicable to human experiments.
3) The United States, by knowingly supporting and funding the hazardous experiments in which plaintiffs were unwitting subjects is liable for the consequent injuries they suffered.

Velma Orlikow had been admitted to the Allan Memorial Institute on November 7, 1956, suffering from *post partum* depression. She was referred to Cameron by a Winnipeg physician. In Orlikow's case, Cameron prescribed psychic driving treatment and used LSD as a disinhibiting agent on fourteen occasions. Of her LSD experience, Orlikow recalls feeling like a squirrel in a cage, having thoughts of suicide, of shrinking like Alice in Wonderland, and of being unable to get down from her hospital bed. Of Cameron she says:

> All the nurses and doctors were in awe of him. No one ever hinted to me that his methods were unusual. I just kept doing everything he told me. I wanted so much to get well.

Orlikow still has violent mood swings and is unable to concentrate sufficiently to read — a favourite pastime. Jean-Charles Pagé talked to her once over the phone. "She is the same as me, " he said. "The same problems."

The lawsuit was eventually joined by eight other former patients of Cameron's and a three-sided battle began with Rauh and his plaintiffs on one side, the American government on another, and the Canadian government on a third.

In 1977, before the lawsuit was filed, the CIA, the U.S. Justice Department and the Canadian government all agreed that the MKULTRA program had been improper, at times illegal, and a violation of democratic principles. Everyone felt that the CIA had a legal and moral responsibility to contact the institutions which may have been compromised and the individuals who may have suffered from unwitting experiments. After attempts to identify former patients proved unsuccessful, and the CIA's role in Cameron's research remained inconclusive, their resolve waned. CIA Director Stansfield Turner didn't report back to the Senate committee within the three month limit he had promised. When Orlikow launched her suit, everyone took apart their political stances and erected their legal positions, a sturdier and less polite construction.

The American government adopted the position that:
1) the CIA had not solicited Cameron's grant application
2) the patients had all given informed consent for their treatment
3) Cameron was doing the research anyway, and
4) the CIA was simply buying goods off the shelf

When points one and two were disproven in the course of investigation, U.S. authorities fell back on points three and four and held firm. They stated that they had no legal responsibilities to the Canadian plaintiffs.

Joe Rauh was sixty-nine years of age when he filed the lawsuit in 1980. He is an imposing figure — tall, white haired, and bow-tied — and, he has an impressive record as a liberal mover and shaker. In the 1930s he played a role in Franklin Roosevelt's New Deal reforms. In the 1940s he helped found the civil liberties group Americans for Democratic Action. A decade later he defended playwright Arthur Miller at the McCarthy trials. Rauh was given one of the pens used to sign the 1964 Civil Rights Act, a gift from President Lyndon Johnson in recognition of his pivotal contribution. He has defended everyone from Lillian Hellman to the paperboy who was ousted by police from the lobby of the building where Rauh has his law office. He is the champion of liberal causes in Washington; a list of his morning's calls includes the likes of Senator Edward Kennedy, and Tip O'Neill.

Rauh's small firm — Rauh, Lichtman, Levy and Turner — occupies offices at the corner of Connecticut Avenue and Avenue K, a short walk from the White House. There are four partners and a secretary. The youngest of the partners, Jim Turner, has done much of the leg work in the case. This will be the last case of Rauh's estimable career; he has taken on the CIA.

Rauh met most of the plaintiffs for the first time in 1986; the rest he has communicated with only by phone. The plaintiffs have contributed little more than their case histories and their depositions. One of them, Florence Langleben, has died. With the possible exception of Orlikow, the rest are too poor to contribute money and too frail or disabled to travel. Rauh has logged seven thousand hours on the case ("One million dollars in billings") and is out of pocket some twenty thousand dollars in operating and travel expenses.

Rauh has the weight to exercise the court room dramatics of another generation. He likes to tilt at the moral conscience of his opponents. "Look friend," he told CIA psychologist John Gittinger when taking his deposition, "you and I are both pretty close to our Maker and let me tell you that I think you have done something terrible, but lying about it today, you ought to think about that."

*　　　*　　　*

At the outset, the legal case seemed to have much going for it. The plaintiffs were undeniably in poor shape, the Canadian government was enraged, the U.S. government regretful, the CIA contrite. Media on both sides of the border condemned the "experiments." The American news program "60 Minutes" did a story on it, and Canada's counterpart "The Fifth Estate" broadcast two stories. Every major newspaper and magazine in Canada published an article on it and the case was featured prominently in *The New York Times* and *The Washington Post*. Public sentiment was overwhelmingly in favour of the plaintiffs. The Canadian government seemed to be a passive partner in the suit, lobbying for the rights of its citizens and recognition of the sovereignty violation.

The case stalled. By 1985, it still hadn't come to trial. The CIA had filibustered at every juncture and refused to release documents on the grounds of national security. Media coverage had petered out, and Rauh was ailing — arthritis in his hips required the use of a brace and a cane. One plaintiff had died and others were frail and fading. Rauh's rhetoric aimed at the Canadian government's inaction on the issue had long since alienated them as an ally. "I don't understand your government," he said, "if a *Canadian* doctor had been performing secret experiments on American citizens, the marines would be across the border before you could blink. Are they scared of us?"

The political mood in the U.S. had not helped the case. America had gone from the introspection of Jimmy Carter's presidency and his Executive Order to promote accountability in intelligence agencies to the jingoism of Ronald Reagan's sporadic leadership and an intelligence community that was supplying covert aid to the Nicuarguan "contras." The CIA wanted to appear tough," said an official at the Canadian Embassy, gauging the political climate, "If they give in to 'torte terrorism' they may be perceived as being soft." America wanted to present an image of strength.

There was also the legal precedent to consider. If the plaintiffs won their case against the CIA, it could leave the Agency vulnerable to the claims of every foreign citizen who felt they had been mistreated by the CIA over the last thirty years; a substantial list. Though the case of Frank Olson's LSD induced suicide was cited, it does not qualify as a legal precedent for unlawful Agency activities. The seven-hundred-and-fifty-thousand-dollar settlement that the Olson family received was awarded by an Act of Congress and, as such, does not constitute a legal settlement. A victory for the Canadian plaintiffs would be a first.

*　　*　　*

A key to all three sides of the issue was the apology(s). External Affairs Minister Allan MacEachen stated that the U.S. government had expressed regret for the CIA action in Canada on at least four occasions; August 1977, September 1977, late 1978 and February 1979. Rauh considered this as an admission of guilt, and pressed the Canadian government for proof of the apologies to use as evidence in court.

John Hadwen, director general of the Canadian Bureau of Security and Intelligence Liason was the recipient of one of the apologies. "I called in a representative of the U.S. Embassy on September 26, 1977, to make representations regarding the issue of CIA funding to the Allan Memorial Institute," he stated. "I know that the official summoned to meet with me expressed regret. His regret certainly applied to the CIA funding of the research in Montreal without our knowledge, but I also believe he expressed to me regret at the nature of the program."

The U.S. official who expressed regret, CIA chief of station in Ottawa, Stacey Hulse, agreed on August 17, 1984, to appear voluntarily to have a deposition taken by Rauh and Turner. In September, CIA lawyer Scott Kragie informed Turner that he now represented Hulse and that he would obtain a court order prohibiting his client from testifying on the grounds of national security. Rauh protested: "What national security? What the hell does an apology have to do with national security?"

When Rauh and Turner went to Ottawa to take Hadwen's deposition, two CIA lawyers were present, preventing Hadwen from identifying Hulse as the official who proffered the apology. "Everyone in the room knew that it was Stacey Hulse who made the apology to him," Rauh said. "I've never heard of one country giving another extra-legal right over one of its own citizens. They're letting the CIA run the whole show."

The Canadian government offered Rauh the opportunity to talk to C. F. Hooper and A. P. Sherwood, two other Canadian officials who had noted expressions of regret from the Americans. Rauh and Turner declined. "It wasn't worth it," said Turner. "The CIA objected at every turn with Hadwen. We can't get the corroborating details we need. It would be a waste of time."

Stanley Zuckerman, councillor for public affairs at the American Embassy in Ottawa, stated that there was no American record of any apology. He explained that any "oral expressions of disappointment" which had been conveyed had been in response to the embarassment the Canadian government suffered as a result of the situation and was not concerned with any possible CIA activities.

Richard Smith, an official at the U.S. Embassy and an accused apologist, further qualified the apology issue, "I never expressed regret," said Smith. "I think the situation is regrettable, but that's different, isn't it?"

Later debates took into account the fact that regrets may have been expressed but "regret" and "apology" were not the same thing; an expression of regret was not tantamount to apology. Whatever the semantic nuances of the situation, no one appeared to have anything in writing. "Even if a letter [containing an apology] were found, it couldn't be made public," said Dyllis Buckley-Jones, a spokesperson for External Affairs Minister Allan MacEachen's office, "because information provided by the U.S. government in confidence cannot be released without its authority."

Both Joe Rauh and David Orlikow, in his capacity as member of Parliament, requested that all communication between the two governments on the issue be released. The American authorities refused to agree to the release of any U.S. origin documents.

Joe Rauh was convinced that a written apology did exist. "The U.S. won't give it to us because they're covering up their wrongs," he said. "The Canadian government won't give it to us because they're scared of the U.S. government."

In 1984, Canada sent diplomatic notes of protest to the U.S. State Department, addressing the violation of Canadian sovereignty that MKULTRA's covert activity presented as well as the plight of the plaintiffs. The State Department responded stating that they rejected any legal responsibility for funding Cameron on the grounds that the Canadian government had contributed more money to Cameron, in the form of Dominion Mental Health Grants, than the CIA had. If America was guilty, Canada was guiltier. CIA lawyer Scott Kragie boasted, "I'm going to wrap the Canadian government's involvement with Cameron around Joe Rauh's neck."

It was clear by 1985 that Canada had yet to establish a viable [or visible] stance on the whole issue. There were in fact two issues; the sovereignty violation and possible responsibility to the plaintiffs. On the sovereignty issue Canadian officials quietly pursued their charge of violation through diplomatic channels and were quietly rebuffed by the Americans. The plaintiffs were a stickier wicket.

In an attempt to ascertain whether or not the Canadian government had any legal or moral responsibility to the plaintiffs, John Crosbie, Justice minister in the newly-elected Tory government, commissioned Halifax lawyer George Cooper in July 1985 to provide the department with an independant legal opinion. Cooper and his staff interviewed government employees, combed archives, polled government experts and, in the early months of 1986, submitted a report to Crosbie. After some waffling about whether the document would be made public, it was released in May of 1986.

Cooper's impressive document [over one thousand pages long] came to the conclusion that "The Government of Canada bears no legal or moral responsibility for the activities of Dr. Ewen Cameron." Despite being well-argued, Cooper's case was confined by the limits of his mandate, which allowed him to interview only people who had a past or present connection to the government. That effectively ruled out most of Cameron's colleagues, former nurses, psychologists, patients and all of the plaintiffs.

The report argued that Cameron had "acted incautiously but not irresponsibly," that his work was "unsound, but not carried out for any improper purpose."

Cooper's report was substantially undermined by an unsolicited twelve page section which argued the validity of the CIA's case. "The CIA was only involved in funding and was not involved in instigating, directing or controlling Cameron's work." The CIA was, by implication, no more culpable than the Canadian government. Cooper conceded that his inferences were both "tentative and speculative" but nonetheless presented a point-by-point exemplification of the CIA's case.

Cooper's unexplained defence of the CIA was the source of some concern at External Affairs where, ostensibly, they were arguing otherwise. "Cooper definitely exceeded his mandate when he looked at the CIA's role," said an official from External Affairs. The material was damaging to the plaintiffs' case. However, Cooper apparently refused to exise it from the report.

The Cooper report was condemned by Rauh, who stated that first of all, it wasn't an "independant legal opinion" as had been suggested by the Canadian Department of Justice. Cooper was the law partner of Donald McInnes, a Tory member of Parliament in the Mulroney government, an administration which had been rocked by charges of patronage during its first two years in power. Furthermore, much of the report had been drafted by Crosbie's legal staff in the Department of Justice. The Department of Justice, Rauh argued, could not be considered independant since they would be the lawyers facing the plaintiffs should a lawsuit be initiated against the Canadian government.

Citing Cooper's defense of the CIA, Rauh called the report a whitewash, and said that it is proof of collusion between the two governments. "The Cooper report doesn't make a bit of legal difference in my case," Rauh said. "But is sure as hell makes a political difference, and this [Washington D.C.] is a political town." He considered the report to be a clear political statement of where Ottawa stood on the issue. He also accused the Canadian government of stabbing its own citizens in the back.

Scott Kragie, lawyer for the CIA, applauded the document. "The outrageous story that the plaintiffs have told us is so far from the truth that letting facts out will dispose the notion that Cameron was running a Frankenstein laboratory." He said it would be a boost for his case.

Justice Minister Crosbie neither endorsed or denounced the contents of the report. He welcomed any further information on the case from any informed source, distributed the report to libraries across the country and reserved judgment. "It's not my job to pass judgement on Dr. Cameron," he said. He later said that the government may help the nine plaintiffs, despite the findings of the Cooper report.

Cooper's findings suggest that the Department of Justice supported the CIA's legal case while External Affairs was shuffling after the U.S. State Department trying to elicit an apology for CIA wrongdoing. The report brought a number of facts to light but failed to present the Canadian government with a united position. What the report did was to reinforce the belief, at least by the media, that Ottawa's funding of Cameron in the form of Mental Health grants was equivalent to the CIA's covert, possibly illegal, funding of what they held to be brainwashing experiments. Cooper's report is constructed largely as a legal defense for his client, the government, should one prove necessary. There is always the possibility that one or more of the plaintiffs could attempt to sue the Canadian government for their funding of Cameron. It provides a biased legal overview but lacks the authority or information to make moral judgements.

*   *   *

Joe Clark, minister for External Affairs in the Mulroney government, discussed the plight of the plaintiffs and the sovereignty violation in private meetings with U.S. Secretary of State George Schultz in Washington on May 20, 1985, again in Kuala Lampur on July 11, 1985, and in Calgary on October 28, 1985. In the course of their meetings Schultz indicated that he felt the plaintiffs didn't have a case and that the CIA would be vindicated. The State Department reaffirmed the position they had expressed earlier; they didn't owe these people anything, but if they did, then surely the Canadian government owed them more. Schultz suggested that Clark send down a lawyer to review the CIA's case and see for himself.

On March 3, 1986, Mark Jewett, a senior official in the Department of Justice was dispatched to Washington to review the case. Rauh heard that he was coming and requested an audience to present his case. Jewett reviewed the CIA's case and then spent three hours talking with Rauh and Turner before flying back to Ottawa with his conclusions. He submitted a report on his trip, the contents of which have not been disclosed, and the issue of the plaintiffs has not been raised in diplomatic meetings since.

"Read the society pages," Rauh said, brandishing a copy of the *Washington Post*. "I keep telling everyone around here to read the society pages, that's where everything happens in this town." Canadian Ambassador

Allan Gotlieb had invited former CIA director, and the impetus behind MKULTRA Richard Helms to a party at the Embassy. Further information was provided in the Style section of *The Washington Post* and now, Rauh said, "Everybody in the capital assumes Canada doesn't give a tinker's damn about what the CIA had done in Canada."

Prime Minister Brian Mulroney had assured Rauh in a letter that Allan Gottlieb "had intervened at the highest possible levels in the U.S.A. administration" on the plaintiffs behalf. Rauh wrote back criticizing Mulroney's lack of action and the duplicity of the Canadian government that still claimed to be helping the plaintiffs when it was in fact damaging their chances. All the government's efforts on behalf of the plaintiffs had been in secret, Rauh argued, while their public stance was one that supported the CIA.

"I keep asking every Canadian I meet why your government is acting this way," Rauh wrote in a letter to Mulroney dated June 2, 1986. "Some say it's the usual Canadian fright of the Big Brother to the south, aggravated by the fright of the CIA. Others suggest it is Canada's now admitted involvement with Dr. Cameron that holds you back. Still others say Dr. Cameron has to be protected to preserve the good name of Canada's intellectual flagship, McGill University. Many others keep muttering about your father-in-law, Dr. Dimitri Pivnicki [Dr. Pivnicki was a resident at the Allan in the 1960s and still practices there as a psychiatrist but did not work with Cameron], an avid Cameron disciple who still practices at the Allan Memorial Institute and wonders whether he has improperly influenced your government policy. I still do not know the answer to the question 'Why?' But one thing I do know — it's hell of a note when a seventy-five year old U.S. civil liberties lawyer cares more about these injured Canadian citizens, now in the twilight of life, than their own government."

Rauh's letter to Mulroney seems to have resulted in the complete eradication of any Canadian government support of Joe Rauh. "Joe has alienated a lot of supporters in this government with his public attacks," said a Canadian official. His increasingly scathing comments on the Canadian government's cowardice and fence sitting eroded most of the goodwill he had enjoyed at a bureaucratic level at the outset of the case.

Rauh sees the case in very clearly defined terms of good and evil; the plaintiffs are victims, the CIA is a nasty piece of work and Dr. Ewen Cameron was a cruel and unethical quack who tortured his patients. One is either with Rauh or against him. The American government sees the situation in roughly converse terms, and the Canadian government would just like everyone to go away happy.

The Canadian government is still considering a form of compensation to the plaintiffs despite George Cooper's recommendations. "We're not totally heartless here," said an official. But there is the question of whose budget the money would come from. Health and Welfare is a likely candidate but an unwilling source of funds. "No one wants to dig a million dollars out of his budget," said the officials.

After ten years of government investigations, senate hearings, legal manoeuvring and public commentary, one thing appears to be agreed upon; it is not the CIA that is on trial, it is Ewen Cameron.

Establishing a doctor's competence or lack thereof — his guilt or innocence — in a court of law is largely a process of lining up prestigious and contrary experts who offer their opinions. Rauh has taken the affidavits from a variety of medical heavyweights, including Robert Jay Lifton, a brainwashing expert and author of the book *The Nazi Doctors*, and is using the taped comments of the late Donald Hebb. The CIA has assembled a similar list that includes Dr. Robert Cleghorn, Canadian Psychiatric Association President Dr. Frederick Grunberg and Dr. Fred Lowy. Widely divergent testimony on Dr. Cameron will be entered as evidence.

Within the medical profession, there is a great reluctance to testify against a colleague. In fact, there is a reluctance to testify, period. The legal profession has been held responsible for the epidemic of medical litigation and the subsequent inflating of medical insurance premiums. The trial will attempt to prove that the plaintiffs did [or did not] suffer damage as a result of treatment given twenty-five years ago. "No doctor could prove that any damage incurred was the result of treatment twenty-five years ago," said Dr. John Davis, an Allan alumnus. "Only a lawyer could do that," he said contemptuously.

There is no shortage of doctors who are critical of Cameron's work; some publicly, others only in anonymous interviews. But few are willing to come forward to testify. One reason is that, like Dr. B., most agree that overall, he was a great benefactor, and often, despite his misguided research, he was a source of personal inspiration. In courtroom testimony, nuances are of little value. In offering his services to testify for the plaintiffs, a doctor would be committing himself to delivering a one-sided, damaging condemnation of Cameron's work and by implication, Cameron himself. The prevailing feeling is that the courtroom does not lend itself to the anaylsis of a complex situation.

Furthermore, the public perception of the plaintiffs as unwitting victims of medical treatment has made rather less of an impression on doctors who have treated thousands of mental patients over the course of their careers. "All patients at the Allan were voluntary. If they didn't like the treatment, why didn't they leave?" asked one doctor. They suggest that opportunism has played a part in the lawsuit. [If someone offered me one million dollars, I'd join the lawsuit myself.] Doctors also stated that none of the plaintiffs complained about their treatment when they were *at* the Allan and, furthermore, that Joe Rauh is a civil rights fanatic whose reading of the situation doesn't allow for shadings. "A lot of these people were very sick. They were desperate," said one doctor. Cameron may not have helped them but he tried to help them. Every doctor has his failures.

The CIA has also had problems in recruiting expert medical witnesses. Despite ongoing attempts at presenting an image of crisp professionalism and new openness [as dictated by Carter's Executive Order] they have again been caught selling arms to foreign countries and providing their own unique interpretation of foreign policy. To speak on Cameron's behalf involves aligning oneself with the CIA.

Anticipating their lack of appeal, Agency lawyer Scott Kragie has tried different recruiting approaches. A Montreal doctor who wrote a letter to the Montreal *Gazette* defending Cameron was contacted by Kragie and invited to testify in Washington. The doctor declined but said that Kragie was welcome to use the letter as evidence. Kragie said the letter wasn't any use in court and that he could subpoena the doctor if he had to. The doctor consulted a lawyer, found that he couldn't be subpoenaed, and told Kragie flatly that he wasn't going to Washington. "He said he could put pressure on me to come and testify," said the doctor. As yet, he has heard nothing further from Washington.

As expert witnesses for the CIA, Grunberg, Cleghorn and Lowy are repeating their performance of their roles as expert witnesses in the Cooper report, where they discussed Cameron and the ethical milieu of the 1950s. Grunberg stated that he would say nothing further than what he is already on record as saying in the report. Though he considers the covert activities of the CIA to be reprehensible, he is in an awkward alliance with them in order to defend Cameron. The perception in the psychiatric fraternity is that

Ewen Cameron is on trial, not the CIA, and it is his integrity that they are defending, not his work.

Doctors prefer to police themselves. They feel they are best qualified for the job. If a psychiatrist is accused of malpractice, he is investigated and if found guilty, he will be chastised, or fired without references but he is rarely taken to court. "If a psychiatrist is a threat to the community," said a former Allan doctor, "then it is more likely that something will be done. Otherwise there is a natural tendency to want to protect your own group, your own friends. It's human nature."

*　　　*　　　*

Joe Rauh retired in January, 1987, on his seventy-sixth birthday. The arthritis in his hips required surgical attention and two operations were complicated by a mild heart attack and a bleeding ulcer. His poor health prompted his retirement. The case has still not come to trial.

It is doubtful, said colleague Jim Turner, that he will be back to fight the case in court. Turner is on his own now. He is a shrewd and able lawyer and has done much of the paperwork since the suit's inception, but, Turner comments, "I'm not Joe Rauh."

It is clear that after a decade of unsuccessfully pursuing an apology from the U.S. for a violation of sovereignty, that Canada will never receive one. Two American administrations and four Canadian governments have batted the issue back and forth and there is no public record of any change in the American position. The American view is that MKULTRA activity may have been a violation but it was a violation of an unwritten agreement and as such, not worth an official apology. As Dr. Omond Solandt noted, the Americans had been caught covertly funding Canadian scientists before MKULTRA and no diplomatic action had been taken. The work was either stopped or turned over to the Canadian Defence Research Board for funding. The Canadian government doesn't feel that the CIA's covert funding is enough of an incident to warrant a lawsuit before the World Court at The Hague. The official government stance is "Since May [1966], the Government maintained its position with U.S. Government that CIA funding represented [a] violation of sovereignty and that matter should be resolved through a fair out of court settlement."

The CIA has managed to manoeuvre itself into the background; its actions are no longer at issue; all emphasis is on Ewen Cameron.

The causes of action in the lawsuit address two things; that Sid Gottlieb, the man who gave Frank Olson LSD, should not have been put in charge of an unwitting drug testing program, and that Ewen Cameron was not a responsible researcher and the CIA shouldn't have funded him.

For his part in Olson's death, Sid Gottlieb received a letter from CIA director Dulles stating that he had exercised "poor judgement." The letter was hand-delivered to Richard Helms who told Gottlieb that the letter was "not a reprimand and no personnel file notation was being made." The incident didn't damage his career. As an Agency man, Gottlieb was considered to be a good soldier, a man willing to do "the tough things that had to be done."

The pressure from Senate sub-committees on the CIA to divulge information and make reparations for MKULTRA activities has dissipated into a host of new priorities for both Senators and the CIA. The issue was brought into the open in 1977, condemned roundly and resulted in a reorganization of American intelligence agencies. That, from a political perspective, was enough. It is clear that no new information on the CIA will surface at this point. The outcome of the lawsuit will have to depend on an interpretation of Ewen Cameron's work. Was it responsible research or hazardous experiment?

CHAPTER FOURTEEN

CONCLUSIONS

From its earliest days, science has been an arena in which man has striven for two goals; to understand the world and to achieve recognition for his personal efforts in doing so.

Betrayers of Truth:
Fraud and Deceit in the Halls of Science
William Broad and Nicholas Wade

The Plaintiffs

In the fall of 1986, a demonstration was held for the "Allan Memorial Victims" in Ottawa. The demonstrators were members of an *ad hoc* coalition formed by a number of interest groups including The Disabled Women's Network (DAWN), the Psychiatric Alternative Network, Action Against Militarism, and Humane Awareness with Respect and Dignity (HARD). None of the plaintiffs attended, though two of them sent letters of support. Rauh contributed the letter he sent to Prime Minister Mulroney to be read at the demonstration. There were about fifteen protesters in all.

The demonstrators intended to make a statement in front of the American Embassy on Wellington Street, then cross over to Parliament Hill, read the letters, listen to the speeches of two members of Parliament invited to address them, and sing the familiar songs that have graced demonstrations for decades. At one p.m., Don Weitz, one of the organizers of the demonstration and the editor of the anti-psychiatry magazine *Phoenix Rising* addressed the gathering. Dr. Bonnie Burstow, a psychiatrist and a patients' rights activist, moved through the small crowd offering support. A television crew filmed only a few minutes of footage, uncertain about the news value of such a small demonstration.

After twenty minutes, the demonstrators were politely rousted from their place in front of the American Embassy by a police officer who explained that they were blocking pedestrian traffic. The demonstrators moved to Parliament Hill, walking in a tight circle and carrying placards. A microphone was set up on the steps, and one of the protestors picked it up and talked wildly about Africa for a few seconds. Bonnie Burstow took the microphone from her and reminded everyone of their mandate to talk only about the Allan Memorial patients. The woman retreated to one side, smiling and talking gaily about castration.

The invited members of Parliament arrived, and David Orlikow spoke to the fifteen people for about sixty seconds. A colleague, Svend Robinson, member of Parliament for Burnaby, talked for five minutes and drew an enthusiastic response from the small group. Afterwards, the MPs walked back up the Hill.

A press conference for the demonstrators was scheduled to take place in a press room in the bowels of the Parliament Buildings at four p.m. It was booked for them by Dan Heap, member of Parliament for Spadina. The room was lit by television lights and there was a cluster of microphone stands at the front. By four-fifteen p.m., no one from the press had arrived. After half-an-hour a man dressed in the calculated tones of a television reporter arrived and stood in the doorway. He announced that he was commandeering the room to deliver a live feed to Halifax.

"We booked this room," Don Weitz argued, "Dan Heap booked it for us. This is a press conference. We have something to say."

The man surveyed the pressless room. "I *am* the press and I don't give a shit what you have to say."

*   *   *

The historical solution for treating the mentally ill was to shut patients up in an asylum, and, subsequently, their families would never mention their condition. To some extent, patients are still treated that way. They remain poorly understood, difficult to deal with and, for the most part, are avoided. A middle class mentally-ill patient usually returns home after his release from an institution and is accepted back into the family with varying degrees of success. The rest of deinstitutionalized patients belong to a disenfranchised underclass that remains disorganized and politically impotent. Even with the organizational efforts of a network of support groups, it has not been possible to assemble an effective lobbying effort to help them. Few former patients want to advertise their illness, many are incapable of contributing constructively to a political movement, and some, like the smiling demonstrator who talked of castration, make unpredictable allies in the effort to promote awareness of the plight of the mentally ill. Society was not ready to deal with them when they were deinstitutionalized in great numbers in the 1960s, nor will it likely be so in the future. A large number of those referred to as the "homeless," are deinstitutionalized patients.

When a group of U.S. politicians attempted to publicize the plight of the homeless, they spent a night on the streets. A critic succinctly pointed out that it would have been of greater benefit to the homeless if the politicians had invited some of them into their own homes for the night. But the discomfort of sleeping on a subway grate is preferable to playing host to a group of unwashed, unwell strangers.

Only nine plaintiffs came forward to identify themselves as former patients of Cameron and to sue the CIA. The Royal Victoria Hospital's reluctance to search their files for similar cases isn't the only reason for this small representation. Dozens of patients (or their relatives) were able to identify themselves as unwitting participants in Cameron's experiments in the wake of the media attention given to the revelations of the late 1970s and early 1980s. Various former patients requested, and received, their case histories from the Royal Victoria. Of these, some felt that they had no complaint with Cameron's treatment at the time of their illness and still maintain that opinion. For others, especially the relatives of depatterned patients, there is still a tremendous amount of anger and resentment, but their emotional reserves have been depleted. They reason that any action on their part would simply open old wounds.

When mental illness strikes a family member, it is a debilitating experience, and to expose it to the scrutiny of the courts and the media is simply too much for most families to contemplate. Also, it is now no longer possible to join in the existing lawsuit because the statute of limitations has long since expired; new litigants would have to hire a lawyer and proceed on their own. Suing the Allan or the CIA could be emotionally and financially draining and the seven-year struggle of the existing plaintiffs is hardly an encouraging precedent.

Mental illness remains a private matter. There is little solidarity even among the plaintiffs. They have hardly spoken to one another in the seven years since the lawsuit was filed, despite the fact that six of them live in the same area.

The Psychiatric Profession

There is a joke in the psychiatric profession: two psychiatrists approach each other in a hallway and say "Good morning." As they pass, each thinks, "I wonder what he meant by that?" This joke touches on the very nature of the psychiatric profession and how it analyzes itself; quietly, carefully and with a touch of paranoia.

Laughlin Taylor, psychologist and one-time Allan worker, described psychiatry from the historically suspicious position of his own profession:

> Psychiatry is a difficult field, . . . for the most part, they don't know what they are doing. They can't even identify and classify the disease processes they're working with. They're very limited in what they can do with a lot of patients. They do something and the condition goes on. It's terribly inexact. But you can't blame the people who are in the field for the inexactness of it. At least they've had the courage to get involved with it. Mind you, I don't always think it's courage.

Ambition pervades their conversations, their judgements, and their perspectives. As a group they are weened on the "publish or perish" dictum of academia and most have a trail of published papers behind them. In broad academic terms the quantity of papers published is more important than quality, though in stricter scientific circles, the opposite is often true.

Psychiatry was not founded on carefully laid foundations and further knowledge was rarely added in well-wrought increments. More often, progress was the result of chance; serendipity has produced as many breakthroughs as scientific method.

In the 1950s psychiatrists were optimistic and boastful, and cures were announced regularly. Various mental disorders, including schizophrenia, were pronounced by Montreal newspapers, and by local doctors as cured; Cameron among them. Many psychiatrists who practised during these years are nostalgic for what they have termed the romantic/heroic era of psychiatry and few people personified the qualities of that time as much as Ewen Cameron. Cameron was the zeitgeist of that era and his spirit and his integrity are being protected by his peers. Psychiatry is an insular profession.

The CIA

The CIA's MKULTRA program was denounced in the 1950s by the Inspector General of the CIA and Agency medical personnel as improper, unethical and possibly illegal. The stated aims of MKULTRA — to provide a defence against Communist brainwashing techniques — evolved into a wide ranging and sinister operation that was clearly out of control. Despite overwhelming evidence provided by Harold Wolff of the SIHE, that the Communists did not possess any miraculous brainwashing methods, MKULTRA continued to pursue activities that violated the rights of both U.S. and Canadian citizens. During the 1950s the CIA distanced itself from its original function — to act as an intelligence gathering agency for the President — and became, increasingly, an unaccountable, autonomous force. And despite attempts to curb its power and promote accountability (Carter's Executive Order) it remains largely autonomous today. Protesting U.S. policy in Central America in front of the CIA's headquarters in Langley, Virginia, Daniel Ellsberg recently said, "This building is filled with people who know what they're doing is wrong."

Was Cameron's Work Unethical?

In a recent interview, Peter Roper, a former Allan psychiatrist, commented that the medical profession has established a system of checks and balances that ensure, careful selection of applicants to medical school, rigorous training of candidates, and an adherence to the principles of the Hippocratic oath. It is a system that generally weeds out the lazy and the unintelligent and rewards the ambitious, but it offers no guarantees. Career pressures can present situations where a doctor's personal ambitions may be in conflict with a patient's best interests.

Ethical questions have always been subject to broad interpretation and very few doctors are prepared to level the charge of unethical behaviour at a peer. Dr. Clifford Scott observed that, in the medical world, one must be tolerant of what other doctors do unless it is illegal. But the legality of an action is determined by the courts and few doctors are likely to initiate a lawsuit against a colleague. That is the patient's job. "Whistle blowers" are a rarity in the medical profession and they do it at the peril of their own career.

The failure of this system to guarantee patient rights has resulted in increasingly stringent guidelines to regulate the practices of the medical profession. Doctors now complain that they are hamstrung by codes and committees, and that, as a result, some patients are unable to get adequate care.

Examining Cameron's experimental work in the context of the Nuremberg Code of 1947 and subsequent codes, it is clear that some of the work was unethical. It is equally clear that in the context of those codes, much of the psychiatric research at that time was unethical. The gap between any professional code of ethics and actual professional conduct did not significantly narrow until those codes became law in the early 1970s. In the 1950s, an Allan psychiatrist recalled, "You did what you thought was right. Things were much simpler then."

A breach of professional ethics by a medical researcher usually arises from a conflict between the two distinct roles of a clinical investigator. As a clinician he should be concerned solely with his patient's care. As an investigator he is motivated by scientific curiosity and ambition. The legal interpretation of unethical behaviour is largely a question of determining how far the investigator has encroached upon the clinician's turf.

Although the ethical codes in existence in the 1950s held no binding legal powers *per se*, they were used as a guideline for determining malpractice in litigation. In a survey of the legal literature published in that decade, Irving Ladimer wrote:

> For any legal process, a reasonable consensus can be found
> containing the elements of a professional ethical code as a
> basis for considering liability or justification in fact situations
> involving research on human beings.

It was acknowledged though, that a violation of an existing code did not imply legal impropriety unless that violation was also against public policy — i.e., what everyone else was doing. A legal position finally rested on a loosely defined code of behaviour that doctors had created. And that is Cameron's chief defense, that his work conformed with the practices of other clinical investigators.

However, in reality it did not conform. Depatterning was practiced by only a very few colleagues, was condemned by most, decried by Aubrey Lewis as "barbarous," and discontinued when Cameron left the Allan. Much of his experimental work was dismissed by his peers, ridiculed by residents, and was rejected by at least one funding agency (the DRB). In assessing Cameron's experimental treatments, even his staunchest supporters concede that he went too far, that, in fact, he exceeded the standard of the time. It is ridiculous to transport the rigorous medical ethics of today back to 1957 to assess Cameron's work. But neither is it fair to justify Cameron's work on the basis of his worthwhile intentions, a nostalgia for the time, or the enlightened bent of his humanist philosophies. He was neither a corrupt nor evil man, but he *was* an impatient and ambitious man. In the political arena those qualities led to success, in the experimental world they did not, and his humanist preachings were not always enough to ameliorate the singlemindedness of his research. Cameron's work, examined in the context of the time and outside the context of his considerable achievements, was unethical.

As a philosopher, Cameron was an elegant counterpuncher. He held social conventions up to the light and exposed their flaws. His philosophies and the administrative innovations that resulted from them are still being implemented in Quebec. In March, 1987, the need for community mental health centres was cited by Quebec Health Minister Therése Lavoie-Roux, a program Cameron had lobbied for forty years ago.

The claim that "overall, Cameron was a great benefactor" is true, especially from the profession's standpoint. From the patient's perspective, opinion remains divided, often violently so.

Initiative, boldness, and even ruthlessness are qualities which are admired if they are part of a successful venture. Wilder Penfield, Egas Moniz, and Ugo Cerletti were all bold men — many would say imprudently so — but their research was successful. You are allowed a number of casualties if success is achieved. They are balanced against the hundreds of future lives that can be saved or improved as a result. Failure in research doesn't make the same allowances.

"It took Cameron six months to get something into the literature and everybody else five years to get it out," said Elliot Emmanual, a Montreal psychiatrist who once unfavourably reviewed an article Cameron had written. Cameron published sixteen papers on psychic driving and depatterning. They are, for the most part, untruthful, redundant and exclamatory. If he couldn't produce a breakthrough in the laboratory, he would produce it in print. Donald Hebb states:

... [Cameron] thought, in his egotism that *he* ought to be the person making these discoveries ... He was the victim of his own kind of brainwashing — he wanted something so much that he was blinded by the evidence in front of his eyes. Cameron stuck to the conventional experiments and paper writing for most of his life but then he wanted that breakthrough. That was Cameron's fatal flaw — he wasn't so much driven with wanting to know — he was driven with wanting to be important — to make that breakthrough — it made him a bad scientist. He was criminally stupid.

The mentally ill and their families are desperate for help, and that desperation is often translated into trust invested in their doctor. As Heinz Lehmann pointed out, in the 1950s, neither the patients nor their relatives cared if patients were given research drugs. Anything could be tried to make them better. They trusted the doctor to do his best. Cameron exploited that trust and, in pursuing his experimental goals, devastated a number of lives.

The question arises in psychiatry of who the profession is for; the patients or the psychiatrists. There is an element of smugness still in the profession, and a clinical aloofness that comes with having to deal with thousands of disturbed patients. "No one likes giving electroshock," said an Allan psychiatrist, "but after giving a thousand of them, you get used to it."

The broad issue behind Cameron's depatterning treatment was medical ethics, but there is also a human issue; memory. Many of the depatterned patients experienced a significant memory loss that never returned. The professionals talked of percentages. Memory was discussed as a physical property; losing twenty percent was equated to having limited movement in an arm or a leg.

Yet memory is the substance of a person's life. Without it, he is rudderless. Spanish film director Luis Bunel wrote in his memoirs:

You have to begin to lose your memory, if only in bits and pieces, to realise that memory is what makes our lives. Life without memory is not life at all ... Our memory is our coherence, our reason, our feeling, even our action. Without it, we are nothing ...

Cameron confronted behaviour in his work but he rarely considered the personality. He wanted to get his patients functioning and get them out of the institute. Cameron spoke to many audiences on the subject of building a better society, talking enthusiastically about individual rights and freedoms. But he was unable to incorporate those words into his own research. He worked to free society of stale dogma and created his own in the process. "He was," said a colleague, "a prisoner of his own dogma."

SOURCES

Chapter One

The biographical information on Ewen Cameron is taken from *The Montreal Star*, July 7, 1943; "Looking back on 21 Years; D. Ewen Cameron M. D. — a pioneer in Canadian Psychiatry" by Dorothy Trainor, July 20, 1965; "The Great Psychiatric Betrayal" by Val Ross, *Saturday Night*, June, 1979.

Information on the CIA is from *The New York Times* article, "Private Institutions Used in CIA Effort to Control Behaviour," August 2, 1977; *The Search for the Manchurian Candidate,* John Marks, 1980; background information on Adolf Meyer is taken from *The History of Psychiatry: An Evaluation of Psychiatric Thought and Practice from Prehistoric Times to the Present*, Alexander, Selesnick, 1966. The announcement that Cameron had won the Adolf Meyer Memorial Award appeared in the Montreal *Gazette*, April 27, 1957.

Information about Cameron's arrival in Montreal is taken from interviews with Dr. T. E. Dancey. Information on Cameron's early administrative work is taken from his papers: "An Address on the Opening of the Allan Memorial Institute," July 12, 1944 printed in the *Bulletin* of the Montreal Medico-Chirurgical Society; "The Day Hospital: An Experimental Form of Hospitalization" printed in *The Modern Hospital*, 69:60-2; "An Open Psychiatric Hospital" printed in *The Modern Hospital*. Further information came from interviews with Dr. Robert Cleghorn, Dr. Brian Robertson, Dr. Heinz Lehmann and Dr. Carlo Bos.

The information on Ravenscrag is taken from *The Montreal Star*, July 7, 1943.

The description of the Allan development is taken from interviews with Alena Valdstyn, Dr. Clifford Scott, Dr. J. R. Unwin and an untitled speech Cameron gave to the Allan nurses on the development of the institute, supplied by Alena Valdstyn; "History of the Growth and Development of the Allan Memorial Institute 1943-1955" Ewen Cameron from the Allan Memorial Library.

Chapter Two

Information on the Nuremberg Trials is taken from: the court transcripts of Trials of War Criminals Under Control Council Law, November 30, 1945; Medical reports from the British psychiatrists (November 19, 1945), American psychiatrists (November 20, 1945), Russian psychiatrists (November 17, 1945) and the Russians and Dr. Jean Delay (November 16, 1945); Cameron's personal notes on the trial; Cameron's papers, "Additional Psychiatric Comment on the Rudolf Hess case" and "Nuremberg and Its Significance," January 19, 1946; letter to Ewen Cameron from Heinz Lehmann dated October 8, 1947; Evaluation of the Rorschach Records of 16 Leading Nazis Tried at Nuremberg, undated, by Heinz Lehmann; letter to Cameron from W. Donald Ross, September 19, 1947, all taken from the McGill University Archives.

Further information came from *The Psychiatric Tragedy of Rudolf Hess* by Clifford Scott and interviews with Dr. Scott; *The Second World War: The Grand Alliance*, 1950, Winston Churchill.

Discussions of experiments in Nazi concentration camps is taken from *The Nazi Doctors*, Robert Jay Lifton. Further information came from a memorandum from the United Nations War Crimes Commission, research office titled "Medical Experiments on Human Beings," September, 1945, taken from the Public Archives in Ottawa.

The government's position on Nuremberg is presented through the minutes of the United Nation's War Crime Commission, July 18, 1945; an Office of War Information Memorandum titled "Special Guidance on Justice Jackson's Report," June 7, 1945; and excerpts from a Canadian government memorandum addressing the Nuremberg Trials dated, November 21-28, 1945.

Henry Beecher's article "Ethics and Clinical Research" appeared in the *New England Journal of Medicine*, June, 1966.

Chapter Three

Discussion of Ewen Cameron's religious stance arose in interviews with Dr. Brian Robertson, Dr. Clifford Scott, Dr. Humphry Osmond and several others who wished anonymity.

The religious foundation of psychiatry is taken from Heinz Lehmann's paper, "No More Surprises in Psychiatry?" supplied by Dr. Lehmann. Information on Quebec 1940-1965 is taken from *Dream of Nation* by Susan Mann Trofimenkoff (Macmillan, 1982); *The Independance Movement in Quebec 1945-1980* by William D. Coleman (University of Toronto Press, 1984); *Quebec: Social Change and Political Crisis* by Kenneth McRoberts and Dale Posgate (McClelland and Stewart, 1980); *Canada, Quebec and the Uses of Nationalism* by Ramsey Cook (McClelland and Stewart, 1986); and interviews with Jean-Charles Pagé.

Cameron's comments on good and evil are taken from "Behavioural Concepts and Psychotherapy" printed in *The Psychiatric Quarterly*, 1949, 24:227-42. His address to the Canadian Dietetic Association, titled "The Recognition of Harmful Personalities" was printed in *The Canadian Dietetic Association Journal*, June, 1947.

The description of Cameron's run-in with the Anglican Church is taken from accounts in the Montreal *Gazette*, "Dr. Cameron Stirs a Controversy," April 28, 1951; "The Philosophy of Dr. Cameron," May 2; "Moralistic Attitude to Behaviour Makes Us Reds, Says Psychiatrist," April 25; "Bishop Dixon to Condemn Remarks of Allan Psychiatrist, Synod Told," April 27; "Man's Recovery Powers Not Enough, Says Bishop," May 4; "Dr. D. Ewen Cameron's Position Fundamentally Atheistic — Bishop," May 4. The *Windsor Daily Star* published Health and Welfare Minister Paul Martin's comments under the headline "Martin Tells Psychiatrists to Halt Attacks On All Religions," June 6, 1952.

Cameron's opinions on the experimental methods are from his papers: "Mensuration in the Psychoses," *American Journal of Psychiatry*, July, 1933; "The Current Transition in the Conception of Science" printed in *Science*, 1948; "The Experimental Method in the Study of Human Behaviour; Central Problems," printed in *Psychopharmocological Methods: Proceedings of a Symposium of the Effects of Psychotropic Drugs on Higher Nervous Activity*, 1963.

Additional information came from interviews with Dr. Robin Hunter, Dr. Robert Cleghorn and from Dr. Cleghorn's papers which appeared in "The Opinion of George Cooper Q.C., Regarding Canadian Government Funding of the Allan Memorial Institute in the 1950s and 1960s."

Chapter Four

Background on the Linguaphone Company is taken from correspondence between Dr. Lloyd Hisey and Max Sherover (October 19-22, 1948); two articles in *Time* magazine, "Deeper . . . Deeper . . . Dee . . .," March 20, 1950, and "Learn While You Sleep," February 2, 1948; "Dormiphonics: A New Language Learning Technique" by Max Sherover, printed in *The Modern Language Journal*, October, 1950; correspondence between Dr. Hisey and Dr. Charles Elliot (March 3 — September 14, 1948).

Descriptions of psychic driving are taken from Cameron's papers, "Psychic Driving" printed in the *American Journal of Psychiatry*, January, 1956; "Psychic Driving: Dynamic Implant," *Psychiatric Quarterly*, 1957; "Effects of the Repetition of Verbal Signals Upon the Reorganization of the Schizophrenic Patient Subsequent to Intensive Physical Treatments" printed in *Report of the Eleventh International Congress for Psychiatry in Zurich*, September, 1957; "A Further Report on the Effects of Repetition of Verbal Signals Upon Human Behaviour," printed in *The Canadian Psychiatric Association Journal*, 1960; "Automation of Psychotherapy," printed in *Comprehensive Psychiatry*, 1964.

Brainwashing material is taken from *The Search for the Manchurian Candidate* by John Marks (McGraw Hill, 1980); "Psychiatrists Develop Beneficial Brainwashing" appeared in *Weekend Magazine*, Volume 5, number 40, 1955.

Information on the origins of electroshock is taken from *The History of Psychiatry: An Evaluation of Psychiatric Thought and Practice from Prehistoric Times to the Present* by Franz Alexander and Sheldon Selesnick, 1966.

The Page-Russell treatment is outlined in the paper, "Intensified Electrical Convulsion Therapy in the Treatment of Mental Disorders" by L. G. Page and R. J. Russell printed in *The Lancet*, April 17, 1948.

Descriptions of depatterning are taken from Cameron's papers, "Production of Differential Amnesia as a Factor in the Treatment of Schizophrenia" printed in *Comprehensive Psychiatry*, 1960; "Treatment of the Chronic Paranoid Schizophrenic Patient" printed in *The Canadian Medical Association Journal*, 1958; "The Depatterning Treatment of Schizophrenia" printed in *Comprehensive Psychiatry*, 1962. Further information was provided by former residents and nurses from the Allan.

Comments on Cameron's work were taken from interviews with Dr. T. E. Dancey, Dr. Brian Robertson, Dr. Clifford Scott, and Dr. Eddie Kingstone.

Chapter Five

Information on the CIA's BLUEBIRD program is taken from *The Search for the Manchurian Candidate* by John Marks (McGraw Hill, 1980). The meeting at the Ritz Carlton Hotel is described through interviews with Dr. Omond Solandt and Dr. T. E. Dancey and with the aid of two separate accounts of the meeting; one from Dr. James Tyhurst who took the minutes for the Defense Research Board and the other from the CIA (either Haskins or Williams).

Hebb's work was described in interviews with Dr. Muriel Stern, and the papers that were published, "Changes in Perceptual Function After Isolation" by B. K. Doane, Winston Mahatoo, W. Heron and T. H. Scott; "The Effects of Exposure to a Monotonous Environment" by Woodburn Heron; "Cognitive Effects of Perceptual Isolation" by T. H. Scott, W. H. Bexton, W. Heron and B. K. Doane. Further information came from "Annual Report — Contract DRB X-38, Experimental Studies of Attitude" by D. O. Hebb, W. Heron and W. H. Bexton and correspondence between Omond Solandt and the Minister of Defence (January 25, 1954). All material came from the Public Archives in Ottawa.

Correspondence between Dr. Hebb and N. W. Norton, Director for the Operational Research Group at the DRB from March 6, 1952 to May 8, 1956, was obtained from the Public Archives in Ottawa.

Chapter Six

Information on the CIA's program is taken from *The Search for the Manchurian Candidate* by John Marks (McGraw Hill, 1980). Further information is from the depositions of Sidney Gottlieb and John Gittinger, both from the office of Rauh, Lichtman, Levy and Turner in Washington, D.C.

The discussion of LSD is from correspondence between Dr. K. Royal Stewart, Medical Director for Sandoz Pharmaceuticals and the Directors of psychiatric institutions across Canada. The historical perspective is taken from "The Currect Status of LSD as a Therapeutic Tool: A Summary of the Clinical Literature on LSD" presented at the American Psychiatric Association Annual Meeting, May 8, 1962, by Gustav R. Schemiege. Use of LSD at the Allan came from interviews with various former Allan staff, including Dr. Eddie Kingstone.

Dr. Raymond Prince described his work with the Yoruba in an interview. MKULTRA material came from a CIA memorandum titled "MKULTRA subproject 121," August 17, 1960.

The CIA Inspector General's comments on MKULTRA appear in the minutes from the Joint Hearing before the Select Committee on Intelligence and the Sub-committee on Health and Scientific Research of the Committee of Human Resources, United States Senate, August 3, 1977.

Chapter Seven

The information on funding is taken from annual reports on individual projects and Health and Welfare document, "A Brief Report on Mental Health in Canada 1948-1955," Mental Health Division, July 21, 1955, taken from the Public Archives of Canada, Ottawa. Further information came from the Allan Memorial Institute accounting records and Cameron's personal papers found in the McGill University Archives.

Omond Solandt's comments were taken from interviews. The Rockefeller Foundation's assessment of Cameron appeared in *The Search for the Manchurian Candidate* by John Marks (McGraw Hill, 1980). John Gittinger discussed Cameron in his deposition taken on behalf of the plaintiffs Mrs. David Orlikow *et al*, January 19, 1983. Descriptions of Cameron's work comes from interviews with Ed Levinson and Cameron's application for a grant from the Society for the Investigation of Human Ecology. Eve Libman and Laughlin Taylor were interviewed by researcher Heather Moe.

Donald Hebb's comments are taken from "Plaintiff's Memorandum in Opposition to Defendant's Motion for Summary Judgement," supplied by Rauh, Lichtman, Levy and Turner.

Cameron's first published psychic driving paper funded by SIHE money was "Repetition of Verbal Signals: Behavioural and Physiological Changes" with L. Levy, L. Rubenstein and R. B. Malmo printed in *The American Journal of Psychiatry*, 115(11):985-991, 1958.

Robert Cleghorn's comments on Cameron's recruiting abilities appear in excerpts from his memoirs published in "The Opinion of George Cooper, Q.C., Regarding Canadian Government Funding of the Allan Memorial Institute in the 1950s and 1960s." Robert Jay Lifton is quoted from his affidavit, plaintiffs exhibit number two, Mrs. David Orlikow *et al* versus the United States of America.

Lyman Kirkpatrick is quoted from the minutes of the Joint Hearing before the Select Committee on Intelligence and the Sub-committee on Health and Scientific Research on the Committee on Human Resources, U.S. Senate, August 3, 1977.

Harry Truman is quoted from *Years of Trial and Hope* by Harry Truman (Doubleday, 1956); *The Washington Post*, December 22, 1963, and; *Off the Record: The Private Papers of Harry S. Truman*, edited by Robert H. Ferrell (Harper and Row, 1980).

Chapter Eight

The information comes from interviews with Jean-Charles Pagé, his book, *Les Fous Crient au Secours* (Edition Jour, 1961) and "Rapport de la Commission D'Etude des Hopitaux Psychiatriques," Bédard, Lazure, Roberts.

Chapter Nine

Much of the information came from interviews with Alena Valdstyn, former Head of Nursing at the Allan and Karralynn Schreck.

Robert Cleghorn's comments are taken from interviews and from statements that appeared in the "Opinion of George Cooper, Q.C., Regarding Canadian Funding of the Allan Memorial Institute in the 1950s and 1960s."

Cameron's quotes are taken from two papers: "The Experimental Method in the Study of Human Behaviour; Central Problems" (1963), and "Effects of Repetition of Verbal Signals Upon the Behaviour of Chronic Psychoneurotic Patients" (1959).

Material on indigenous psychiatry is taken from interviews with Dr. Raymond Prince and his paper, "Indigenous Yoruba Psychiatry." Further material is taken from interviews with Dr. Frédérick Grunberg, Dr. Heinz Lehmann and Dr. Humphry Osmond.

Chapter Ten

Descriptions of depatterning are taken from Cameron's papers: "Treatment of the Chronic Paranoid Schizophrenic Patient" printed in *The Canadian Medical Association Journal* 78:92-96, 1958; "Production of Differential Amnesia as a Factor in the Treatment of Schizophrenia" printed in *Comprehensive Psychiatry*, 1:26-34, 1960; "The Depatterning Treatment of Schizophrenia" with J. G. Lohrenz and K. A. Hancock, printed in *Comprehensive Psychiatry* 3(2):65-76, as well as Cameron's personal notes, "Notes on Sensory Deprivation," March 30, 1960.

Dr. Cleghorn described his experience with depatterning in two interviews. Schwartzman and Termansen's paper "Intensive Electroconvulsive Therapy: A Follow-up Study" appeared in the *Canadian Psychiatric Association Journal*, Volume 12, 1967.

Cameron's quote on repetition is from his paper "Adventures with Repetition" printed in *Psychotherapy of Perception*, 1965. Dr. Fred Lowy's comments are taken from an interview. Robert Cleghorn's remarks are from his excerpted memoirs which appear in "The Opinion of George Cooper, Q.C., Regarding Canadian Government Funding of the Allan Memorial Institute in the 1950s and the 1960s." Further information is taken from interviews with Dr. J. R. Unwin, Dr. John Davis, Rock Robertson and Alena Valdstyn. The information on the Bédard Commission is taken from "Rapport de la Commission D'Etude des Hopitaux Psychiatriques" by Dominque Bédard, Denis Lazure, and Charles Roberts, published by the Minister of Health for the Province of Quebec, 1962. Jean Gregoire's proposal is outlined in correspondence between Gregoire and Dr. G. E. Wride, of the department of National Health and Welfare in Ottawa, December 15, 1962.

Chapter Eleven

The information is taken from an interview with Dr. Brian Robertson.

Chapter Twelve

The information is taken from an interview with Dr. Heinz Lehmann.

Chapter Thirteen

The information on the Senate hearings is taken from minutes from the Joint Hearing before the Select Committee on Intelligence and the Subcommittee on Health and Scientific research of the Committee on Human Resources, United States Senate. Ninety-fifth Congress, first session, August 3, 1977.

Quotes of Canadian members of Parliament were obtained from the *Hansard* for Thursday, August 4, 1977, 14:40.

The information on the American military research at Canadian institutions was taken from correspondence between the Department of External Affairs and the Defense Research Board, and memorandums from the DRB and the office of the Judge Advocate dating from January 22, 1952 to July 5, 1955. The documents were made available through the Public Archives in Ottawa. Further information was gained through interviews with Dr. Omond Solandt, Chairman of the DRB from 1947 to 1956, and through records of interviews he had given Joseph Rauh and George Cooper.

Carter's Executive Order refers to Executive Order 12036 filed January 25, 1978 with the office of the Federal Register.

Information on the progress of the case through diplomatic channels is from correspondence between the Department of External Affairs and the U.S. State Department, memorandums from External Affairs and correspondence between the CIA and various Canadian officials. All were made available through External Affairs.

The search for patient records and lack of success is documented by a letter from Allan director Maurice Dongier to the Bureau of Consular Services at External Affairs, May 22, 1979, interviews with External Affairs officials and repeated inquiries at the Royal Victoria Hospital.

Information on the lawsuit was obtained through documents made available by Joseph Rauh pertaining to civil action 80-3163 Mrs. David Orlikow *et al* vs. the United States of America, interviews with Joseph Rauh and James Turner and plaintiff Jean-Charles Pagé.

The information on the apology comes from External Affairs memorandums; John Hadwen's statement of June 14, 1984, legal documents obtained from Joseph Rauh — Plaintiffs' Opposition to Defendants' Motion for Continuance of Deposition. Stanley Zuckerman's comments were taken from his letter to the *Globe and Mail*, May 7, 1984. Richard Smith's comments are taken from Jeffrey Simpson's April 25, 1984, article in the Toronto *Globe and Mail*.

Information on External Affairs Minister Joe Clark's meetings with U.S. Secretary of State George Schultz is taken from External Affairs documents and interviews with officials in External Affairs.

Chapter Fourteen

Daniel Ellsberg's comment was published in an AP story headed "Hundreds arrested at CIA protest" published in the Montreal *Gazette*, April 28, 1987.

Hebb's quote is from "Plaintiff's Memorandum in Opposition to Defendant's Motion for Summary Judgement" Civil action number 80-3163 from the office of Rauh, Lichtman, Levy and Turner.

Bunvel's quote is from *The Man Who Mistook His Wife for a Hat*, by Oliver Sacks (Summit Books, 1985).